THE SUPREME SOURCE

The *Kunjed Gyalpo*
The Fundamental Tantra of Dzogchen Semde

THE SUPREME SOURCE

The *Kunjed Gyalpo*

The Fundamental Tantra of Dzogchen Semde

Chögyal Namkhai Norbu
Adriano Clemente

Translated from Italian into English by
Andrew Lukianowicz

Snow Lion Publications
Ithaca, New York USA

Snow Lion Publications
P. O. Box 6483
Ithaca, NY 14851 USA
607-273-8519
www.snowlionpub.com

Published by arrangement with Casa Editrice Astrolabiao - Ubaldini Editore.

Originally published as *La Supreme Sorgente*, Rome, 1997.

ISBN 1-55939-120-0

Printed in Canada on acid-free recycled paper.

Library of Congress Cataloging-in-Publication Data

Namkhai Norbu, 1938-

The supreme source: the Kunjed Gyalpo, the fundamental tantra of Dzogchen Semde / Chögyal Namkhai Norbu, Adriano Clemente; translated from Italian into English by Andrew Lukianowicz.

p. cm.

ISBN 1-55939-120-0

1. Tripiṭaka. Sūtrapiṭaka. Tantra. Sarvadharmamahāśāntibodhicittakulayarāja —Criticism, interpretation, etc. 2. Rdzogs-chen (Rñiṅ-ma-pa) I. Clemente, Adriano. II. Lukianowicz, Andrew. III. Tripiṭaka. Sūtrapiṭaka. Tantra. Sarvadharmamahāśāntibodhicittakulayarāja. English. IV. Title.

BQ2180.S257N36 1999

249.3'85—dc21

99-30399
CIP

Table of Contents

Reading the *Kunjed Gyalpo* you will often come across the word "I": "I am the nature of all phenomena," "I am the root of existence," and so on. This "I" is your true state: the primordial Buddha, the supreme source of manifestation. Try to understand the meaning of *Kunjed Gyalpo* reading it in this light.

—Chögyal Namkhai Norbu

Foreword

The *Kunjed Gyalpo* (*Kun byed rgyal po*)[1] can be considered the fundamental tantra of Dzogchen, a teaching that according to tradition has been transmitted for over two thousand years from teacher to disciple. Its aim is to awaken each individual to his or her true nature: the primordial state of enlightenment, which can be compared to a mirror on whose surface the multiplicity of the phenomena of existence is reflected. Introducing this knowledge is the teacher's task, while understanding it deeply and integrating it into one's existence is the disciple's task: only when this has been accomplished do the traditional texts becoming living words, precious pointers along the timeless journey towards the supreme source.

Dzogchen, in fact, can be deemed the pinnacle not only of all the Buddhist paths of realization, as has often been asserted by Tibetan teachers, but also of the various spiritual methods and teachings of other traditions. The aim of each path, either directly or indirectly, is to overcome the dualistic condition in order to attain the ineffable dimension of the absolute: precisely this dimension is the primordial state to which the true Dzogchen teacher introduces the disciple.

It was this fact that inspired me to make available, albeit not in its entirety, to readers interested in the spiritual quest in general and in Tibetan Buddhism in particular, a basic text of Dzogchen: the *Kunjed Gyalpo*, or *All-creating King*. Rendered "Supreme Source" in the present work, it is a tantra whose title comprises simultaneously the meanings of the teacher, of the primordial state communicated by the teacher to the disciple, and of the knowledge that blossoms in the latter. The choice of this text, which in its present version derives from the eighth century but whose origin may be far more ancient, is also due to its universal message, which places it among the great spiritual scriptures of all the ages, comparable to classics such as the *Bhagavad Gītā*.

The present work is structured in three parts. The first part describes the origin and basic principles of Dzogchen as stated in the traditional texts of the Dzogchen Semde, of which the *Kunjed Gyalpo* is the fundamental scripture. A large part of the material is drawn from the *Vairo Drabag* (*Bai ro 'dra 'bag*), the biography of the great Tibetan teacher and translator Vairocana, who introduced the Semde and Longde series[1] of Dzogchen from India and Oḍḍiyāna to Tibet in the eighth century. In fact, the first five chapters of this biography constitute a veritable history of the origin of Dzogchen.

The second part of this work consists exclusively of oral teachings given by Chögyal Namkhai Norbu: a brief introduction to the fundamental aspects of Tantra[2] and Dzogchen, followed by a succinct exposition of the most salient points of each of the eighty-four chapters of the *Kunjed Gyalpo*. These teachings were given by Chögyal Namkhai Norbu in Sardinia at the end of 1977 and the beginning of 1978, when he gave the transmission of and an oral commentary to this tantra. Readers who are not familiar with Tibetan Buddhism are advised to first read the chapter on "The Fundamental Principles of Tantra and of Dzogchen." However it would be useful for readers to have at least some general knowledge of Hīnayāna and Mahāyāna Buddhism.

The third and last part contains extracts from the *Kunjed Gyalpo* selected to enable readers to approach the extraordinary message of this text yet avoiding plunging them into details that are difficult to understand without a certain knowledge in the various fields within sutra and tantra. The *Kunjed Gyalpo* is a text committed to writing primarily for the benefit of Buddhist practitioners, and consequently its language and terminology are largely those of sutric and tantric Buddhism. It is important to bear this in mind while reading this text.

In all the gnostic traditions, the absolute is the equivalent of the ineffable, of that which transcends word and thought. For example, a famous invocation by Jigmed Lingpa reads that "even the Buddha's tongue is weak to explain this point [i.e., the absolute condition]."[3] This does not mean, however, that words have no value. Since ancient times, knowledge of Dzogchen has been communicated by means of three types of transmission: direct, that is, from mind to mind; symbolic, through the use of gestures, objects, or riddles; and oral, through spoken language. Nubchen Sangye Yeshe, one of the first Tibetan teachers of Dzogchen, wrote: "Just as to look for gold in the dark we need a lamp, so to discover the true meaning [of the absolute] in one's mind and to cultivate recognition of it we need the lamp of words and scriptures to shed light for us.... 'The lamp of names and of words illuminates the gold of true meaning,' states the *Supreme Peak*."[4]

This work is dedicated to the spread of the Dzogchen teachings in the West, with the hope that future generations too might have the good fortune to meet a living source of knowledge such as the teacher Chögyal Namkhai Norbu, the true Kunjed Gyalpo, has been and still is for me.

Adriano Clemente
June 1996

This edition of The Supreme Source *has been revised and partially enlarged from the original Italian edition published in 1997.*

Chögyal Namkhai Norbu
Photo by Liane Graf

Preface

The fundamental scriptures of the Dzogchen teachings are divided into three categories, called *gyüd*, *lung*, and *mennag*.

The *gyüd*, or tantras, are texts that explain the fundamental principle of the teaching of "total primordial perfection" or Ati Dzogpa Chenpo in its entirety, presenting fully the three key points of the base, the path, and the fruit.

The *lung*[5] may form part of a tantra, summarizing its essential point or emphasizing or elucidating a specific aspect in relation to the base, the path, or the fruit.

The *mennag*, or *upadeśa*, are extracts containing special instructions for practices related to the specific points of the base, the path, or the fruit of Ati Dzogpa Chenpo, in extensive or concise form, or they may be texts of instructions derived from the personal experience of realized teachers, written expressly for the benefit of future generations and marked with the seal of secrecy.

The meaning of the word "tantra" is "continuity" or "without interruption," and refers to the condition of infinite potentiality and of uninterrupted manifestation of the energy of our primordial state. The tantras are so called because their express function is to enable one, directly or indirectly, to understand clearly this natural state.

All the principal tantras were revealed in a precise, pure dimension in a particular age, or *kalpa*, by a specific manifestation of the saṃbhogakāya as a teacher who transmitted the appropriate teaching to various Vidyādharas and Siddhas at the final three levels of realization (*bhūmi*) who were present on that occasion as disciples.[6]

As regards the *Kunjed Gyalpo* in particular, the Dzogchen scriptures recount that in a place called "The Womb of Conception" (*Chags 'byung mngal gnas*), in the epoch when the average human life span was eighty thousand years, the teacher Zhönnu Rolpa Nampar Tsewa transmitted to about a thousand non-human yakṣa and rakṣasa disciples the essential teachings of the five root tantras (*rtsa rgyud*), including the *Kunjed Gyalpo*, and of the six secondary tantras (*yan lag gi rgyud*) of the Dzogchen Semde.[7] Hence, we can deduce that these teachings constituted the base of Ati Dzogpa Chenpo in remote ages.

The five root tantras of the Dzogchen Semde have been classified in diverse ways, but on examination of the contents of the various tantras, the list that seems to correspond most closely to the importance of their contents is the following:

1. *The Tantra of Bodhicitta That Is the All-creating King* (*Byang chub kyi sems kun byed rgyal po'i rgyud*).
2. *The Tantra Called "The Secret Wheel Overcoming Concepts"* (*La zlo gsang ba'i 'khor lo zhes bya ba'i rgyud*).
3. *The Great Tantra of Vajrasattva That Equals the Bounds of Space* (*rDo rje sems dpa' nam mkha'i mtha' dang mnyam pa'i rgyud chen po*).
4. *The Tantra of the Total Space of Vajrasattva* (*rDo rje sems dpa' nam mkha' che'i rgyud ces bya ba*).
5. *The Supreme Tantra of the Dimension of Total Perfection of Bodhicitta That Equals Space* (*Byang chub kyi sems rdzogs pa chen po mkha' mnyam klong gi rgyud kyi rgyal po zhes bya ba*).[8]

For each root tantra there are six secondary tantras closely tied to its contents and each secondary tantra has further subsidiary tantras. As it contains in their entirety the contents of all five root tantras of Semde and consequently constitutes their base, the *Kunjed Gyalpo* has been deemed by all the great Dzogchen teachers as the principal tantra of Semde.

Let us analyze the meaning of the name *Kunjed Gyalpo*. The literal translation, "all-creating king," is really a synonym for "Samantabhadra[9]," a term widely used in Dzogchen teachings. The first word, *Kunjed*, "all-creating" or "all-making," may lead one to think of a universal creator, an entity that generates the world through an act of will; however, it must absolutely not be interpreted in this way. Its true meaning denotes our primordial state, that by its own nature contains all the qualities of self-perfection together with the capacity to manifest them without needing to create them, nor rely on any effort. Think of a mirror: the capacity to reflect is a natural quality of the mirror itself, and it is only thanks to this condition that diverse images can appear on its surface uninterruptedly.

At a deeper level, the true meaning of the term *kun*, which means "all," is emptiness, inasmuch as the ultimate nature of all phenomena is the condition of original purity (*ka dag*), or emptiness. *Jed*, a verb meaning "to do" or "to act," refers to the natural energy of emptiness that, being endowed with movement and action, manifests as clarity (*gsal ba*), vision (*snang ba*), and pure instantaneous presence (*rig pa*). The two syllables that compose the word "kunjed" thus directly signify those characteristic principles widely indicated in Vajrayana[10] with the expressions "clarity and emptiness" (*gsal stong*), "vision and emptiness" (*snang stong*), "bliss and emptiness" (*bde stong*), and "presence and emptiness" (*rig stong*).

The term *gyalpo*, or "king," is used to denote the principal tantras, or those scriptures that expound teachings higher than those in other tantras. It signifies the principle of knowledge that corresponds to the total perfection of the primordial state or Ati Dzogpa Chenpo: our authentic, original condition.

In conclusion, as this tantra discloses the nature of Kunjed Gyalpo, the condition of the primordial state, and indicates in its entirety the path or way to realize it, it not only forms the base and root of all the Dzogchen teachings but also presents the final goal of all the paths of realization.

For these reasons, those who have the opportunity to study and reflect on this root tantra of Semde and to apply perfectly the principle of knowledge that it expounds, need do nothing more. However, in cases where this is not possible, then understanding just one part of this text will guide us surely towards authentic knowledge of Ati Dzogpa Chenpo, and consequently will be of immense benefit.

Several years ago, for the benefit of some students who showed great interest in the contents of this tantra, I gave oral explanations, dwelling on its principal points. My student Adriano Clemente, who has studied under me for a long time and has by now acquired a good measure of experience, has collected them and edited them in the form in which they are presented in this book. I am certain that they will serve to open the eyes of all those who wish to discover the state of knowledge of Kunjed Gyalpo, and I hope this may truly happen.

Chögyal Namkhai Norbu
December 1995

PART ONE

The Origin and Teachings of Dzogchen Semde

Samatabhadra
Drawing by Glenn Eddy

1 The Origin of Dzogchen: from Oḍḍiyāna to Tibet

I. THE ORIGIN OF THE TRANSMISSION OF DZOGCHEN

Dzogchen, an abbreviation of *Dzogpa Chenpo*, is a Tibetan term that means total completion, or perfection: the original state, or condition, of every living being whether or not they are aware of it. *Dzogchen* is one of the various names, and currently the best known together with *atiyoga*, or "yoga of primordial knowledge" (*gdod ma'i rnal 'byor*), of a very ancient teaching that clearly and directly communicates the nature of this original state. Examination of the literature in Tibetan currently available reveals that the Dzogchen teaching existed in Tibet at least as early as the eighth century in both its great religious traditions: Buddhism and Bön. The Dzogchen of the Buddhist tradition derives from the teacher Garab Dorje of Oḍḍiyāna, a region that many scholars have identified as the Swat valley in Pakistan, once a flourishing center of Buddhism. The Dzogchen tantras and teachings he transmitted were subsequently introduced into Tibet during the first spread of Buddhism in the eighth century, and they still form part of the canon of the Nyingma or "ancient" tradition, the *Nyingma Gyüd Bum*. Bön on the other hand had already existed for several centuries prior to the introduction of Buddhism. Although this tradition asserts that its founder, Shenrab Miwoche, who probably lived far earlier than Garab Dorje, transmitted the first Dzogchen teachings, as no written documents of sufficient antiquity are extant, it is difficult to establish the chronological precedence of the Dzogchen scriptures of Bön or of

Buddhism.[11] In any case, study of the scriptures, transmission of the teachings, and realization of the practice have continued to our own day in both traditions. Following this brief mention, let us put aside Bön Dzogchen in order to focus our attention on the origin of Dzogchen as handed down within the Buddhist tradition.

The Tibetan texts that recount the history of the Dzogchen teaching describe a threefold division in its mode of transmission: direct transmission (*dgongs brgyud*), symbolic transmission (*brda brgyud*), and oral transmission (*snyan brgyud*), respectively tied to the three *kāyas*, or fundamental dimensions of existence. These are the *dharmakāya*, or dimension of the essence; the *saṃbhogakāya*, or dimension of the richness of qualities; and the *nirmāṇakāya*, or dimension of the manifestation. Underlying these modes, and in particular the direct transmission, is the notion of an absolute reality present in every being whence the whole manifestation of saṃsāra and nirvāṇa issues forth. Concerning this, in a work on the history of Dzogchen, Chögyal Namkhai Norbu has written:

> Self-arising wisdom, the essence of all the Buddhas, exists prior to the division of saṃsāra and nirvāṇa and is beyond the limits of transmigration and liberation. As it transcends the four conceptual limits[12] and is intrinsically pure, this original condition is the uncreated nature of existence that has always existed, the ultimate nature of all phenomena. It cannot be identified with a stable and eternal substance allowing the assertion "It is thus!" and is utterly free of all the defects of dualistic thought, which is only capable of referring to an object other than itself. It is given the name ineffable and inconceivable "base of primordial purity" (*ye thog ka dag gi gzhi*), beyond the conceptual limits of being and non-being. As its essence is the purity of original emptiness, it transcends the limits of being an eternal substance: it has nothing concrete and no specific characteristics to display. As its nature is self-perfection, it transcends the limit of nothingness and non-being: the clarity of light is the pure nature of emptiness. Thus, this natural condition of primordial enlightenment, which is the immutable state of dharmakāya, does not entail subdivision into saṃsāra and nirvāṇa. Self-arising wisdom, primordially empty, is in a condition similar to space, and it pervades all beings without distinction, from glorious Samantabhadra down to the tiniest insect on a blade of grass. For this reason the total state of dharmakāya, the inseparability of the two truths, absolute and relative, is called "the primordial Buddha"....
>
> Even though in the condition of the base there is no separation or duality between saṃsāra and nirvāṇa, when its primordial

> energy manifests, it becomes the common ground of liberation and of delusion. Consequently, according to the guise it assumes, it is designated as nirvāṇa or saṃsāra, just like a vase that, even though it has no name, can be referred to in various ways according to the language one speaks.[13]

But then, one might ask, how does saṃsāra arise? How does one enter the dualistic vision that is the cause of transmigration? The text continues by explaining that:

> If, at the moment the energy of the base manifests, one does not consider it something other than oneself and one recognizes one's own state as the indivisibility of essence, nature, and potentiality of energy, the movement of energy self-liberates.... Understanding the essence that is the very nature of primordial enlightenment, one finds oneself always in this state: this is called "Samantabhadra," or "Immutable Light" (*'od mi 'gyur*), this itself is the "Primordial Lord" (*gdod ma'i mgon po*) perfect in his original condition.... Without color or form, beyond the limit of size, and transcending the duality of abode and of someone dwelling therein, it is the immutable nature of the fourth time, beyond past, present, and future, the infinite space of self-perfection endowed with the five perfect conditions for the transmission of knowledge until the end of time.[14] This is the pure dharmakāya dimension, the essence of the vajra of clear light, that also contains the dimensions of saṃbhogakāya and nirmāṇakāya.[15]

As mentioned, the principle of the three transmissions is closely connected to the three dimensions, or *kāyas*, of the state of enlightenment. In fact, as often explained in the *Kunjed Gyalpo*, it is from these three dimensions that the various types of teachings arise in congruity with the diverse capacities of beings. In particular, there is the explanation that the three series of inner tantras derive from the dharmakāya, the three series of outer tantras from the saṃbhogakāya, and the Mahāyāna and Hīnayāna sūtra teachings from the nirmāṇakāya.

For example, a *History of the Dharma* ascribed to Longchenpa states:[16]

> How does the fundamental nature manifest as pure dimension and as teacher in order to help beings? Because they do not understand the fundamental nature due to ignorance and erroneous conceptions, the beings of the three worlds accumulate actions and passions that produce various kinds of suffering. The Buddhas, who with the eye of omniscience perceive the suffering undergone by beings in the same way as a mother who loves her own son, help them with great compassion by manifesting the dimension of the body, the wisdom that abides therein, and beneficial activities... [The tantra] *The Unified State of Knowledge*[17] says:

> The wisdom of the Tathāgatas tames beings through compassion:
> From the altruistic aspiration of the three kāyas
> Are created the three pure dimensions of the enlightened ones.
> The dimension of the dharmakāya is like space,
> Its name is "total all-pervasiveness,"
> The teacher is Samantabhadra,
> Who transmits the teaching through the non-conceptual dimension and through the three inner tantras.

Furthermore:

> In the Akaniṣṭha[18] palace of [Buddha] Vairocana,
> Like a king, the saṃbhogakāya teaches the Bodhisattvas
> The three series of outer tantras: kriyā, ubhaya, and yoga,
> By means of the symbols of the manifestation it has taken on...

And further:

> South of Jambudvīpa [our world], nirmāṇakāya Śākyamuni
> Took on the form of a śrāvaka and taught various disciples
> The three sections of Sūtra, Vinaya, and Abhidharma,
> Transmitting the teaching through the three analytical vehicles.[19]

The *Vairo Drabag*, which is believed to relate an ancient tradition, speaks of the transmission of the teaching through four kāyas or dimensions: *svabhāvikakāya*, or dimension of the fundamental nature, dharmakāya, saṃbhogakāya, and the secret kāya, or dimension (*gsang ba'i sku*). However, this subdivision takes into consideration only the transmission of the Tantra and Dzogchen teachings.[20]

II. THE TWELVE PRIMORDIAL TEACHERS

The traditional texts assert that the promulgation of the Dzogchen teaching is not limited to the human world. For example, the tantra *The All-surpassing Sound* (*sGra thal 'gyur*) explains that it is found in no less than thirteen solar systems (*thal ba*) as well as our own, and describes minutely, albeit cryptically, the location of these worlds and the characteristics of the beings that inhabit them.[21] Much better known, on the other hand, is the tradition that states that Garab Dorje was preceded by twelve teachers (*ston pa bcu gnyis*), described in the texts as nirmāṇakāya manifestations of the primordial Buddha Vajradhara.[22] They lived in different times and places, from the remote epoch when the average life span was incalculable (a kind of mythical golden age) until the appearance of Śākyamuni Buddha in our Kali Yuga. Although they probably derive from a single ancient tradition, at times the lists of teachings transmitted by the twelve teachers do not concur. Moreover, some sources contain interesting details not found in others. For this reason, rather than quoting directly from one text, there follows a summary drawn from various sources which discuss this subject.[23]

1. At the time when the life span was incalculable, in the divine dimension called Gaden Tsegpa (Joyous Pagoda), all beings had bodies of light composed of the substance of the elements. They were born miraculously, did not wear clothes, and shone by their own light. To transmit the teaching to them, Buddha Vajradhara manifested as a white, eight-year-old child in the center of a golden, thousand-petalled lotus: his name was Khyeu Nangwa Samgyi Mikhyappa (Supreme Child Inconceivable Vision). On each petal of the lotus there appeared an emanation identical to the central one, and thus there formed one thousand emanations heralding the appearance of one thousand Buddhas in that fortunate kalpa. In the sky there appeared six million four hundred thousand stars heralding the appearance of an equal number of Dzogchen tantras. The seventeen stars that shone brighter than the others heralded the seventeen principal tantras.[24] To the thousand Buddhas present as disciples, he taught the tantra *The All-surpassing Sound* (*sGra thal 'gyur*) with the voice of the bird of the deities, and the two divine Bodhisattvas Nyima Rabtu Nangwa and Gajed Wangchuk gathered the teachings.

2. Gradually the life span started to diminish and the first tenuous passions arose, causing the decline of merit, and the light of beings abated day after day. Thus came the epoch when the life span was ten million years. In the dimension called *Sahā* the beings were now born from five-colored eggs composed of the substance of the elements. They were perfectly endowed with the senses and all the limbs, and were as vigorous as sixteen-year-old youths. Tall as arrows, they were dressed in leaves and surrounded by a luminous aura. They all had miraculous powers and few passions, did not encounter material obstacles, and their food was of the substance of the four elements. Buddha Khyeu Wöd Mitruppa (Child Imperturbable Light) manifested as one of them. With the voice of Viṣṇu "with five tufts," to two hundred thousand ḍākinis,[25] as a sign that in future an equal number of female beings would be liberated thanks to his teachings, he taught the five tantras of the Body, of the Voice, of the Mind, of the Qualities, and of the Activities.[26]

3. Due to the passions, the light continued to abate, and the life span shortened further to one hundred thousand years. At that time,

beings born from heat and humidity[27] fell victim to the first illnesses, caused by the imbalance of the elements, and started to eat plants. In a place called Trödsher Düpa Wödkyil Pungpa (Mass of Light that Gathers Humidity) there was born among them Buddha Jigpa Kyoppai Yid (Mind that Protects from Fear). To six hundred thousand Bodhisattvas, as a sign that in future an equal number of male beings would be liberated thanks to his teachings, he taught *The Emptying of Saṃsāra* (*'Khor ba dong sprugs*), *The Peacock's Entwined Neck* (*rMa bya mjing snol*), *The Exhaustion of the Four Elements* (*'Byung bzhi zad pa*) and other tantras, barely whispering them, like the buzzing of bees conveyed on the wind.[28]

4. The life span became even shorter, and the passions were becoming ever stronger. Beings' bodies lost their light and thus the sun and the moon appeared. When the average life span had become eighty thousand years, because of desire and attachment the sexual organs sprouted forth: at first, looking at each other was enough to satisfy desire, then it became necessary to hold each other's hands, and finally beings coupled and procreated. Hence beings started to dress in cotton or in tree-bark and to eat the fat of the earth;[29] however, their avarice was such that after a while it was all consumed. So they started to eat rice, but since the feeling of I and mine became ever stronger, hatred and pride caused even this food to disappear. In that epoch, in the place called Chagjung Ngaldu Nangwa (Apparition in the Womb of Conception) Buddha Zhönnu Rolpa Nampar Tsewa (Young Manifestation of Compassion) was born from the uterus, like everybody else, in the form of a ten-year-old child. To one thousand yakṣas he taught eleven tantras: the five root tantras and six secondary tantras of Semde.[30]

5. When the average life span became sixty thousand years, in the dimension of the Thirty-three Gods, the Buddha Sixth Vajradhara was born as a divine Bodhisattva. In the enchanting garden of the Young Doctor ('Tsho byed gzhon nu) he transmitted to the seven heroic Buddhas of our epoch[31] teachings on the six, three, and eighteen pāramitās that embraced methods both with and without effort, including the tantras of Dzogpa Chenpo. After having remained among the devas for seventy-five years he left his testament to his disciple Norzang and entered parinirvāṇa where he was absorbed in samādhi for seven thousand years.

6. After seven thousand years he reawakened, and moved by compassion towards beings, he was reborn as the son of a yakṣa and a fierce *ḍākinī* in the dimension of the Cemetery of the Secret Manifestation in

the terrifying place of the yakṣas northeast of Mount Meru.[32] It was the epoch when the average life span was sixty thousand years. He had the appearance of a frightful dwarf with three faces and six hands that held the worlds of the six classes of beings,[33] and his name was Zhönnu Pawo Tobden (Young Powerful Hero). He taught to the seven Bodhisattvas "having the force of clouds" (so called because they listened immersed to the navel in clouds) and to countless ḍākinīs, devas, and nāgas the *Tantra of the Spontaneous State of Pure Presence* (*Rig pa rang shar*) and other tantras.[34] He remained among them for a thousand years, and after having left his testament to the yakṣa Legchöd,[35] he entered parinirvāṇa. He remained in samādhi for one hundred thousand years.

7. When the average life span had become ten thousand years, he reawakened from his samādhi and was reborn in the dimension of the rākṣasas on earth in a place to the west where there were many Bodhisattvas. He was called Trangsong Tröpai Gyalpo (Wise Wrathful King) and in the cave that spontaneously radiated the sound "rulu" he transmitted to ten million rākṣasas the "ten tantras to subjugate gross negativities" and other teachings.[36] He left no testament, and at the end of his life he became reabsorbed in samādhi. He remained so for fifty thousand years.

8. Then the average life span became five thousand years, and in the place on this earth called Vulture Peak he was reborn in a royal family and was named Ser Wöd Tampa (Supreme Golden Light). At the age of twenty-five, before a *stūpa* he cut his own hair, taking the vows by himself. Then he transmitted the Vinaya[37] and Prajñāpāramitā teachings to countless śrāvakas.

9. When the average life span became one thousand years, in the land called Yui Minmachen (With Turquoise Eyebrows) in northern Mongolia, near a bodhi tree[38] that had grown next to a self-arisen stūpa, Tsewe Rolpai Lodrö (Intelligence Manifestation of Compassion) was born. To his disciples—countless Bodhisattvas that had achieved the eighth bhūmi,[39]—he transmitted the "seven special tantras," including *The All-creating King* (*Kun byed rgyal po*) and *Total Space* (*Nam mkha' che*).[40] He remained there one hundred and twenty years.

10. When the average life span became five hundred years, from the world of the Thirty-three Gods, Buddha Kāśyapa the Elder chose to take birth in the human world to alleviate the suffering of old age.

So in the place called Vulture Peak, he gave many teachings, including the anuyoga scriptures,[41] to seven disciples who had taken on the form of arhats. He remained there seventy-five years and then went to practice asceticism, remaining in the lotus posture for seven years. At the end of his life he left no mortal remains, dissolving into a body of light. He left his testament to the brahmin Gön Sem.

11. When the average life span became three hundred years Buddha Ngöndzog Gyalpo (Perfected King), the son of a brahmin expert in the Vedas, was born at Vajrāsana (Bodhgaya). To the Bodhisattvas Mañjuśrī, Avalokiteśvara, and Vajrapāṇi and to other disciples he transmitted all the teachings regarding the real condition and other tantras.[42] After having taught for twenty-five years, he entered parinirvāṇa manifesting the ordinary signs of death in order to display to his disciples of lower capacity the truth of the suffering of birth, old age, sickness, and death.

12. When the average life span became one hundred years, Buddha Śākyamuni was born as the son of King Śuddhodana. At Varanasi and other places he taught the four noble truths and the diverse gradual paths and accomplished twelve great deeds.[43]

In this way the primordial Buddha took on twelve forms in order to transmit the teaching in accordance with the infinite conditions and capacities of beings.

III. GARAB DORJE

Garab Dorje is the teacher who transmitted the teachings and tantras of Dzogchen currently available to us. All the sources unanimously declare that he was born after Buddha Śākyamuni's parinirvāṇa, or final passing, although they do not agree on the precise date. In any case, the majority set this great teacher's birth about three hundred and sixty years after the Buddha's death, in the second century B.C.E.[44] However, if we accept the tradition which asserts that Garab Dorje's first disciple, Mañjuśrīmitra, was a pandit at the Buddhist university of Nālandā expert in the field of Yogācāra or Cittamātra philosophy, then the most likely hypothesis is that they met no earlier than the fourth or fifth century C.E.[45] In any case, he lived in an age when Mahāyāna Buddhism was already developed and widely promulgated. His message aimed at enabling people to understand the ultimate meaning of the Buddha's teaching, both sūtras and tantras, centered on the recognition of the true nature of existence beyond the principle of cause and effect, only attainable by means of the path free of effort characteristic of Dzogchen atiyoga.

In Dzogchen there are two different lineages that, starting from Garab Dorje, reach Śrī Siṃha, the teacher of the eighth-century Tibetan translator Vairocana. These are the Semde lineage, which counts over twenty teachers from Mañjuśrīmitra to Śrī Siṃha and then on to Vimalamitra, and the Longde and Mennagde lineage, which from Mañjuśrīmitra directly reaches Śrī Siṃha.[46]

The Semde lineage is of particular interest for historical research, because most of the teachers listed come from Oḍḍiyāna, the birthplace of Dzogchen and many other tantric cycles. The lineage also includes the famous teacher and philosopher Nāgārjuna (c. second century C.E.), but we can do no more than repeat the traditional version.

Let us return to Garab Dorje, whose original name (presumably in the language of Oḍḍiyāna) according to some sources was Vajra Prahe.[47] His biography is found in diverse Tibetan texts, some of which, particularly those belonging to the Mennagde tradition, have already appeared in English.[48] The version given below, which diverges from the others in certain details, is based instead on the Semde tradition as related in the *Vairo Drabag*.[49] As in the case of all nirmāṇakāyas, or realized teachers, who elect voluntarily to reincarnate for the benefit of beings, the narration of Garab Dorje's deeds starts in another dimension, in the celestial abode of the Thirty-three Gods.

In the abode of the Thirty-three Gods, the deva Zangkyong had five hundred and one sons, among whom Kunga Nyingpo was celebrated for his physical ability and intelligence. While the other children passed their time playing, singing, and dancing in the parks, Kunga Nyingpo preferred to sit alone in a retreat hut practicing the "vajra recitation."[50] Thus he became known as Lhai Sempa Lhagchen (Divine Son with Superior Mind), contracted to Sem Lhagchen. In the "month of miracles" (the first month) of the female water bull year, he had marvellous dreams that predicted the appearance of the teaching "beyond effort," that he would attain complete realization and in future would be reborn in the human world as regent of all the Buddhas. When the king of the devas came to know of this, he implored the Buddhas to promulgate the teaching "beyond effort," reminding them that until that moment, only the teachings that required effort had been transmitted. Moved to compassion, the Buddhas of the ten directions gathered like clouds in the sky and in unison asked Vajrasattva to impart the teaching. From his heart Vajrasattva emanated Vajrapāṇi, and consigning to him a flaming wheel made of precious materials exhorted him thus:

> The secret meaning of non-dual wisdom
> Is primordial enlightenment beyond action and effort.
> The right path of the great "middle way"
> Is what you will have to teach!

Vajrapāṇi promised to fulfil his task and answered:

> The total space of Vajrasattva
> That cannot be expressed in words
> Will be difficult for me to explain.
> But for the good of those who do not know it
> I will seek to indicate it in words
> So that they might understand it!

Then Vajrapāṇi went to the Tathāgatas of the five families to resolve his last doubts concerning the base and the fruit.[51] First, he headed east, where Buddha Dorje Sangwa of the Vajra (Indestructible)[52] family was teaching a tantra to a retinue of disciples inseparable from himself, and asked him:

> If the nature of mind is like the vajra
> Whence do birth and cessation arise?

Dorje Sangwa answered:

> In the immutable vajra of the nature of mind
> Neither birth nor cessation exists.
> Birth and cessation derive from dualistic thought!

Then Vajrapāṇi went south to Buddha Rinchen Zhab of the Ratna (Jewel) family and asked him:

> If the nature of bodhicitta
> Is not produced through the effort of causes and conditions,
> How can the fruit of the qualities manifest?

Rinchen Zhab answered:

> Just like the *dagshaka* jewel,
> Cause and effect are self-perfected in the primordial base:
> All is self-arising in the supreme essence.
> If you understand its secret,
> The manifestation of the fruit is like the rays of the sun!

Then he went west to Buddha Padmai Wöd of the Padma (Lotus) family and asked him:

If the nature of mind is pure as a lotus
Whence do the impurities of the dualism of subject and object arise?

Padmai Wöd answered:

Just as a lotus growing in the mud
Is not sullied by dirt,
The essence of bodhicitta
Is not defiled by saṃsāra:
Saṃsāra derives from dualistic thought!

Then he went north to Buddha Trubpa Nangwa of the Karma (Activity) family and asked him:

If the nature of mind is beyond effort,
How can one act for the benefit of others?

Trubpa Nangwa answered:

If you understand self-arising wisdom
Beneficent acts arise spontaneously!

Finally Vajrapāṇi arrived at the center. As soon as he saw him, Buddha Vairocana of the Tathāgata family exhorted him to realize the meaning of secret wisdom. When Vajrapāṇi asked him to explain this meaning to him Vairocana said:

Listen, Sattvavajra!
The nature of secret wisdom
Is the non-duality of Buddhas and sentient beings.
Like the sky, it pervades everything.
There is no distinction between ignorance and wisdom.
Understanding and not understanding are a single path.
The essence of secret wisdom
Is the purity of the clear light of presence,
It is the thought that abides in the state of wisdom,
It is the precious treasure of the spontaneous, original condition.
The self-arising state, without needing to seek it, has always been pure.
Secret wisdom manifests in the variety of phenomena,
But it cannot be identified with concepts.
If the meaning of self-perfection of the magical apparition
Is always clear beyond concepts—this is the view!

So after having obtained the essence of the atiyoga teaching "beyond effort," Vajrapāṇi went to the world of the Thirty-three Gods and conferred on Sem Lhagchen all the empowerments (or initiations) and transmissions of Dzogchen, crowning him "regent" of the Buddhas. In this way the teaching was promulgated in the world of the devas.[53]

The *Vairo Drabag* proceeds with the narration of the birth of Garab Dorje on earth and then recounts his encounter with his first predestined disciple, pandit Mañjuśrīmitra.

This is the story of how the teaching "beyond effort" was promulgated in the human world. In the land of Oḍḍiyāna, northwest of India, in the Dhanakosha region on the banks of Lake Kutra, King Dhahenatalo lived in Dorje Lingphug. His son was called Thuwo Rājahati. He also had a daughter called Barani[54] who was endowed with all the desirable qualities, of pure mind, and sincerely dedicated to the altruistic aspiration to enlightenment. Free of defects and of malice, she renounced the world and received the vows of a *bhikṣuṇī* (Buddhist nun) which she scrupulously observed. Having forsaken male company, she lived with five hundred nuns. In the female wood bull year at dawn on the eighth day of the first summer month, she dreamed that all the Tathāgatas emanated a light that all at once took the form of a sun and a moon. The sun penetrated her head and dissolved downwards, while the moon penetrated her feet and dissolved upwards. In the morning, absorbed in thought she went to bathe in the lake, and while immersed in the water, looked eastwards. At that moment Vajrapāṇi transformed himself into a golden-colored duck while Sem Lhagchen became absorbed in the letter *HŪṂ*. Then he emanated four more ducks, and together with them, dove into the water. Immediately afterwards, the four ducks flew up returning to the sky, while Vajrapāṇi, in the form of a duck, approached the princess, pecked her lightly three times upon the breast so that she was penetrated by a luminous *HŪṂ*, then flew away and disappeared. The princess was very amazed and revealed her dream and the episode with the duck to the king and his court. Her father explained that it heralded the appearance of the emanation of a Buddha. After nine months had elapsed, a nine-pronged vajra made of precious materials emerged from the princess's breast. When the vajra opened it gave birth to an extraordinary child holding a vajra in his right hand and a scepter made of precious stones in his left, who recited *The Total Space of Vajrasattva* and other texts. While everybody was rejoicing, the brahmin expert in examining signs predicted that the child would become a nirmāṇakāya teacher of the supreme vehicle and named him Garab Dorje.

As a child Garab Dorje displayed his mastery in games and sporting contests. Some time passed, and shortly before he was to accede to the rule of the kingdom, Vajrapāṇi appeared to him, conferring on him the Dzogchen empowerments, consigning to him all the scriptures, and enjoining all the guardians of the teaching to protect him.[55] Thus, Garab Dorje instantaneously and effortlessly realized the state of enlightenment of "total perfection," essence of the Buddhas of the three times. As well as understanding perfectly all the teachings based on cause and effect, he realized the meaning of all the root tantras of Dzogchen transmitted by Samantabhadra and the secondary scriptures. At this time he started to teach and to transmit the empowerments of Dzogchen to special disciples.[56]

IV. MAÑJUŚRĪMITRA

At that time there was a brahmin who was an emanation of Mañjuśrī, whose name was Nyingpo Drubpa, the son of Palden Dekyong and of Kuhana. He was a bhikṣu learned in the five branches of knowledge[57] and in all the teachings based on cause and effect, and was the foremost among the five hundred pandits of that age. When he heard that the nirmāṇakāya Garab Dorje was transmitting a teaching that transcended effort and the principle of cause and effect, Mañjuśrī appeared to him and said, "In the land of Oḍḍiyāna to the northwest, at Dorje Lingphug, in the region of Dhanakośa on the banks of Lake Kutra near the great cemetery Serling Hechen Dalwa there is the nirmāṇakāya Garab Dorje. He is an emanation of Vajrasattva, who all the Buddhas have empowered as a lamp of the teaching beyond effort. His marvellous teachings called atiyoga can bestow the opportunity to attain enlightenment effortlessly and instantaneously. Go to him and collect his teachings!"

In the meantime, the other pandits, who were convinced that there could not be a teaching superior to the one based on cause and effect, had decided to confute Garab Dorje to make evident his heresy. Nyingpo Drubpa, who secretly wished to display the teacher's eminence, feigned agreement. When the pandits met to decide who was to depart for Oḍḍiyāna, many complained about the long distance and the difficulties of the journey, so that only seven volunteered and set off on the journey, headed by Nyingpo Drubpa.

When they reached Dorje Lingphug, the seven pandits started to praise the excellence of the teaching of cause and effect and to debate upon the three piṭakas,[58] but they could not defeat Garab Dorje. The discussion then moved on to the inner and outer Mantrayāna vehicles, but in this case too, the pandits could not match Garab Dorje's knowledge. Finally, the pandits upheld the position of the causal vehicles, while Garab Dorje maintained the view of atiyoga beyond cause and effect, and they were not able to refute him. At this point, Nyingpo Drubpa consulted the other pandits to discover if they wished to ask Garab Dorje for teachings. Some said they felt remorse for having sought to confute him, while others, though they wished to do so, did not have the courage to make this request. So they decided first of all to confess their negative deed. They went to the teacher, prostrated at his feet, and circumambulated him. Nyingpo Drubpa, who regretted having dared to debate with the teacher, burst into tears and was preparing to cut off his tongue to atone for his transgression. But Garab Dorje read his thoughts and spoke thus in his sacred voice:

> The total bliss of self-perfection, equality beyond the limits of a school,
> Is the essence of the bodhi of all phenomena.
> However, beings of the six worlds perceive it as an object and are conditioned by attachment,
> The mutegpas[59] confine it within a limit and uphold the mistaken concepts of eternalism and nihilism,
> While the eight Buddhist vehicles have a dualistic view of it.
> Getting attached to their own partial views
> And dividing and limiting the dimension of equality,
> They disdain what they already have and seek something else.
> They neglect the natural state and then try to obtain it through effort.
> Even though they already possess enlightenment, they turn it into something conditioned by time.
> They do not understand equality and uphold the partial view
> To which they are attached with all their might: how pitiable they are!
> So liberate yourselves from the poison of attachment and from sectarian views
> And enter the path of equality, beyond the limits of a school!

Then he continued, saying: "Nyingpo Drubpa, cutting off your tongue will not serve to purify your negative deed. If you wish to atone for your transgression, write a book on the teaching that transcends the law of cause and effect!"

Subsequently, when the other less fortunate pandits had left, Garab Dorje transmitted knowledge to Nyingpo Drubpa through symbols, and he instantaneously achieved perfect understanding. Nevertheless, in order to entrust to him the totality of the teachings, Garab Dorje conferred on him the complete empowerment of Dzogchen and transmitted to him all the scriptures contained in the twenty thousand sections pertaining to the Nine Spaces,[60] giving him the name Mañjuśrīmitra. In conclusion, Garab Dorje summarized the essence for him in the following words:

> The nature of mind is the original Buddha,
> Without birth and cessation, like the sky!
> When you understand that all phenomena are equality beyond birth and cessation,
> Meditating means letting this condition be as it is, without seeking!

Then Mañjuśrīmitra gained perfect understanding of the meaning of the primordial state and expressed his realization thus:

> I am Mañjuśrīmitra
> Who has obtained the siddhi of Yamāntaka![61]
> Having understood the complete equality of saṃsāra and nirvāṇa,
> The wisdom of omniscience has arisen in me!

Then he wrote *The Bodhicitta of Pure Gold*[62] and collected all of Garab Dorje's teachings.[63]

As we have just read, the *Vairo Drabag* mentions that Garab Dorje transmitted knowledge to Mañjuśrīmitra through symbols, what is known as "symbolic transmission" (*brda brgyud*). Another account of Mañjuśrīmitra's meeting with his teacher, drawn from the *Dorje Sampa* or "Vajra Bridge" tradition of the Dzogchen Longde[64] recounts in detail the way this transmission took place.

Wondering whether a method existed that could enable one to understand instantaneously the ultimate nature of phenomena and attain enlightenment in a single lifetime, Mañjuśrīmitra decided to consult the pandits of the University of Nālandā. The pandits learned in the philosophy of the sūtras did not utter a word, but the experts in Mantrayāna answered: "Here there is nobody who has realized the ultimate nature of phenomena, but to the west in Oḍḍiyāna in the region of Dhanakośa on the banks of a lake there is a great cemetery called Serling Hechen Dal. Living in a retreat cave there called Sergyi Traphug Yuwachen, is the teacher Garab Dorje, also known as Semdag Lhai Pu (Divine Son of Pure Mind). His body is visible but intangible. He alone knows the method that grants understanding of the ultimate nature instantaneously and the attainment of enlightenment in a single life." Then Mañjuśrīmitra asked, "Is it difficult to get there?" They answered, "It is an extremely arduous journey that takes thirteen months.

Furthermore, the route is beset by traps laid by evil ḍākinīs and yakṣas, and inhabited by wild beasts and poisonous snakes. Were it not for these risks, we too would go there!" But Mañjuśrīmitra thought: "Even if I encounter obstacles such that I lose my life, it is not important: by offering my mind to the teacher, I will receive nothing but blessings. I have no doubts, I will go!"

Having set off, he did not encounter any dangers and after thirteen months he reached his destination safe and sound. He found himself in a place full of rocks and wild beasts. Here he saw a man in monk's robes with his long hair bound on top of his head, holding a bow and five arrows. Immediately he thought, "He must be the teacher, nobody else could possibly live in this place." Having no doubts in this regard, he offered him a maṇḍala of gold, prostrated at his feet three times, and circumambulated him seven times. Then he asked him, "I beseech you to awaken in me the knowledge you possess!" The teacher remained silent. Mañjuśrīmitra asked him again twice more, but the teacher left without answering. Ardently wishing to receive the teachings, he did not get discouraged and followed him to the great cemetery. There he continued offering him a maṇḍala three times every day and three times every night, prostrating and circumambulating, and every month he repeated the same request, but the teacher remained silent. After thirteen months had passed in this way, Mañjuśrīmitra thought: "I am certain the teacher does not want to accept me," and overcome by desperation, he pulled out his razor, convinced that it was better to cut his throat and die than to be denied the teachings. That very moment the teacher called him in a loud voice. When Mañjuśrīmitra appeared before him, the teacher asked: "What is it you want?" "I wish to understand the ultimate nature instantaneously and to attain enlightenment in a single life!" he answered. "Haven't you understood yet?" "No!" answered Mañjuśrīmitra. Then Garab Dorje pronounced the symbolic syllables *A HA HO YE*,[65] and for seven days their natural sound continued without interruption. Mañjuśrīmitra understood: "This means that primordial purity is unborn, uninterrupted, and non-dual." Then Garab Dorje pronounced *SURYADHARA* and intuitively Mañjuśrīmitra understood that it meant: "Turn your gaze towards the sun!" Gazing at the luminous disc, he understood that the sun is beyond the three times and transcends the limits of rising and setting, shining and fading, because it is always unchanging: thus he realized that just this is the true nature of self-perfection that everybody has. Because of these symbols, in that very moment, Mañjuśrīmitra realized the supreme siddhi and consequently obtained the ordinary ones.[66]

In conclusion, it is worth mentioning that according to the *Vairo Drabag,* the other lineage teachers who saw and heard Garab Dorje teach during his lifetime were King Dhahenatalo, Prince Thuwo Rājahati, Princess Barani, Lui Gyalpo Jogpo, Nödjingmo Changchubma, and the first Kukurāja.

V. THE LINEAGE OF TEACHERS FROM OḌḌIYĀNA AND INDIA

The *Vairo Drabag* narrates pithy biographies for each teacher from Oḍḍiyāna and India of the Dzogchen Semde lineage, up to Śrī Siṃha and Vimalamitra, and also gives the essential teachings that awoke ultimate understanding in them together with the songs with which they expressed their realization, translated in their entirety below.[67]

1. Dhahenatalo

King Dhahenatalo was the son of King Helubhadhe and of the brahmin lady Tsönden. He was a direct disciple of nirmāṇakāya Garab Dorje from whom he received the essence. He then asked Mañjuśrīmitra for the complete teachings. Mañjuśrīmitra summarized their essential meaning for him thus:

> Bodhicitta is the five great elements.
> It is space, which does not manifest, but is all pervading;
> It is the wisdom of earth that perfects the mind as Buddha;
> It is the wisdom of water that washes away the traces of thoughts;
> It is the wisdom of fire that burns the concepts of subject and object;
> It is the wisdom of air that makes one proceed without moving a step.
> The ultimate nature of mind manifests in the five elements.
> If you understand that there is no dualism between mind and the elements,
> Do not correct your meditation, let everything arise and abate by itself!

Then King Dhahenatalo perfectly understood the meaning of the primordial state and expressed his realization thus:

> I am Dhahenatalo.
> My mind is like celestial space;
> Celestial space has no center or border;

Bodhicitta has no center or border.
Meditating means being undistracted
In the ultimate nature that knows no center or border.

In this way he realized the essence and obtained the power of longevity.

2. Thuwo Rājahati

Prince Thuwo Rājahati (or Rājahasti), the son of King Dhahenatalo and of Queen Tsöngyal, received the transmission of the essence from nirmāṇakāya Garab Dorje. He then asked his father for the complete teachings. King Dhahenatalo summarized their essential meaning for him thus:

Bodhicitta is the Buddhas of the three times:
Buddhas of the past were born from it;
Buddhas of the present abide in it;
Buddhas of the future will be enlightened in it.
The state of the Buddhas of the three times is one's own mind.

Then Prince Thuwo Rājahati perfectly understood the meaning of the primordial state and expressed his realization thus:

I am Prince Thuwo Rājahati.
Understanding that bodhicitta is pure presence that has no origin,
I have become the holder of the transmission of Samantabhadra Vajrasattva.
Without undertaking the path, I have attained simultaneously the three levels of enlightenment.[68]
My state is equal to that of the Buddhas of the three times!

3. Barani

Princess Barani[69] received the transmission of the essence from nirmāṇakāya Garab Dorje. Then she asked her brother, Thuwo Rājahati, for the complete teachings. Thuwo Rājahati summarized their essential meaning for her thus:

Not being composed of aggregates, mind neither develops nor declines;
Neither being born nor dying, it cannot be killed or split up.
As everything is ultimately nothing but mind, its very nature is dharmakāya:
If you understand, this is the state of enlightenment!

Then Princess Barani perfectly understood the meaning of the primordial state and expressed her realization thus:

I am Princess Barani.
Bodhicitta is without the duality of arising and ceasing.
Understanding that my mind is beyond arising and ceasing,
In it I have found the state of the Buddhas of the three times.
In the dimension of knowledge, the limits of union and separation do not exist!

4. Nāgarāja

Lui Gyalpo Gawo (Lui Gyalpo Jogpo) was the emanation of a Bodhisattva who lived among the nāgas,[70] operating for their benefit. When he learned that the marvellous Dzogpa Chenpo, essence of all the teachings, had appeared in the human world, he reincarnated. His father, Apardharmujñāna, was a *cāṇḍāla*, or outcaste, his mother's name was Gyatso. Lui Gyalpo (Nāgarāja) met Garab Dorje while the latter was still alive and obtained the ripening empowerments[71] from Prince Thuwo Rājahati. Then he asked Princess Barani for the essence of the teachings. She summarized their essential meaning for him thus:

Joyfully delight in the uninterrupted vision of the objects of the six senses!
Whatever you enjoy, bodhi will blaze more and more.
When one has obtained the power of supreme presence and become familiar with it,
Meditating means leaving the six sense consciousnesses free and relaxed!

Then Lui Gyalpo perfectly understood the meaning of the primordial state and expressed his realization thus:

I am Lugyal Gawo.
Without needing to be forsaken, the emotions are the five great wisdoms.[72]
Without needing to be removed, the three poisons[73] are the perfection of Body, Voice and Mind.
Without needing to be eliminated, saṃsāra is the path that leads to the bliss of bodhi.
Thus has the state of knowledge of the Buddhas of the three times arisen in me.

5. Nödjyinmo Changchubma

Nödjyinmo Changchubma,[74] the daughter of King Sidsung, was endowed with all desirable qualities, great faith, and wisdom. She asked Lui Gyalpo Gawo for the essence of the teachings. He summarized them for her thus:

Bodhicitta is the victory banner that never wanes.
As it does not change in the three times, it is indestructible,

As it wins the war against saṃsāra, it is the victory banner.
If you understand, this is supreme knowledge!

Then Nödjyinmo Changchubma perfectly understood the meaning of the primordial state and expressed her realization thus:

I am Nödjyinmo Changchubma.
Enlightened from the origin,
Mind itself is Bhagavan, the great spontaneously-arising state:
Saṃsāra has always been utterly pure.
Understanding mind, I have discovered the state of enlightenment!

6. Metsongma Parani

The father of the prostitute (Metsongma) Parani[75] was a *śūdra*[76] named Bhahuta, her mother was Gaden Dhari. Endowed with wisdom and keen intelligence, fully qualified for the Great Vehicle, she asked Nödjyinmo Changchubma for the essence of the teachings, who summarized them for her thus:

From the origin, there is no duality between Buddhas and sentient beings.
If you understand, this is supreme knowledge.
Realize that your non-dual mind is dharmakāya.
Apart from this there is no other meditation!

Then Metsongma (Parani) perfectly understood the meaning of the primordial state and expressed her realization thus:

I am the prostitute Parani.
As mind is neither male nor female,
When one understands bodhicitta, the supreme view,
Sexual union does not disturb its nature.
As mind is beyond birth and death, even if you kill it, it does not die.[77]
As all of existence is nectar, from the beginning there is no place for purity and impurity!

7. Khenpo Rabnang

The Kashmiri Khenpo Rabnang,[78] son of King Bhibhi Rahula of Kashmir and of Śila Kumāra, was the most learned pandit of his country. He asked Metsongma Parani for the essence of the teachings. She summarized them for him thus:

Bodhicitta is the fruit that does not derive from a cause;
Bodhicitta is the secret instruction that does not derive from the scriptures;

Bodhicitta is enlightenment that does not stem from the mind;
Bodhicitta is space that does not manifest visibly.
As it has no color, it cannot be pointed to saying: "Here it is!"

Then Rabnang perfectly understood the meaning of the primordial state and expressed his realization thus:

I am Khenpo Rabnang.
From the great emptiness of the nature of mind
Arise all animate and inanimate phenomena,
Nevertheless, mind does not increase nor diminish.
I have understood that great dharmakāya is the spontaneous arising and abating of phenomena!

8. Khenpo Mahārāja

Khenpo Mahārāja[79] was born in Oḍḍiyāna; his father was Śrīrāja and his mother was Tragden. At Torchogchen in Oḍḍiyāna he became a great khenpo learned in all five branches of knowledge. As he aspired after the essential meaning he asked the Kashmiri Khenpo Rabnang for the essence of the teachings. Khenpo Rabnang summarized their entirety for him thus:

The nature of mind is enlightened from the beginning,
There is nothing else on which to meditate.
Yet, one cannot understand this "object of meditation" with the intellect;
Meditating means not being distracted from the nature of mind!

Then Mahārāja, the khenpo of Oḍḍiyāna, perfectly understood the meaning of the primordial state and expressed his realization thus:

I am Mahārāja!
Meditating on mind, I have transcended the object of meditation.
Scrutinizing the mind, one sees nothing.
But precisely perceiving this "nothing to see" is "seeing."
Meditating means not being distracted from the meaning of "nothing to see"!

9. Gomadevī

Princess Gomadevī, endowed with all the desirable qualities, strongly sought the essential meaning and asked the Khenpo of Oḍḍiyāna, Mahārāja, for the essence of the teachings. He summarized their entirety for her thus:

The state of the single sphere is beyond the three times and the duality of union and separation,

The state of single self-liberation is beyond treading a gradual path,
The ultimate nature is not the object of experience and cannot be bound within the limits of words.
When one understands "limitlessness" one transcends the object of meditation!

Then Princess Gomadevī perfectly understood the meaning of the primordial state and expressed her realization thus:

I am Gomadevī.
The five aggregates are the five Tathāgatas
And the five elements are their consorts,
The spheres of sense perception are the male and female Bodhisattvas,
The ground-consciousness is Samantabhadrī,
The mental consciousness is Samantabhadra.[80]
This is the siddhi of the non-duality of the male and female deities!

10. Atsantra Āloke

Atsantra Āloke,[81] the son of Rishi Paratsa and of Zhönnu Dejed, had deep knowledge of the teachings based on cause and effect. Aspiring ardently after the essential meaning, he asked Princess Gomadevī for the essence of the teachings. She summarized their entirety for him thus:

Aspiring after the levels of realization and liberation means deviating from bodhi,
Aspiring to obtain happiness is the great suffering,
Aspiring to attain the state beyond thought is another thought:
If you understand this, do not seek anything else!

Then Atsantra Āloke perfectly understood the meaning of the primordial state and expressed his realization thus:

I am Atsantra Āloke!
Having perfectly mastered the method of "elimination," I have interrupted the flow of birth.
Having perfectly mastered the method of "union," I have severed the limit of cessation.
Having perfectly mastered the method of beneficial deeds, I have realized the absence of effort.
Having perfectly mastered the method of the siddhis, I no longer depend on the outside.
Having perfectly mastered the method of meditation, I remain in my state without correcting it!

11. The First Kukurāja

The First Kukurāja, Lord of Dogs, whose father was Kukurāja Gatu and whose mother was Dawa Dachen, was a bhikṣu learned in the five branches of knowledge and particularly expert in the eighteen mahāyoga tantras of Mantrayāna. Aspiring after the essential meaning, he asked Atsantra Āloke for the essence of the teachings. The latter summarized them for him thus:

> It is thought that creates the duality of mind and object;
> It is wisdom that perceives them as non-dual.
> Meditation means understanding there is nothing to enter into or to exit from.
> Not grasping what appears is the state of self-liberation!

Kukurāja perceived without any shadow of doubt the state of self-liberation of his mind and of all the phenomena of vision. Then he perfectly understood the meaning of the primordial state and expressed his realization thus:

> I am Kukurāja!
> Being without birth or death, mind itself is Vajrasattva.
> The dimension of Vajrasattva's body pervades the whole universe
> And not even the sky can be an example of it.
> Meditating means not being distracted from this understanding!

12. Rishi Bhashita

Rishi Bhashita,[82] whose father was Rishi Kumāra and mother Dzinma, was expert in the seven divisions of the Vedas. Wanting to perfect his wisdom and aspiring after the essential meaning, he asked the "Lord of Dogs" Kukurāja for the essence of the teachings. Kukurāja summarized their entirety for him thus:

> Bodhicitta beyond arising and ceasing
> Is vision that appears even though it has no self-nature.
> Bodhicitta beyond meditation
> Is the perfect conduct of the yogin who rests in bliss!

Rishi Bhashita perceived the nature of "absence of effort" of his mind. Then he perfectly understood the meaning of the primordial state and expressed his realization thus:

> I am Rishi Bhashita!
> The five elements are perfectly contained in the dimension of space,

> The nine vehicles have their root in atiyoga,
> The Buddhas of the three times have their root in bodhicitta.
> Understanding bodhicitta is enlightenment, total perfection.
> Thus the nature of mind is Buddha, beyond all efforts.
> Having neither center nor border, it is all pervading.
> Not subject to birth and cessation, it is the great siddhi:
> There is no other "ultimate nature" on which to meditate!

13. Metsongma Dagnyidma

The prostitute (Metsongma) Dagnyidma,[83] intuiting that all the phenomena of existence abide in the deep womb of the Mother,[84] aspired after the essential meaning, so she asked Rishi Bhashita for the essence of the teachings. He summarized their entirety for her thus:

> Not thinking of anything at all
> Is to understand the great discriminating wisdom.
> Not grasping anything with concepts
> Is the sign of having realized meditation!

Then Dagnyidma perfectly understood the meaning of the primordial state and expressed her realization thus:

> I am the prostitute Dagnyidma!
> The sky of the five elements, consorts of the five Tathāgatas,
> Is itself the dimension of Samantabhadrī,
> The universal ground is Samantabhadrī.
> Understanding it, one discovers it is inseparable from space.
> Bodhicitta is like the sun rising in space:
> Understanding the nature of mind is the best meditation!

14. Nāgārjuna

Nāgārjuna, a bhikṣu learned in the five branches of knowledge, had absorbed the three piṭakas and also knew perfectly many teachings "of the fruit" of Guhyamantra. He was seeking the ultimate meaning of total perfection beyond effort, so when he met bhikṣuṇī Dagnyidma he asked her for the essence of the teachings. With these words Dagnyidma summarized their entirety for him:

> Analyzing, even analyzing emptiness, is nevertheless still illusion.
> Getting attached, even getting attached to a deity, is slavery.
> Thinking, even thinking of dharmakāya, is judging.
> Meditating, even meditating on the absence of thought, is conceptualizing!

Then Nāgārjuna perfectly understood the meaning of the primordial state and expressed his realization thus:

I am Nāgārjuna!
Beginningless dharmakāya, not being composed of aggregates, is happiness.
The voice that is without interruption and transcends the very concept of "voice," not having material characteristics, is happiness.
The mind of wisdom that transcends the very concept of "mind," not having either birth nor death, is happiness.
I have understood that bodhicitta is total bliss!

15. The Second Kukurāja

The Second Kukurāja, whose father was Gyuhenagatama and mother Mahintsarma, was a khenpo endowed with great faith and wisdom, expert in all the teachings based on cause and effect. Aspiring after the essential meaning, he asked Nāgārjuna for the essence of the teachings. Nāgārjuna summarized their entirety for him thus:

Emptiness is the absence of the dualism of subject and object,
Understanding is simultaneous with the dissolution of names and definitions.
If it is not conceptualized, this state is emptiness:
Abiding in it is meditation on emptiness!

Then the Second Kukurāja perfectly understood the meaning of the primordial state and expressed his realization thus:

I am Khenpo Dhahuna!
I have understood that the five aggregates and the five elements
Are the male and female deities of the various families in union.
Their non-dual condition is bodhicitta, the universal ground.
All of existence is the pure maṇḍala of the enlightened ones!

16. Mañjuśrībhadra, the Second Mañjuśrīmitra

The second Mañjuśrīmitra, who was the son of Rishi Lahina and of Tsuggi Gegmo, was expert in the vehicles based on cause and effect. Aspiring after the essential meaning, he asked the Second Kukurāja for the essence of the teachings. The latter summarized their entirety for him thus:

Even if one gives a name to mind, it is beyond all names.
However many examples one may use for it, it is beyond all examples.
It is non-dual, transcends thought, and cannot be fixed in a concept.

> Meditating means remaining in the dimension of knowledge
> without conceptualizing or getting distracted!

Then Mañjuśrīmitra perfectly understood the meaning of the primordial state and expressed his realization thus:

> I am Mañjuśrībhadra!
> Continuing the practice started in previous lives,
> I have realized my wish, cutting mind at its root:
> Now I no longer have any doubts that the fruit of perfect enlightenment
> Is not something other than my state!

17. Devarāja

Rishi Bhahi and his wife Bhagula Tsogyal had a very intelligent son, endowed with all the finest qualities. They named him Devarāja. He sought the essential meaning, so when he met Mañjuśrībhadra, he asked him for the essence of the teachings. Mañjuśrībhadra summarized their entirety for him in these words:

> The vastness of space is beyond center and border,
> But not even this can be taken as an example for understanding bodhicitta:
> If you understand bodhicitta, which cannot have examples,
> Meditating means remaining in a condition free of effort!

Then Devarāja, the "king of gods," perfectly understood the meaning of the primordial state and expressed his realization thus:

> I am Devarāja!
> These instructions on total bliss that derive from the scriptures
> I have placed in the depth in my mind, and they will not leave my lips.
> The essential meaning of atiyoga, the state of Samantabhadra,
> Is dharmakāya never separate from understanding!

18. Buddhagupta

Buddhagupta[85] was a bhikṣu learned in the five branches of knowledge, particularly expert in the mahāyoga teachings of Mantrayāna. Seeking the essential meaning beyond effort, he met Devarāja and asked him for the essence of the teachings. Devarāja summarized their entirety for him in these words:

> The nature of mind, being beyond union and separation, is great eternity:
> As pure presence arises in mind, it itself is supreme presence.
> As it does not know saṃsāra, it is the supreme nectar.
> Being without center or border, it is the great maṇḍala.

Then Buddhagupta perfectly understood the meaning of the primordial state and expressed his realization thus:

> I am Buddhagupta.
> From the beginning, one's own mind is total bliss:
> Hidden from those who do not know it, it is the great secret!
> Understanding the state of enlightenment beyond effort is the best meditation;
> Enlightenment transcends meditating and not meditating!

19. Śrī Siṃha Prabata

Śrī Siṃha Prabata, the son of King Drubjed and of Nantaka, was a great bhikṣu who had studied at the feet of five hundred pandits and had become learned in the five branches of knowledge. Aspiring after the essential meaning, he asked Buddhagupta for the essence of the teachings. Buddhagupta summarized their entirety for him in these words:

> This nature of mind that never manifests
> Is always present in the phenomena of vision.
> When one discovers the immutable root of mind,
> No enlightenment remains to be obtained elsewhere!

Then Śrī Siṃha perfectly understood the meaning of the primordial state and expressed his realization thus:

> I am Śrī Siṃha.
> Bodhicitta that transcends the limits of concepts
> Has no material abode but pervades the whole universe.
> The wisdom of pure presence beyond all limits,
> Not even Vajrasattva can define it by saying: "It is thus!"

20. Kungamo

Bhikṣuṇī Kungamo, the daughter of Chamka and of the prostitute Patu, was learned in the five branches of knowledge. Seeking ardently for the essential meaning, she eagerly set off on her quest. On meeting Śrī Siṃha she asked him for the essence of the teachings. Śrī Siṃha summarized their entirety for her in these words:

> Like someone who never feels like doing anything,
> Leave everything as it is!
> Possessing the force of this presence
> Is the state of enlightenment.

Then Bhikṣuṇī Kungamo perfectly understood the meaning of the primordial state and expressed her realization thus:

> I am Bhikṣuṇī Kungamo.
> Just as all streams

Flow together into a great river,
So all the teachings of the nine vehicles
Flow together in Dzogpa Chenpo!

21. Vimalamitra

Bhikṣu Vimalamitra,[86] the son of King Dhahenatsadu and of Siṃha Sripitika, was learned in the five branches of knowledge. Seeking the essential meaning, he met Śrī Siṃha and asked him for the essence of the teachings. Śrī Siṃha summarized their entirety for him in these words:

> Without having to be forsaken, the five poisons are the five great wisdoms.
> Without having to be eliminated, saṃsāra is totally pure from the beginning.
> If you understand that enlightenment is your own mind,
> There is no other meditation!

Then Vimalamitra perfectly understood the meaning of the primordial state and expressed his realization thus:

> The ultimate nature of phenomena, being inconceivable, is immense space—
> The space of the nature of mind that transcends all thoughts.
> Bodhicitta, which cannot be thought,
> Is not found by meditating on the ultimate nature of phenomena:
> Whether one meditates or not, it is present from the beginning and cannot be lost.
> Meditating means abiding in the state of equanimity without thinking!

Thus ends an outline of the history of the teachers of the lineage.[87]

VI. ŚRĪ SIṂHA

Without doubt, the person of greatest historical importance in the introduction of Dzogchen into Tibet was the teacher Śrī Siṃha. Active in Oḍḍiyāna in the eighth century, he transmitted the Semde and Longde teachings to the Tibetan translator Vairocana. As we have just read in the *Vairo Drabag*, he was the disciple of Buddhagupta and the teacher of Bhikṣuṇī Kungamo and of Vimalamitra. The Longde and Mennagde traditions, on the other hand, recount that he was the direct disciple of Mañjuśrīmitra, and the account of their meeting reported in the Mennagde texts has already been translated into English.[88] However the version recounted in the Longde "Vajra Bridge" texts is quite different and particularly significant, reiterating certain themes that we have already encountered in the biography of Mañjuśrīmitra. Here follows a slightly abbreviated version.

Śrī Siṃha wondered whether, besides the methods of accumulation and of purification[89] that predicate the duration of several lives for the achievement of self-realization, there existed a teaching that enabled one to understand the ultimate nature in an instant and to attain enlightenment in a single lifetime. When he asked the sages of Nālandā, the pandits expert in Mantrayāna told him: "Seven generations ago the teacher Mañjuśrīmitra asked the same question and so he met Garab Dorje. If now you head south to the Betai Ling region, in a city called Palyön Thamched Jungwa you will find the teacher Mañjuśrīmitra; he has what you are seeking!" "Is it difficult to get there? And how long will it take?" he asked. "The journey is very long and it takes about thirteen months to get there. Also, the way is beset with evil ḍākinīs and yakṣas, with poisonous snakes and wild beasts." Śrī Siṃha hesitated a moment, then asked: "Is there a short cut?" "There is a way to get there underground, but it is not without danger because there are poisonous snakes and the dwellings of evil spirits." "Is there no protection against all this?" "For protection against the snakes and spirits you should travel with your body smeared with a special oil (*maghita*) and carry a lamp of human fat. And, as you will always be in the dark, you will need a torch."

With difficulty Śrī Siṃha obtained all that was necessary and departed. After travelling for six months in the dark, he reached Betai Ling, the city that had been indicated to him, without encountering any obstacles. Here he asked where the teacher lived and a local inhabitant told him, "We know that a certain Mañjuśrīmitra lives in our city, but we have no idea what he looks like!" Others told him the same thing. So, the whole seventh month, he continued to look for him everywhere, but without success.

Once, when he was near a fountain, he saw an old woman coming to fetch water and asked her whether she knew the teacher. The old woman, without answering, was about to set off again, but when she tried to lift her jar, she could not pick it up from the ground. Śrī Siṃha was using his magical powers. Then the woman pronounced the formula *CITTA ABHIPRASALA* and ripped open her chest, displaying in her heart the maṇḍala of the nine deities of the Yangdag cycle.[90] At that point, Śrī Siṃha asked her again whether she knew the teacher Mañjuśrīmitra, and she answered, "Of course! Only I know him, he is my brother!" Then she sealed her chest, picked up her jar of water, and started walking back home followed by Śrī Siṃha.

When they reached the old woman's house, Śrī Siṃha saw a man dressed like a monk with his hair tied on top of his head, ploughing a field, pulling his plough with the yoke on his shoulders. The woman pointed at him, saying, "That's him!" But Śrī Siṃha was in doubt, thinking: "The teacher Mañjuśrīmitra should look like a pandit or yogin. This man seems an ordinary religious layman: could he possibly be the teacher?"

After a while, Śrī Siṃha asked for some food, and the man answered, "We haven't got any food here, go and beg from my wife in town!" When he got to town, Mañjuśrīmitra's wife told him: "Today, I haven't got any tsampa,"[91] then she took seven sparrows she had bought at the market, and after having cooked them with all their feathers, she served them with rice. But Śrī Siṃha said: "As I am a bhikṣu, I am not allowed to eat meat, especially the meat of animals killed expressly to feed me." The woman exclaimed, "Very well!" and after having put the seven sparrows in the palm of her hand, she blew on them and made them fly free in the sky. Śrī Siṃha thought, "If this woman has such magic powers, chances are that man really is the teacher Mañjuśrīmitra!" But he decided he wanted to check further. When evening fell, as he had to find a place to sleep, he was allowed to stay at the wife's house. The man, who looked like a monk, but actually was the teacher, soon arrived and asked his wife, "Did you give him the food?" She answered, "I offered it to him, but he didn't eat it." The teacher said, "As he likes!"

The next morning, Śrī Siṃha started reading aloud *The Net of the Magic Manifestation of Vajrasattva.*[92] At first, the teacher listened without rising, then he stood up and continued listening until Śrī Siṃha had finished. He then told him: "Not only do you not understand the real meaning, you don't even understand the superficial meaning of the words!" Śrī Siṃha thought: "Is he really the teacher, then?" His wife, who had gone, returned from the market where she had bought a woman's left arm, still fresh and with five bracelets fastened on it. She cooked and served it up, but Śrī Siṃha exclaimed, "I am a bhikṣu and cannot eat meat, especially not human meat, man's nor woman's." The teacher took hold of the arm and snapping his fingers, made it disappear into the sky enveloped in a mass of light. In that instant, Śrī Siṃha understood that the person before him was truly Mañjuśrīmitra. He offered him a maṇḍala of gold, prostrated at his feet, and circumambulated him three times, then asked him: "I beseech you to awaken in me the knowledge you possess!" The teacher remained silent. Śrī Siṃha repeated the ritual three times, but the teacher made no answer at all.

Discouraged, Śrī Siṃha thought: "The teacher does not want to teach me; it is better for me to leave!" At that moment the teacher called aloud: "Śrī Siṃha, come here!" Śrī Siṃha got up and saw Mañjuśrīmitra lying down in the dirt, and thinking that he wanted him to sweep away the dirt, he started vigorously cleaning the floor, sweeping it with a broom eighteen times. Finally, exhausted by his exertion, he lay down to rest. He noticed that on the teacher's cushion there was an attractively colored fruit with an enticing fragrance. Thinking the teacher wanted him to eat it, he took a bite and tasted eight different, delicious flavors. But as soon as he had finished eating it, he started to feel sick, vomit, and began to pass out, fearing that he was dying. Seven times he formed the thought: "Even if I die, it does not matter! At the beginning, when the teacher was ploughing the field with the yoke on his shoulders, he was teaching me through symbols, but I did not understand; even if I die, it does not matter! When he had the meat of the small birds served to me, he was transmitting knowledge to me through that symbol, but I did not understand; even if I die, it does not matter! When I had finished reciting the text, he transmitted knowledge to me through his symbolic words, but I did not understand; even if I die, it does not matter! When he had the woman's arm served to me, he was transmitting knowledge to me through that symbol, but I did not understand; even if I die, it does not matter! When I offered him the maṇḍala, prostrating and circumambulating, and the teacher did not answer, I did not understand the symbol of his silence; even if I die, it does not matter! When I decided to go away, and the teacher called me back to sweep the floor, I did not understand the symbol; even if I die, it does not matter! Finally, when I ate the fruit, I did not understand the symbol; so even if I die, it does not matter now!"

At that moment, Śrī Siṃha stopped vomiting and regained consciousness. He looked up and saw the teacher standing nearby, who asked him, "What is it you want?" "I need a method that will enable me to gain understanding in an instant and to attain enlightenment in one life!" "Have you still not understood?" the teacher asked him. "No, teacher!" Śrī Siṃha answered. "I have taught you from the very first moment; you did not understand! When I was ploughing the field, I taught you the true meaning of method and prajñā.[93] When you were served the meat of the sparrows, through that symbol I taught you the ultimate nature of the six aggregate consciousnesses.[94] When you were reciting *The Net of the Magic Manifestation,* I taught you that all phenomena are beyond explanation. When you were served the woman's arm, the fact that it was the left arm represented prajñā, while the bracelets symbolized the five wisdoms. When you offered me the maṇḍala, prostrated, and circumambulated me, but I remained silent, I was teaching you that all phenomena are beyond word, thought, and definition. When you decided to leave because you had not understood, to purify the eighteen sense elements,[95] I made you sweep the floor eighteen times. Seeing you still had deep and subtle dualistic hindrances tied to the idea of subject and object, I made you eat the fruit: your attachment to its color and its fragrance symbolized attachment to the external world. Your attachment to the fruit's delicious flavor the moment you took a bite of it symbolized attachment to the conceptual mind that constitutes the inner subject. When you were ill due to the hindrances tied to the dualism of subject and object, while you were suffering and you thought seven times that it did not matter to you that you were dying, you purified the obstacles and were healed."

Then Mañjuśrīmitra transmitted to him the meaning of the unborn, of the uninterrupted, and of the non-dual, pronouncing the symbolic syllables *A HA HO YE*, and Śrī Siṃha had the experience of the natural sound of the ultimate condition of phenomena that lasted seven days. When he reawakened from this state, he saw his teacher beside him. To keep him from forgetting the meaning of what he had communicated to him, Mañjuśrīmitra transmitted to him the symbolic word *ABANDHARA*. Śrī Siṃha understood that it meant "Look towards the center of the sky!" So at dawn, while the planets and stars were setting and the clouds and mist were fading, he turned his gaze into space in front of him, neither up nor down. Then he understood that, just as space is not produced by causes and does not depend on conditions in order to manifest and cannot be defined in any way, so, the true nature of mind is not produced by causes, does not depend on conditions, and has no substance that can be limited by definition. Śrī Siṃha thus obtained the supreme siddhi and consequently the ordinary siddhis, purifying all his karma and its residual traces.[96]

VII. THE TIBETAN TRANSLATOR VAIROCANA

The transmission of the teachings of the lineage of Oḍḍiyāna then passed from Śrī Siṃha to the Tibetan translator Vairocana, who lived in the eighth century and is famous as one of the seven "trial" monks ordained at Samye by Śāntarakṣita.[97] It was Vairocana, in fact, as mentioned above, who introduced to Tibet the Tantras and instructions of the Semde and Longde series. The teachings of the Mennagde, on the other hand, were transmitted to Tibet by the teacher Padmasaṃbhava and later by Vimalamitra.[98]

The story of Vairocana, in its various extant versions, unfolds through the following salient points. He was found as a child by King Trisong Deutsen thanks to Padmasaṃbhava's clairvoyance. He became expert in Sanskrit and other Indian languages, and consequently, though still in his youth, was selected to undertake the journey to Oḍḍiyāna. With his travelling companion Tsang Legdrub, he reached Oḍḍiyāna and received the Dzogchen teachings from Śrī Siṃha, then returned to Tibet by means of the skill of "fast walking"[99] and started translating the Dzogchen scriptures. Shortly afterwards, due to being slandered he was exiled to a border zone in east Tibet, where he met Yudra Nyingpo, his foremost disciple. After several years, through the intercession of Vimalamitra he was allowed to return to Tibet where he completed many translations. Some of his deeds have already been translated into English,[100] so there follows only the more notable episodes regarding Vairocana's meeting with his teacher Śrī Siṃha, as narrated in the *Vairo Drabag*, considerably abridged in some parts.

At the time of King Trisong Deutsen, thanks to the presence of teachers such as Śāntarakṣita and Padmasaṃbhava and qualified Tibetan translators, many texts belonging to the teachings based on the principle of cause and effect had been translated. Padmasaṃbhava informed the king that in India there was a teaching beyond the principle of cause and effect called Dzogpa Chenpo, whose texts had not yet been brought to Tibet. So, following Padmasaṃbhava's advice, the king sent two of his most important translators to India: Pagor Vairocana and Tsang Legdrub. With great exertion and self-sacrifice, after having endured robbery and beatings and other misfortunes and overcome no less than sixteen tests of courage and endurance, the two translators finally arrived in India. Here they were told that the most learned teacher of the time was Śrī Siṃha, so they decided to go to Dhahena, in Oḍḍiyāna, where he lived. When they arrived in front of the teacher's house at Dhahena they asked an old woman, who was the warden, for permission to meet him, and the teacher, revealing that their meeting was predestined, answered that he would receive them at midnight. At the appointed time, Vairocana and Legdrub prostrated and paid homage to Śrī Siṃha, offering him gold and telling him of King Trisong Deutsen's wish: to receive the atiyoga teaching "beyond effort." The teacher explained that due to a dispute between Dagnyidma and Kungamo, all the pandits had experienced bad dreams, so they had decided to hide the atiyoga texts at Bodhgaya and not to divulge the teachings they contained. Consequently, the king of Oḍḍiyāna had commanded that the pandits' decision be obeyed, warning that all teachers who gave these teachings were at risk of being punished or executed. Śrī Siṃha, however, was aware that the time had come for these teachings to be promulgated in Tibet and promised that in some way he would help the two translators. He said, "First of all, go and receive the teachings on cause and effect from other pandits, then go and receive the Mantrayāna teachings on the fruit; only then, in secret and at midnight, will I transmit to you the instructions of Dzogpa Chenpo." So, after having studied the teachings based on cause and effect and having received all the tantric initiations, the two translators returned and sat at Śrī Siṃha's feet. Together with the teacher, they miraculously recovered the original atiyoga texts and, while by day they continued to follow the Mantrayāna teachings, at night they were initiated into the Dzogchen teachings.[101]

In his room Śrī Siṃha put an earthenware cauldron on three big stones, surrounded it with a net, and then went inside. He had the opening closed with a big lid on which a pan full of water was placed. A pipe ran through a hole in the cauldron, then crossed through a cleft in the wall and out of the house; it was through this tube that Śrī Siṃha's words would pass. Vairocana and Legdrub remained outside, wearing big deerskin hoods, a load on their shoulders, and a stick [i.e., pretending to be wayfarers]. At midnight, they prepared to listen to the teachings: Legdrub wrote them in goat's milk on white cotton, while Vairocana memorized them instantaneously, hiding them in his heart.

Thus, as a sign that the Dzogchen teaching would be promulgated in Tibet, Śrī Siṃha first taught *The Cuckoo of Presence*. As a sign that everything is perfectly contained [in the primordial state], he taught *The Great Potency*; to express the meaning of meditation, he taught *The Six Spheres*; to express the conclusion of the views and meditations of all the vehicles, he taught *The Great Garuḍa in Flight;* to show the superiority of atiyoga over the other vehicles, he taught *The Victory Banner that Does Not Wane.*[102] Then he asked, "Noble sons, are you satisfied?" to which the translators answered, "We are happy."

To show the fundamental unity of all the philosophical views, he taught *The Wish-fulfilling Jewel;* to show the excellence of the Dharma and of the teachers' instructions, he taught *The Supreme Lord;* to show the need to understand the defects and qualities of the lower and higher vehicles, he taught *The All-penetrating King;* to demonstrate that it is necessary to base oneself on the three discriminating wisdoms, he taught *The Jewel in Which All Is Unified;* these are the four minor teachings. To show that all knowledge must be based on the instructions of the teachers, he taught *Infinite Bliss;* to show that the fruit is included in the Body, Voice, and Mind, he taught *The Wheel of Life;* to show that it is necessary to base oneself on the example, meaning, and characteristic sign, he taught *The Infinitesimal Sphere of Mind* and *The King of Space;* these are the four middle teachings. Then, to show how to help others through the provisional meaning, and the definitive meaning he taught *The Encrusted Ornament of Bliss;* to show that it is necessary to discern all the vehicles, he taught *The All-embracing State;* to avoid the arising of logical contradictions, he taught *Pure Gold in Ore;* to show that behavior and samaya are the yogin's heart, he taught *The Supreme Peak;* these are the four higher teachings. Finally, to demonstrate the need to distinguish between a mistaken teaching and a valid one, he taught *The Marvellous.* Śrī Siṃha asked: "Are you satisfied?" The two translators answered: "Not yet, because we would like to receive the tantras and instructions linked with these eighteen texts." So the teacher transmitted the eighteen tantras together with the instructions and specific introductions to knowledge. Then he asked again: "Are you satisfied?" At this point Legdrub answered: "I am satisfied!" and, wishing to show the king the teachings he had obtained, he decided to leave. However, during his return journey he fell down a precipice and died at the age of forty-four.

Vairocana, however, replied that he was not satisfied and lay down flat on his face for three days without getting up. Seeing him in that state, Śrī Siṃha asked him: "Are you disappointed because your friend has left?" Vairocana answered: "Thanks to common karma we two friends met like wayfarers at an inn who then proceed each their own way: why then should I be disappointed?" "Then are you ill?" the teacher rejoined. "Yes, I am ill!" replied Vairocana. "What is the matter?" asked the teacher. Then Vairocana explained the reason for his illness in the following song:

I am Vairocana
And have no illnesses due to external causes.
I am suffering because I have heard but have not yet understood!
I am suffering because I have seen but have not yet grasped!
I am suffering because I have tasted but am not yet satisfied!
The cause of my illness lies in the eighteen Semde texts:
I am pained at not yet having found certainty in my own state!
I ask you for a definitive medicine
For this illness that afflicts me!

"I have taught you everything," answered the teacher. "Why are you in despair?" Then Vairocana sang:[103]

I am in despair at a dangerous pass
Because the bliss of self-arising wisdom is caught in the closely woven net of latent tendencies.
I am in despair at a dangerous pass
Because the view beyond limits is hindered by karma and dualistic thoughts.
I am in despair at a dangerous pass
Because spontaneous, effortless meditation is obscured by the states of torpor and agitation.
I am in despair at a dangerous pass
Because conduct beyond accepting and rejecting is hindered by desire and effort.
I am in despair at a dangerous pass
Because the path that knows no treading is hindered by quotations and reasoning.
I am in despair at a dangerous pass
Because the state of the Buddhas of the three times is hidden by the doubt of thoughts.
I am in despair at a dangerous pass
Because the state of spontaneous perfection and of the non-action of Dzogchen cannot be communicated by signs and meanings.
I am in despair at a dangerous pass
Because the self-perfection of the three kāyas of the fruit is so difficult to introduce.
I am in despair at a dangerous pass
Because in spite of the empowerment of the direct introduction, I have not understood the enlightenment I naturally possess.

The instructions of the eighteen sources of Semde
Have not enabled me to overcome these eight dangerous passes!

The teacher smiled contentedly, taught him *The Space of the Ocean*, and then asked him, "Now are you satisfied?" Vairocana answered, "No." Then Śrī Siṃha transmitted to him the tantras and instructions of the Longde, but when he asked him, "Are you satisfied?" Vairocana again answered that he was not. So then he taught him many texts and instructions of the series of Tantras and other teachings, but still Vairocana was not satisfied. Finally, he taught the series of *Brahmin-tantras for Discerning the Real Meaning* and the series of *King-tantras to Overcome Concepts*[104] as well as many essential instructions. "Are you satisfied?" asked Śrī Siṃha yet again, and Vairocana answered: "I would like to receive the introduction to direct self-liberation in order to understand the true way to apply all the teachings I have received without relying on effort."

So Śrī Siṃha transmitted to him the direct introduction and consigned to him all the scriptures of the Semde and Longde, including the five root tantras and twenty-five branch tantras of the Semde together with the specific instructions of the teachers of the lineage.[105] Finally, Vairocana realized the state of self-liberation, his conceptual thought dissolved due to the "six spheres" and he understood definitively the "Buddha" condition of his mind through the "five greatnesses."[106] Full of gratitude towards his teacher, he offered him some verses in thanks. Śrī Siṃha advised him: "The instructions I have given you have the power to enable you to understand all of saṃsāra and nirvāṇa and actually to perceive their essence. So take care of them as if they were your own eyes. They are the root of all the teachings, the peak of all the vehicles, the essence of the mind of all the enlightened ones; take care of them as if they were your own life and your own heart. As they are the source of all the siddhis, the supreme siddhis and the ordinary ones, take care of them as if they were the wish-fulfilling gem."[107] Then he transmitted to him other teachings tied to tantra and to medicine and recommended he return to Tibet as soon as possible because the other pandits were jealous of him. Finally, he informed Vairocana that his friend had died during the return journey and advised him to learn the art of "fast walking" in order to avoid dangers during his journey.

After his return to Tibet, Vairocana started translating the first five Semde texts and other scriptures, including the *Kunjed Gyalpo*,[108] and teaching them in secret to the king. But the pandits in India sent a calumnious message, spreading the rumor that Vairocana had not discovered authentic teachings in India and that, on the contrary, he had brought to Tibet magic formulas of the mutegpas with the aim to destroy the kingdom. The king, instigated by envious ministers, did not know how to resolve the problem. But Vairocana, aware of a predestined link he had with the small kingdom of Gyalmo Tsawarong in east Tibet, asked the king to exile him there and advised him to invite from India the greatest pandit of the time, Vimalamitra. So he departed, and after having overcome some difficulties, was received with great honor in the kingdom of Tsawarong, where he found his predestined disciple Yudra Nyingpo, the reincarnation of his former companion Legdrub, to whom he transmitted all the teachings he had received from Śrī Siṃha.[109] It is through this lineage that the empowerments and instructions of the Dzogchen Semde have been transmitted down to our own day.

2 DZOGCHEN SEMDE AND THE *KUNJED GYALPO* TANTRA

I. THE SERIES OF PRIMORDIAL BODHICITTA

According to the traditional texts, at the moment of his passing away Garab Dorje manifested as a body of light and entrusted to his disciple Mañjuśrīmitra a small casket containing his testament in three aphorisms, subsequently known as "the three statements that strike the essence":

> **Directly discover your own state.**
> **Remain without any doubt.**
> **Achieve confidence in self-liberation.**[110]

On the basis of these three statements, Mañjuśrīmitra divided the teachings transmitted by Garab Dorje into the three series of Dzogchen: Semde, the series of bodhicitta or "nature of mind," the primordial state; Longde, the series of "space"; and Mennagde, the series of "secret instructions," or upadeśa. The starting point, as mentioned above, is the principle of direct introduction indicated in the first of the three statements. The teacher introduces the nature of mind, that is, the state of primordial bodhicitta, to the disciple, and the latter must recognize or "discover" it in a direct, non-conceptual manner. The teachings that explain the meaning of the primordial state and contain instructions that enable its recognition are mainly contained in the Semde series.

After having recognized one's own state, it is necessary to eliminate all doubts about it, not in a merely intellectual way, but rather through experience: instantaneous pure presence or recognition, called *rigpa*, must ripen and become more stable thanks to the various Longde methods tied to particular experiences of contemplation.

Finally, the practitioner's task is to integrate the state of knowledge into all his or her daily activities and to develop that capacity to the point of unifying the energy of the physical body with the energy of the outer world. This is the aim of the practices of the third and final series, the Mennagde, the supreme realization of which lies in the manifestation of the "rainbow body," the total re-absorption of the material elements into the pure energy and luminous essence of the primordial state.[111] In substance, these three phases correspond to three aspects of the Dzogchen teaching: "understanding" (*rtogs pa*), "stabilizing" (*brtan pa*), and "integrating" (*bsre ba*). One should not think, however, that the practice of Dzogchen must necessarily start with Semde and end with Mennagde; total realization can also be achieved by practicing only one of the three series, inasmuch as each of them is a path complete in itself. It is simply a matter of understanding which aspect receives greater emphasis in one series rather than another and knowing how to embark on the path that will be most beneficial in terms of one's capacity.

The Mennagde series, in particular, was kept secret at the time of the first promulgation of the teachings in Tibet, when the "official" Dzogchen teaching consisted mainly of the Semde series.[112] Moreover, the Semde and Longde literature belongs almost exclusively to the "oral" tradition, or *kama*, while numerous cycles of Mennagde teachings, marked by the name *Nyingthig* or *Teachings of the Innermost Essence*, belong to the "rediscovered treasures," or *terma*, genre.[113]

Let us return to the Semde series. *Sem*, literally "mind," in this case is an abbreviation of *changchubsem*, the Tibetan for bodhicitta, a key term in the teachings found in this series. *Chang* means "pure" or "purified"; *chub* means "perfect" or "perfected": the nature of mind, pure and perfect from the beginning, the true primordial state of each individual. It is knowledge of this state that is transmitted by the teacher at the time of the direct introduction, and when it is comprehended and becomes living presence, it is called *rigpa*: instantaneous, nondual, pure presence. To demonstrate the importance of the term *bodhicitta*, many Semde tantras attach the word as a prefix before the actual title, and it appears that in ancient times the term was used to designate the Dzogchen Semde teachings in their entirety.[114]

In Mahāyāna Buddhism the term *bodhicitta* designates the mind (*citta*), or intention addressed to the attainment of enlightenment (*bodhi*), and at the same time the fundamental nature of mind that is the very essence of enlightenment. However, used as a technical term, in general it denotes the cultivation of a positive state of mind which is motivated by compassion and based on the aspiration to realize one's potential for the benefit of all beings. In particular, the sūtras speak of relative and absolute bodhicitta based on the philosophical notion of the two truths. Relative bodhicitta entails training the mind in the altruistic aspiration towards enlightenment while absolute bodhicitta is direct or intuitive knowledge of the true nature of phenomena, that is, emptiness, or *śūnyatā*.

In Tantra the term *bodhicitta* assumes a more specific connotation. The essence of enlightenment or "Buddha-nature," revealed in the sūtras of the third turning of the Wheel of Dharma,[115] is equated to the subtle essence (*thig le*) of the human body, the coarse aspect of which is present in the seminal fluid and in the ovum. Thus in Tantra, bodhicitta is recognized as the seed of the manifestation of the infinite maṇḍalas and deities who are all already contained in potentiality in the energy structure of the physical body itself, what is known as the "vajra body." However, in spite of this underlying recognition as its base, tantric practice entails visualization and commitments of body, voice, and mind to achieve the transformation of the energies of impure vision into the pure dimension of the maṇḍala and of the deities.

And lastly, in Dzogchen, the primordial state of bodhicitta is the source of all the manifestations of energy: it is not only a condition of emptiness as in the sūtras, nor does it depend on the transformational methods of the Tantras for its realization. The way to cultivate and to reintegrate one's existence into this state is called "self-liberation," remaining in pure non-dual recognition without being conditioned by the flow of thoughts. Reasoning and analysis can be useful in order to distinguish illusory phenomena from subtler and deeper concepts, but they no longer serve when it is a matter of directly encountering the ultimate nature of one's mind. After having treated the gradual and non-gradual sutric traditions (Indian and Chinese, respectively) and the mahāyoga system, *Light of the Eyes for Contemplation*, one of the earliest and most important Dzogchen Semde texts, written by the great Tibetan teacher Nubchen Sangye Yeshe in the ninth century, introduces Dzogchen thus:[116]

> Atiyoga is the supreme vehicle, the peak of all yogas and the mother of all Buddhas. It is called *Dzogpa Chenpo* (Total Perfection) because it discloses in detail the meaning of the spontaneous and natural perfection of all the infinite phenomena so that it can be understood in its nakedness. The essence of this excellent treasure, universal forebear of all the paths, is a spontaneous and natural state that must be perceived, or recognized, directly, without intervention by the conceptual mind; it must disclose itself clearly to one's instantaneous pure presence. But how does one gain access to this knowledge? In the path of the supreme yoga there is no object of knowledge based on the scriptures to be analyzed by one's intellectual faculty. Why so? From the very beginning without changing their skin or their color, all the phenomena of existence are in the natural state of enlightenment within the dimension of the single sphere of self-arising wisdom. Who could identify something concrete therein to examine? Who could ever adduce any reasons? What philosophical conclusion could ever be drawn, and on the basis of what cognitive means? The truth is, that, being inseparable, the essence of everything cannot be conceived by the mind.[117]

The great eleventh-century teacher and scholar of the Semde tradition, Rongzom Chökyi Zangpo, presented Dzogchen in the following way in his work *Access to the Great Vehicle*:[118]

> Even though there are numerous treatises pertaining to the Dzogpa Chenpo tradition, its fundamental meaning can be subsumed in four points: the nature of bodhicitta, the qualities of this nature, the factors that obstruct its presence, and the way to make it continuous. In effect, by knowing its qualities and the factors that obstruct its presence, automatically one understands its nature; one also understands its qualities and, accordingly, the factors that obstruct its presence dissolve. So, even if other texts do not explicitly give explanations using these four points, they will never stray from them.
>
> In brief, as for the first point, that is, the nature of bodhicitta, all outer and inner and animate and inanimate phenomena are bodhicitta that cannot be reduced to dualism. As they are the nature of the fundamental essence of purity and totality, they are the primordial state of enlightenment: natural perfection that is not produced by effort and cannot be realized by correcting oneself or by using the antidotes of a path.
>
> As for the second point, that is, the qualities of bodhicitta, on a golden island the word "stone" does not even exist, for everything is gold. In like manner, for the totality of outer and inner phenomena contained in the universe not even the words "saṃsāra," "lower states," and the other things we consider as

defects, exist. Everything shines as the ornament of the uninterrupted energy of Samantabhadra (Always Good), and precisely this is the quality of the state of enlightenment.

The third point, that is, the factors that obstruct the presence of bodhicitta, refers to all the views and forms of conduct [that precede those of atiyoga], starting from the worldly paths that do not at all understand or that misconstrue the true condition to those who follow the lower [Buddhist] vehicles. These factors are divided into thirty fundamental types.

As for the fourth point, that is, the way to make [the presence of] bodhicitta continuous, practitioners endowed with higher capacity realize supreme awareness of the natural and authentic state of absolute perfection and abide in a condition of total equanimity.

These words, which illustrate Dzogpa Chenpo, are expressed in a simple, rough way, but in reality they are as subtle and deep as space. Conversely, that which is explained in the lower vehicles is expounded in subtle and elaborate language, yet it remains something rough and coarse, like a pile of dust. It is for this reason that understanding Dzogpa Chenpo requires an open, deep, and subtle mind.[119]

In Kathog Monastery in east Tibet, its founder, Ka Tampa Desheg (1122-1192), perhaps the last great protagonist of Dzogchen Semde, established a college for the study and practice of the Semde texts in particular and the kama tradition in general.[120] However, over the centuries, this institution dwindled on account of the spread of the Mennagde termas, and nowadays it is difficult to meet teachers proficient in the meaning of these ancient texts, though fortunately their transmission has been kept up within the kama literature tradition.

II. THE SEMDE SCRIPTURES

The fundamental Dzogchen Semde scriptures mainly comprise twenty-one texts, eighteen of which, termed the "eighteen major *lungs*" (*lung chen bco brgyad*), are tied to empowerments and instructions handed down from the time of the teachers from Oḍḍiyāna. Diverse sources give lists of the eighteen texts (which were listed above in the biography of Vairocana) that do not exactly concur. This is also the case for the identification of the first five texts translated into Tibetan. Longchenpa gives the following list:

1. *Rigpai Khujug, The Cuckoo of Presence*
2. *Tsalchen Trugpa, The Great Potency*
3. *Khyungchen Dingwa, The Great Garuḍa in Flight*
4. *Dola Sershün, Pure Gold in Ore*

5. *Minuppai Gyaltsen—Dorje Sempa Namkha Che, The Victory Banner that Does Not Wane—The Total Space of Vajrasattva.*

These are the "first five texts translated."

6. *Tsemo Chungyal, The Supreme Peak*
7. *Namkhai Gyalpo, The King of Space*
8. *Dewa Traköd, The Encrusted Ornament of Bliss*
9. *Dzogpa Chiching, The All-encompassing Perfection*
10. *Changchubsem Tig, The Essence of Bodhicitta*
11. *Dewa Rabjam, The Infinite Bliss*
12. *Soggi Khorlo, The Wheel of Life*
13. *Thigle Trugpa, The Six Spheres*
14. *Dzogpa Chichod, The All-penetrating Perfection*
15. *Yidshin Norbu, The Wish-fulfilling Jewel*
16. *Kundü Rigpa, The All-unifying Pure Presence*
17. *Jetsün Tampa, The Supreme Lord*
18. *Gompa Töndrub, The Realization of the True Meaning of Meditation.*

These are the thirteen "later translated texts" which, together with the first five, form the so-called "eighteen major *lungs*" of Semde.

19. *Kunjed Gyalpo, The All-creating King*
20. *Medjung Gyalpo, The Marvellous King*
21. *Dochu, The Ten Concluding Teachings.*[121]

The eighteen major *lungs* undoubtedly constitute the basis of Dzogchen Semde. The "first five texts translated" seem to enjoy particular esteem, as attested by their appearance, albeit in one case in reduced form, as separate chapters in the *Kunjed Gyalpo*[122] and also in other tantras. Outstanding among these is the *Dorje Sempa Namkha Che* or *The Total Space of Vajrasattva*, which, according to tradition, was recited by Garab Dorje immediately after his birth, and is considered the root *lung* of all the Semde scriptures. This text constitutes the thirtieth chapter (translated in its entirety in the present work) of the *Kunjed Gyalpo* and is paraphrased in various sections of the *Dochu*. It is also referred to at length in fundamental texts such as *Light of the Eyes for Contemplation* by Nubchen Sangye Yeshe, and was used by Rongzom Chökyi Zangpo as a reference in his descriptions of deep and subtle aspects of Dzogchen view and practice in his *Access to the Great Vehicle*.

The *Dorje Sempa Namkha Che* is a short text of only fifty-five quatrains, written in cryptic language that is difficult to interpret. The two commentaries available, the first ascribed to Śrī Siṃha, the second probably written by Vairocana himself,[123] are extremely useful for understanding the general meaning of the various strophes, but in some cases literal understanding of the texts remains doubtful. The *Dorje Sempa Namkha Che* is a *lung* that epitomizes the fundamental points of the state of knowledge of Dzogchen, however the *Nyingma Gyüd Bum* collection embraces nine tantras whose titles also contain the name *Dorje Sempa Namkha Che*.[124]

As well as the twenty-one texts mentioned above, the section of the *Nyingma Gyüd Bum* devoted to Dzogchen Semde contains a vast literature belonging to the various categories of root tantras, explicative tantras, secondary tantras, secret instruction tantras,[125] and so on. Some of these texts are included in the *Vairo Gyüd Bum*, the collection of works and translations by Vairocana, which also contains previously unpublished works of extreme importance, such as the above-mentioned commentaries to the *Dorje Sempa Namkha Che*.[126] The *Nyingma Kama*, on the other hand, contains the texts and instructions on the Semde practice originally handed down by the Oḍḍiyāna teachers and subsequently enhanced in accordance with the experiences of Tibetan teachers. Three practice systems have been handed down to this day and put in writing, known as *Nyang-lug*, or "Nyang's system," *Aro-lug*, or "Aro's system," and *Kham-lug*, or "the Kham system," all systematized about the eleventh century.[127]

The fundamental Dzogchen Semde practice, corresponding to the first of Garab Dorje's three statements, consists in cultivating recognition of one's primordial state through meditation and contemplation methods that entail a sequence of states to be traversed that are necessary in order to stabilize and ripen one's knowledge. However, this does not imply a gradual "recognition" of the primordial state but rather a natural process of evolution and ripening of one's practice. This is indispensable for those without higher capacity in order to accomplish the state in which there is no longer any distinction between meditation session and daily life. To this end, the method most commonly followed on the basis of instructions found in tantras such as *The Secret Lamp of Wisdom*,[128] is that of the four yogas, or four contemplations, which are: (1) calm state, (2) unperturbed state, (3) absolute equality, (4) self-perfection.[129]

III. STRUCTURE AND CONTENTS OF THE *KUNJED GYALPO*

As we have seen, the *Kunjed Gyalpo* is considered the fundamental tantra of the Dzogchen Semde and is found in all the editions of the *Nyingma Gyüd Bum* and the *Nyingma Kama*, as well as being the only text to represent atiyoga in the *Kangyur*, the Tibetan Buddhist canon.[130] Written in the form of a dialogue between Buddha Kunjed Gyalpo and Sattvavajra, the *Kunjed Gyalpo* comprises eighty-four chapters divided into three parts: the root tantra (*rtsa rgyud*), in fifty-seven chapters; the further tantra (*phyi ma'i rgyud*), in twelve chapters; and the final tantra (*phyi ma'i phyi ma'i rgyud*), in fifteen chapters. These three parts are associated with the three wisdoms, or prajñās, described in Mahāyāna Buddhism: wisdom derived from listening, wisdom derived from reflection and wisdom derived from meditation.[131] This is also evidenced from the fact that in the first part of the text, Buddha Kunjed Gyalpo addresses Sattvavajra saying, "Listen!" In the second, "Understand!" In the third, "Meditate!" or "Experience!"

Furthermore, the root tantra of the *Kunjed Gyalpo* addresses people of higher capacity; the further tantra, those of average capacity; the final tantra, practitioners of lower capacity. In this regard, it is handed down that Vairocana himself said, "Some people self-liberate as soon as they perceive the true nature of the mind because they have no need to reflect or meditate. Others self-liberate simply by reflecting on the meaning of absolute equality, so they have no need to meditate. Yet others self-liberate only after having acquired sufficient familiarity with the true nature [through meditation]. This is the reason underlying the divisions [of this tantra]."[132] Nevertheless, it should be borne in mind that the three capacities referred to are in fact three further subdivisions within the "higher capacity" category.[133]

The various chapters of the *Kunjed Gyalpo* are designated *dolung* (*mdo lung*) or concise teachings, and this could lead one to suppose that this tantra is actually a large collection of *lungs*. This would also explain the presence of the "first five texts translated" within the *Kunjed Gyalpo*. The root tantra, which constitutes the fundamental part of the work, consists of five sections each containing ten principal chapters, or *dolungs*, whose list is given in a sequence that differs from the order in which they are found in present-day editions.[134] The five sections of the root tantra, traditionally tied to the principle of the "five greatnesses," or qualities of primordial bodhicitta, are:

1. The teachings on manifestation (*mngon du phyung ba'i mdo lung*), which aim to enable one to understand the nature of existence, related to the principle of the "greatness of the direct manifestation of enlightenment"

2. The teachings that disclose the true nature (*nges par bstan pa'i mdo lung*), which aim to enable one to understand that the nature of existence is Kunjed Gyalpo, related to the principle of the "greatness of enlightenment in the ultimate dimension of phenomena"

3. The teachings beyond cause and effect (*rgyu 'bras 'das pa'i mdo lung*), which aim to eliminate attachment to misconceptions regarding cause and effect, related to the principle of the "greatness of enlightenment in the totality of one's state"

4. The teachings on perfection beyond action (*bya med rdzogs pa'i mdo lung*), related to the principle of the "greatness of enlightenment that proves its own nature"

5. The teachings that establish knowledge (*gtan la 'bebs pa'i mdo lung*), related to the principle of the "greatness of the absolute non-existence of enlightenment."[135]

The *Dochu*, or *Ten Concluding Teachings*, are deemed an explanatory tantra of the *Kunjed Gyalpo* root tantra.[136] In fact, although they do not explicitly comment on the text of the *Kunjed Gyalpo*, its ten chapters do refer directly to the five sections mentioned above. Moreover, each of the ten chapters has an appendix comprising a "comment relating the true meaning" (*don gyi 'grel pa*), presumably authored by Vairocana, with paraphrases of the "first five texts translated," preeminent among which is the *Dorje Sempa Namkha Che* occupying the greater part of the sections.[137] Due to the topics they treat, two other tantras, *The Secret Wheel Overcoming Concepts* and *The Tantra That Examines Aspects of Bodhicitta*,[138] seem to be directly connected with the *Kunjed Gyalpo* and the *Dochu*. In the first of these two tantras, in particular, it is again Buddha Kunjed Gyalpo who personally teaches Sattvavajra.

The root tantra of the *Kunjed Gyalpo*, especially, is of fundamental importance, as it precisely defines the view of the "primordial state" particular to Dzogchen. The two parts following the root tantra deal with aspects relating to the practice and to the integration of knowledge in the totality of the individual's existence. Only these two are included in the *Vairo Gyüd Bum*.[139]

The *Nyingma Kama* contains two crucial texts tied to the *Kunjed Gyalpo*. The first is an extremely concise compendium summarizing the contents of the whole tantra, quoting three chapters in their entirety.[140] The second is the celebrated *Guide to the True Meaning* by Longchenpa. It contains a set of instructions based on an ancient text by Vairocana, unfortunately no longer extant, on the way to apply the state of knowledge expounded in this tantra and the way to integrate it into the three aspects of body, voice, and mind. A translation into English has already been published.[141] Also worthy of note is another work by Longchenpa that has recently returned to light: an extremely useful summary of the *Kunjed Gyalpo* that, as asserted by the author himself, relates the traditional interpretation of this tantra as it was taught by teachers in Tibet in the fourteenth century.[142]

The *Kunjed Gyalpo* thus takes the form of a dialogue between Sattvavajra, who poses the questions, and Buddha Kunjed Gyalpo, synonymous with Samantabhadra, who answers them. The text opens with a description of the absolute dimension of Kunjed Gyalpo, the primordial state of bodhicitta, whence everything manifests: the five elements as the base of saṃsāra and nirvāṇa, the six classes of beings, the various Buddhas, and so on. At the same time the diverse ways of realization arise, which the Nyingma tradition generally divides into nine "vehicles": the three sutric vehicles of the śrāvakas, *pratyekabuddhas*, and Bodhisattvas; the three outer tantric vehicles, kriyā, ubhaya, and yoga; and the three inner tantric vehicles, mahāyoga, anuyoga, and atiyoga.[143]

Atiyoga is the path that leads to the realization of the state of Dzogchen and, as such, is synonymous with it. *Ati* means primordial, and *yoga*, in this context, denotes living, concrete knowledge of the real condition. For the benefit of beings, from the primordial Buddha Kunjed Gyalpo there have issued forth the teachers of the three kāyas, or dimensions (dharmakāya, saṃbhogakāya, and nirmāṇakāya) who transmit the three diverse series of vehicles of realization in accord with the mental endowments and capacities of disciples. According to this classification, the dharmakāya is the source of the three inner tantras, while the saṃbhogakāya and nirmāṇakāya give rise to the three outer tantras and the three sūtra vehicles respectively. Each teaching transmission, moreover, presupposes the conjunction of five factors, called "the five perfect conditions": the teacher, assembly, time, place, and teaching.

The text often mentions another division, that of the "four yogas": sattvayoga,[144] mahāyoga, anuyoga, and atiyoga. In this case sattvayoga encompasses the contents of the three outer tantras, in particular yoga tantra. At times the teachings of the three inner tantras are denoted with terms that point to their specific methods: "creation," "completion," and "total perfection," respectively.[145] In fact, the "creation," method, that entails gradual visualization of the maṇḍala and the deity, is characteristic of the path of transformation of Tantra in general and of mahāyoga in particular. The method of "completion," on the other hand, denotes accomplishment of the practices of creation. Its purpose lies in the re-absorption of the pure dimension of the maṇḍala into the practitioner's inner condition by means of yogic practices tied to visualization of the cakras and channels and to breath control: this method is utilized in particular in the path of anuyoga. Finally, in this view, "total perfection" is the point of arrival of the transformation practice of Tantra, in a certain sense equivalent to the state of Mahāmudrā characteristic of the modern tantric tradition. This "total perfection" or Dzogpa Chenpo, however, is also the natural state of the individual and all the phenomena of existence. If in mahāyoga and anuyoga the means to realize it consist mainly in transformation and in the methods tied to *prāṇa* and to the cakras, in atiyoga the fundamental method is that of self-liberation, the effortless path of the recognition of pure non-dual presence. This is the message that Kunjed Gyalpo transmits to Sattvavajra, and, consequently, to all those to this day who read this tantra.

The tantras tied to the path of transformation must necessarily be based on ten fundamental points, called the "ten natures of Tantra" that constitute the principal means of realization of this path: view, conduct, maṇḍala, initiation, commitment (*samaya*), capacity for spiritual action, sādhana, visualization, making offerings, and mantra.[146] In particular, the *Kunjed Gyalpo* continuously refers to the following ten aspects: view, commitment, capacity for spiritual action, maṇḍala, initiation, path, levels of realization, conduct, wisdom, and self-perfection strictly tied to the principle of the "ten absences" (*med pa bcu*) characteristic of the deep understanding of Dzogchen:

1. There is no view on which one has to meditate.
2. There is no commitment, or samaya, one has to keep.
3. There is no capacity for spiritual action one has to seek.

4. There is no maṇḍala one has to create.
5. There is no initiation one has to receive.
6. There is no path one has to tread.
7. There are no levels of realization (bhūmis) one has to achieve through purification.
8. There is no conduct one has to adopt, or abandon.
9. From the beginning, self-arising wisdom has been free of obstacles.
10. Self-perfection is beyond hope and fear.

These ten points are repeated and explained from various angles in different parts of the book and constitute the fundamental feature that distinguishes Dzogchen from the other paths of realization, which are all, to a greater or lesser degree, bound to the notion of cause and effect. The further tantra, in particular, defines in ten separate chapters the principle of the true understanding of these "ten natures," while the final tantra does the same regarding meditation.[147]

At this stage there is need for a brief annotation on the translation of the term *bodhicitta*, rendered until now in Sanskrit. In the transcripts of the oral teachings given by Chögyal Namkhai Norbu some twenty years ago, I have preferred to adhere to the expression he used at the time: "the state of consciousness," meaning the primordial state of consciousness of each individual. In the translations from the Tibetan, on the other hand, I have used the expression "pure and total consciousness," which is congruent with the literal meaning of the Tibetan term *changchub sem*. For "Kunjed Gyalpo," in the translations of the passages I have almost exclusively used the term "supreme source," which was also expressly suggested by Chögyal Namkhai Norbu for the name of this book as a whole.

To conclude this first part, there follows a list of the eighty-four chapters of the *Kunjed Gyalpo*, based on the division proposed by Longchenpa in his *Summary*.[148]

THE ROOT TANTRA

The ten dolungs on primordial manifestation

1. *The introductory chapter*
2. *The chapter that discloses the manifestation of the ultimate nature*
3. *The chapter that discloses how the origin arose:* Kunjed Gyalpo arose before all phenomena.

4. *The chapter that explains his names*
5. *The chapter that explains the true meaning*
6. *The chapter on the single root:* all phenomena are perfect in the nature of Kunjed Gyalpo.
7. *The chapter that epitomizes multiplicity:* the subdivision of the teachings that originated from the activity of Kunjed Gyalpo
8. *The chapter that explains how all views about the ultimate nature have arisen from it:* all existent phenomena are one single thing in the essential condition, whence the three natures manifest in three distinct aspects.
9. *The chapter on the elimination of the defects related to deviations and hindrances*
10. *The chapter on the manifestation of perfect conditions:* the very nature of Kunjed Gyalpo is the perfect condition.

Longchenpa adds that these ten dolungs "demonstrate the true condition of the totality of existence (essence, nature, and energy) in the same way that sight is restored to a blind man."[149]

The ten dolungs that disclose the true nature

11. *The chapter that demonstrates that the sole root of all phenomena is Kunjed Gyalpo bodhicitta*
12. *The chapter that demonstrates the true nature of the teachings*
13. *The chapter that explains the nature of mind*
14. *The chapter that exacts secrecy towards the unsuitable*
15. *The chapter on the manifestation of the three natures*
16. *The chapter of advice to Sattvavajra*
17. *The chapter on relics*
18. *The chapter that demonstrates that realization cannot be achieved by seeking*
19. *The chapter on self-perfection that transcends seeking*
20. *The chapter that demonstrates how all phenomena originate from Kunjed Gyalpo bodhicitta*

Longchenpa adds that these dolungs "demonstrate the perfect condition of the nature of mind as it is, using logical reasoning, examples, and meanings in the same way that a truthful person relates the contents of a letter."[150]

The ten dolungs beyond cause and effect

21. *The chapter that explains the reasons*
22. *The chapter on the state beyond concepts:* the source of the teachings on perfection beyond action to relax the mind in its original condition (*The Great Garuḍa in Flight*)[151]
23. *The chapter that discloses the state of the sky, the view free of reference point*
24. *The chapter on the unchanging condition of perfection beyond action*
25. *The chapter that demonstrates that one's own mind is the teacher:* the primordial state of each being of the three worlds is the teacher.
26. *The chapter that demonstrates that perfection beyond action is not something on which to meditate* (*Pure Gold in Ore*)
27. *The chapter that discloses the dimension of purity of non-action* (*The Great Potency*)
28. *The chapter that demonstrates that unchanging perfection beyond action cannot be found by seeking it*
29. *The chapter on relaxation in the authentic state*
30. *The chapter on the nature of Vajrasattva, the victory banner that does not wane* (*The Total Space of Vajrasattva*)

Longchenpa adds that these teachings "demonstrate that the nature of mind cannot be altered, achieved, or eliminated; it is just like celestial space."[152]

The ten dolungs on perfection beyond action[153]

31. *The chapter of the six vajra verses:* spontaneous self-perfection beyond action is the nature of Kunjed Gyalpo (*The Cuckoo of Presence*).
32. *The chapter of the four verses of knowledge:* the teaching for the realization of the absolute meaning without needing to act
33. *The chapter that demonstrates the definitive and provisional teachings*
34. *The chapter that concentrates the essence of knowledge:* the teaching that synopsizes the state of knowledge of all the Buddhas
35. *The chapter that demonstrates the system of total perfection:* Dzogpa Chenpo is not known in other teachings, its method transcends the effort tied to cause and effect.
36. *The chapter that demonstrates that all is contained in the Body, Voice, and Mind:* the nature of all phenomena is comprehended in the Body, Voice, and Mind of the state of Kunjed Gyalpo
37. *The chapter of the essential teaching on the state beyond meditation:*

the ultimate nature of total perfection is not something on which to meditate.

38. *The chapter that indicates the deviations and hindrances related to view and behavior*
39. *The chapter on the fundamental essence of the Victorious Ones:* as it is the essence of the Buddhas, the nature of Kunjed Gyalpo is free from errors and hindrances.
40. *The chapter that shows the nature of bodhicitta:* being gradual paths, the vehicles of cause and effect deviate from total perfection and hinder presence.

Longchenpa adds that these teachings "demonstrate that the qualities of self-arising wisdom, that is, of the nature of mind, are already naturally present and self-perfected and that there is no need to seek them. Simply abiding in the state of total relaxation, effortlessly, and without correction or alteration, one achieves realization. Thus, [the true nature] can be compared to the wish-fulfilling jewel."[154]

The ten dolungs that establish knowledge

41. *The chapter on the single essence*
42. *The chapter on the state that cannot be altered:* all phenomena are enlightened in bodhicitta.
43. *The chapter that explains [the nature of] the teacher:* all phenomena are the teacher.
44. *The chapter that demonstrates how total perfection does not give results to those who are unsuitable*
45. *The chapter that demonstrates that there is no view on which to meditate:* in Dzogpa Chenpo the view is not something on which one has to meditate.
46. *The chapter that demonstrates that there is no commitment to keep:* in Dzogpa Chenpo there is no limited commitment to keep.
47. *The chapter that demonstrates that there is no capacity for spiritual action to seek:* in Dzogpa Chenpo capacity for spiritual action is not something that one needs to acquire through effort.
48. *The chapter that discloses how the ground of all phenomena is Kunjed Gyalpo*
49. *The chapter that demonstrates that in total perfection there is no progressing through the levels of realization:* everything is in the state of Kunjed Gyalpo.

50. *The chapter that discloses self-arising wisdom:* the self-arising wisdom of bodhicitta knows no hindrances.

Longchenpa adds that "these teachings smash the huge rocks of erroneous views of the lower vehicles, and at the same time they illuminate the true meaning of the natural state, thus they can be compared to a diamond or to the splendor of the sun."[155]

The three chapters that summarize the essence[156]

51. *The chapter that demonstrates that there is no path to tread:* in Dzogpa Chenpo there is no path to tread in a gradual manner.
52. *The chapter on the immovable, desireless state:* perfection without action is without movement and desires.
53. *The chapter that demonstrates that the nature of all phenomena is the immovable state*

The four chapters that concisely explain the meaning of the words

54. *The chapter that demonstrates that all teachings are contained in the nature of Kunjed Gyalpo*
55. *The chapter that demonstrates that no phenomenon exists that does not derive from bodhicitta*
56. *The chapter in which Sattvavajra declares his understanding of the nature of Kunjed Gyalpo*
57. *The chapter on the entrustment of the teaching*

THE FURTHER TANTRA

The twelve dolungs *that explain understanding* [157]

58. *The introductory chapter on understanding*

The chapters on understanding the true meaning of the ten natures

59. *The chapter on the unborn state:* understanding that the view is not something on which to meditate
60. *The chapter on the commitment that need not be kept:* understanding that the commitment is not something to keep
61. *The chapter on understanding the nature of the three doors beyond action and seeking:* understanding that the capacity for spiritual action is not something to seek

62. *The chapter on understanding that the maṇḍala is not to be created by visualization*
63. *The chapter on the power of understanding the self-arising state:* understanding that there is no initiation to receive
64. *The chapter on understanding that there is no path to tread*
65. *The chapter on understanding that there is no progressing through the levels of realization*
66. *The chapter on understanding that there is no conduct to accept or to reject*
67. *The chapter on understanding that knowledge has no hindrances*
68. *The chapter on understanding that self-perfection cannot be the result of a quest*
69. *The chapter that praises understanding*

THE FINAL TANTRA

The teachings on meditation on the true meaning of the ten natures

70. *The chapter that demonstrates whether or not it is necessary to meditate*
71. *The chapter on the inseparability of view and state of knowledge*
72. *The chapter that demonstrates that one cannot deviate from view and meditation:* the way to abide in the essential condition beyond "maintaining"
73. *The chapter that demonstrates how to abide in the condition "as it is" without acting and seeking*
74. *The chapter that demonstrates how to abide in the fundamental meaning:* how to abide in the essence beyond union and separation
75. *The chapter on the power of pure instantaneous presence*
76. *The chapter on how to abide on the path of the fundamental essence*
77. *The chapter that demonstrates that the true meaning is beyond any progress*
78. *The chapter that demonstrates that in equality there is neither acceptance or rejection*
79. *The chapter on the state that knows no hindrances:* the meaning of the self-arising essence has no obstacles that need to be eliminated.
80. *The chapter that demonstrates how self-perfection is beyond hope and fear*

81. *The chapter that demonstrates the key to the fundamental meaning*
82. *The chapter of praise*
83. *The chapter that indicates to whom the teaching should be transmitted*
84. *The chapter that illustrates the diverse names*

The colophon of the mTshams brag edition states, "*Bodhicitta Kunjed Gyalpo*, the tantra of the view without center or border like space, the supreme meaning of the essence of space: the eighty-four supremely secret dolungs are finished. Translated, revised, and established in their definitive version by the Indian teacher Śrī Siṃha Prabha and by Bhikṣu Vairocana."[158]

PART TWO

AN INTRODUCTION TO THE *KUNJED GYALPO*

An Oral Commentary by
Chögyal Namkhai Norbu

3 The Fundamental Principles of Tantra and Dzogchen

I. THE OUTER, OR LOWER, TANTRAS

In Tibetan Buddhism there are six or four classes of tantras, according respectively to the Nyingma (ancient) or Sarma (modern)[159] classifications, but in substance the fundamental division is between "outer" or "lower" tantras and "inner" or "higher" (*anuttaratantra*) tantras.

The outer tantras comprise the three series of kriyā, ubhaya (called caryā in the modern tradition), and yoga. The starting point is thus the kriyā tantras or "tantras of ritual action," while the final series is the yoga tantras or "tantras of union." In fact there are many differences in both view and practice between these two series of tantras. The ubhaya tantras, literally "neutral tantras," are so called because they share the rules of conduct of the kriyā tantras and the meditation methods of the yoga tantras. Thus the fundamental traditions are two: kriyā and yoga. Kriyā tantra is the general name of a series that encompasses diverse systems of practice. The word *kriyā* means ritual or moral engagement: the characteristic feature of this series of tantras is to attribute great importance to external factors and to moral conduct. The kriyā tantra teachings hinge on the concept of the "deity," but certainly not in the sense of a single creator-god. What, then, is meant by "deity"? A deity is a being who has accomplished realization through this same path. So, all realized beings can manifest in the form of a deity and the deity itself is deemed to be the main means of realization for practitioners, whose task is to prepare themselves to receive that deity's wisdom.

At this point it is useful to explain what is meant by a deity's "wisdom." Before achieving realization, while still on the path, a practitioner ineluctably commits many deeds, good and bad, that in all cases at the moment of realization are transformed into wisdom. Thus, realization does not entail the total annihilation of actions, but only their transformation into wisdom. The function of a realized being's wisdom is to be received by practitioners who are following the same path. For example, if I am practicing the kriyā tantras, this means that I have a precise karmic relationship with these teachings and, consequently, that in a certain sense, I am meant to receive wisdom by practicing this path. However, in order to receive it, I have to prepare myself, for realization depends mainly on oneself and not solely on the power of a realized being. Were the latter the case, a great enlightened being such as Śākyamuni Buddha, endowed with infinite power and boundless compassion, would already have liberated all beings from the suffering of saṃsāra. Yet, even though the fundamental thing is the participation of the individual, the infinite wisdom of a realized being can help a person to awaken because this is its specific characteristic quality. So this point is particularly important in the kriyā tantras, whose practice is based mainly on preparing oneself to receive wisdom.

But how does one prepare oneself? First of all by considering that realized beings are present everywhere and at all times. "Present" for us means something we see with our eyes; this is our limitation. We say that anything that is outside our field of vision "doesn't exist." Realized beings, however, are not subject to the limitations of distance, and if we have prepared ourselves properly, it is always possible to receive their wisdom. If we believe that realized beings are present everywhere, we need to observe determined rules of conduct relative to body, voice, and mind, the three principal aspects of the existence of each individual. Obviously, rules depend on the specific conditions of time and place, and there cannot be a "conduct" that is universally valid. It is we who have to assign limits to ourselves, on the basis of our needs and our attachments.

Thus, to prepare ourselves to receive wisdom, we start with rules relative to the body, for example, shunning alcohol and meat, garlic and onions. This is tied to the principle of purification that is of fundamental importance not only in the kriyā tantras, but also in the other series of tantras. In general, as our vision is dualistic, we continuously commit negative actions which in their turn comprise the main obstacle to realization and lead to the performance of further dualistic actions, without any possibility of getting out of this vicious cycle. To overcome this obstacle, practitioners have to devote themselves to the purification of body, voice, and mind. In terms of the body, it is necessary to perform "prostrations," visualizing the realized beings in front of oneself, or to do physical and breathing exercises. In terms of the voice, it is necessary to recite specific mantras for purification and for the development of clarity while maintaining mental concentration. One might ask, how can a formula consisting of words purify negative actions? In reality, a mantra is not composed of ordinary words, because in its first instance it was pronounced by a realized being that in a certain sense inserted the energy of his or her wisdom into it. Thus, the power of the mantra resides in the sound vibration and not in the written letter: by pronouncing a deity's mantra correctly one is connected with the wisdom of that specific deity. Various kinds of mantras have different functions, and until the accomplishment of realization, they are always useful for overcoming obstacles. Finally, as regards the aspect of the mind, the fundamental point of the kriyā tantras is to focus one's concentration on the realized beings, to receive their wisdom and to awaken. Thus one visualizes the "deity" forms of realized beings, selecting one in particular that becomes the symbol representing the wisdom of all the enlightened ones. Let us take the example of the Bodhisattva Avalokiteśvara, a "deity" whose practice is very widespread in the kriyā tantras. First of all one must understand that Avalokiteśvara is a realized being: practitioners visualize him because they are unable to see him with their eyes, despite the fact he is ever present in front of them. At the same time, with their voice they recite his mantra to ask the "true" Avalokiteśvara, the "wisdom deity," to merge with the visualized image. In general there are three fundamental points in all tantric practice (and not only of the kriyā tantras): mudrā, mantra, and visualization, linked respectively with the body, voice, and mind. Mudrās are hand gestures with diverse functions: tendering offerings such as flowers, perfume, silk clothes, etc., invoking the power of the deity and absorbing it into oneself, and so on. The simultaneous use of mudrā, mantra, and visualization is extremely effective and can markedly increase the practitioners' capacity to enter into contact with the visualized deity. To conclude the practice, practitioners visualize that rays of light, symbolizing wisdom, radiate from the deity and are absorbed into them, empowering them and helping them in their awakening. The traditional texts summarize the contents of the kriyā tantras in this simile: the deity is the lord, or king, the practitioner is the subject. Thus, just as a subject's task is to secure the king's favor, so the practitioner's is to propitiate the deity in order to receive the deity's empowering energy flow.[160]

Let us now pass on to the yoga tantras. The yoga tantras are considered greatly superior to the kriyā tantras, because, unlike the latter, their fundamental point is not that of preparing oneself to receive wisdom. The difference of the deity and the practitioner is no longer that of king and subject: instead now there is a condition of parity and equality. However, as it is considered to be very difficult to accomplish realization without the aid of the wisdom of an enlightened being, the deity still constitutes the principal means of realization. Resuming the example of Avalokiteśvara, instead of visualizing him before us, we imagine ourselves in the form of Avalokiteśvara, and, what is very important, at the center of our body we visualize our consciousness in the form of the letter *HRĪ*, the seed syllable and specific phoneme of Avalokiteśvara. Then we imagine that countless rays radiate from the *HRĪ*, inviting the Avalokiteśvara "wisdom deity" to unite with our own manifestation in his form, or "commitment deity." In this case too, the practice includes the use of mudrā, mantra, and visualization, but the crucial difference lies in visualizing oneself directly in the form of the deity. Regarding conduct, as there is no great emphasis on the deity as an external and omnipresent entity to be worshipped, there are far fewer rules to obey than in the kriyā tantras. The fundamental point here is unification with the deity, the achievement of that state in which the practitioners themselves become the symbol of the deity. Nevertheless, there still remains a clear distinction between the practitioner and the deity: the former is weak and has not yet manifested enlightenment, so that unless he or she unifies with the deity, he or she remains in the ordinary condition. The name *yoga*, or "union," of these tantras derives precisely from the unification of the deity with the state of the practitioner.

As mentioned above, the ubhaya or "neutral" tantras constitute a middle way between the kriyā and yoga tantras. Here the relationship between the practitioner and the deity is compared with that between two friends or siblings. For example, during the meditation, we first visualize Avalokiteśvara in front of us and then ask him to transmit the power of his wisdom, just as in the kriyā tantra practice.

But at the end, instead of only receiving the deity's wisdom in the form of rays of light, the deity unites with the practitioners, who themselves then manifest in the form of Avalokiteśvara. The rules of conduct are similar to those observed in the kriyā tantras. Initially, the ubhaya tantra tradition was not as well known as those of the kriyā and yoga tantras in Tibet, however, it spread widely during the period when the practice of the higher tantras was officially banned after practitioners were accused of taking too literally the instructions contained in the ritual texts.

In conclusion, these three series of tantras—kriyā, ubhaya, and yoga—are classified as "outer tantras" because their means of realization principally comprise an "outer" deity as the object of meditation.

II. THE INNER, OR HIGHER, TANTRAS

Unlike the preceding tantras, those tantras denominated "inner" by the ancient tradition and "higher" by the modern tradition have no concept of an "outer" deity: the deity is only the symbol of the primordial state transmitted by the teacher during the initiation. This series of tantras is mainly known by the general name of *anuttarayogatantra* or "higher yoga tantras" and its literature is far greater than that of the outer tantras. For example, the Kālacakra tantra alone is a system of teaching that is complete in itself and includes numerous principal and secondary texts. This is also the case, albeit to a lesser degree, for tantras such as Guhyasamāja, Cakrasaṃvara and so on. And it is precisely the prevalence of the practice of one tantra or the other that characterizes the different schools of Tibetan Buddhism, which are mainly subsumed in four traditions: Nyingma, Kagyüd, Sakya, and Gelug. In fact, the differences between the various schools rarely lie in issues related to the sutric scriptures, which form the common philosophical framework with few theoretical divergences. Within the modern tantric tradition, the general division among the higher tantras is that of father, mother, and non-dual tantras. Underpinning this classification is the typically tantric view of the entire structure of phenomenal existence, of macrocosm and microcosm, as being in a constant state of equilibrium between two complementary forces. These are the "solar-feminine" force (corresponding to the aspect of *prajñā*, or energy) and the "lunar-masculine" force (corresponding to the aspect of *upāya*, or method). The solar side pertains more to emptiness and the energy that represents the potentiality of manifestation of existence, while the lunar side symbolizes the aspect of clarity and, consequently, that of the more material level of manifestation. Whether a tantra is predominantly tied to the former or the latter aspect determines its denomination respectively as a "father" or a "mother" tantra, while in the non-dual tantras, the two aspects are more balanced. This also refers to the greater or lesser importance attributed to the creation and completion phases, the stages that subsume all practice in tantra.

In the father tantras, for example, the principal means comprises the creation phase, or *kyerim,* that consists in the gradual visualization of the pure maṇḍala dimension. The outer tantras too have the maṇḍala, but with a different meaning and function. For example, if we had before us two maṇḍalas of Avalokiteśvara, one according to the kriyā tantras and the other to the anuttaratantra, they would appear to us to be the same. However, while the kriyā tantra maṇḍala is a representation of the "pure abode" of Avalokiteśvara as an outer dimension to be visualized, the anuttaratantra maṇḍala is a symbol of the inner dimension of the primordial state of the individual.

Just now we mentioned the "pure abode"; what does this actually mean? It is a realized being's pure vision. In fact, one should not think that on the accomplishment of realization, nothing any longer exists. A realized being's vision continues to exist, and this vision represents that being's wisdom and is called that being's "pure abode." However, the higher tantras deem the pure dimension to be already present in potentiality in the intrinsic structure of the individual in the three vajras or "indestructible states" of body, voice, and mind. Everything existing inside and outside is only a symbol of the nature of these three states. Closing the eyes and other senses to external stimuli, in place of his or her ordinary body, the practitioner visualizes the maṇḍala in the form of a celestial palace: at the center resides the deity, the practitioner's primordial state of consciousness. Just as in a palace there can be several people engaged in various activities, the diverse energies and functions within the body are visualized in the form of sundry divine figures: the energy of the human body is recognized as being the same as the wisdom energy of realized beings. Thus all the deities are visualized within one's own dimension in order to attain a pure or "divine" vision of the aggregates, of the elements, of the sense bases, and of everything that constitutes the individual according to the Buddhist notion. This is the fundamental principle of the "transformation" of impure vision into pure vision that is characteristic of the tantric teachings in general and is the crucial point of the practice of the father tantras.

As well as utilizing these practice methods as the base, the mother tantras are mainly concerned with the completion phase, or *dzogrim,* that consists in re-absorbing or integrating the pure maṇḍala dimension within one's "subtle" body composed of the channels, prana, and vital essence (*rtsa, rlung, thig le*). For this reason, the breathing methods and those of concentration on the cakras and channels are indispensable, together with perfect mastery of the kuṇḍalinī energy. In fact, the famous teachings known in the modern tradition as the "Six Yogas of Naropa," especially widespread in the Kagyüd school, belong to dzogrim. These are: *Tummo,* or "inner heat yoga"; *Gyulü,* or "illusory body yoga"; *Wödsal,* or "clear light yoga"; *Milam,* or "dream yoga"; *Bardo,* or "intermediate state yoga"; and *Phowa,* or "transference of consciousness yoga."[161] Originally each of these six yogas constituted the principal means of realization of a specific tantra, and only in a later period were they extracted and condensed in order that practitioners could apply them more easily.

In all the higher tantras, the final point of realization is called Mahāmudrā, the "great symbol" that transcends the separation between saṃsāra and nirvāṇa: everything is integrated in the knowledge of the ultimate nature of reality, a knowledge that comes about through the "symbol" of the deity. Often there is talk of "union," or *zungjug,* a term that can have diverse meanings: it can mean the union of outer and inner vision, the union of subject and object, the union of solar and lunar forces, and so on. In each case, the starting point is the concept of two discrete things to be united or brought together, which is the literal meaning of the Tibetan term *zungjug*. In higher and more direct teachings such as Dzogchen, however, instead of union, one talks of the condition that is "beyond" and "non-dual": knowledge of the primordial state that from the very beginning constitutes the transcendence of dualism.

The ancient tradition has a particular subdivision of the inner tantras in three series: mahāyoga, anuyoga, and atiyoga. The mahāyoga series corresponds by and large to the higher tantras of the Modern tradition in their entirety. The anuyoga series still forms part of the path of transformation, but in a less gradual and more essential way that recognizes the basic principle of the self-perfection of the state of the individual. Atiyoga, finally, does not use the method of transformation and instead directly introduces the practitioner to knowledge of the nature of mind, as we shall see in the next section.

III. DZOGCHEN ATIYOGA

With atiyoga we reach the culmination of the paths of realization: Dzogchen, or "total perfection," whose characteristic path, being based on the knowledge of self-liberation, does not entail any more transformation. In fact, when we understand the principle of self-liberation, we come to recognize that not even the method of transformation of tantra is the ultimate path. The fundamental point of the practice of Dzogchen, called *tregchöd* or "release of tension," is to relax in the state of contemplation, while the way to remain in this state is called *chogshag*, "leaving as it is."

Doing a visualization, a practice of transformation of impure vision into a maṇḍala etc., means "constructing" something, working with the mind, whereas in the state of contemplation, body, voice, and mind are totally relaxed, and it must indispensably be this way. A term used very frequently in Dzogchen is *machöpa*, "not corrected," or "not altered," whereas transformation means correcting, considering that there is impure vision on one side and pure vision on the other. Thus, all that is necessary to enter into the state of contemplation is to relax, and there is no need of any transformation practice. Some people believe that Dzogchen is only the final phase of tantric practice, rather like the Mahāmudrā of the modern tradition, but this is because the arrival point of the path of anuyoga, too, is called Dzogchen. In reality, Dzogchen atiyoga is a path complete in itself, and, as already mentioned above, is not dependent on the methods of the path of transformation.

When we follow the Dzogchen teaching, if we have sufficient capacity, we can start directly with the practice of contemplation. The only really indispensable thing is the practice of guru yoga or "unification with the state of the teacher," because it is from the teacher that we receive the direct introduction to knowledge.

The original atiyoga tantras, such as the *Kunjed Gyalpo*, often assert that the characteristic feature of Dzogchen is the absence of the ten requisites of the practice of Tantra: initiation, mantra, maṇḍala, visualization, and so on. Why are they absent in Dzogchen? Because they are ways of correcting or altering the true nature of the individual, but in reality there is nothing to change or to improve, all that is necessary is to discover the real condition and to remain relaxed in that state. So it is important to understand that the word *Dzogchen* refers to the state of the individual and that the purpose of the Dzogchen teaching is to enable one to understand this condition.

In general, the Dzogchen teaching is explained through three fundamental aspects: the base, the path, and the fruit. The base is the primordial state of the individual and is further explained through the principle of the "three wisdoms," or three natural conditions: essence, nature, and energy. One of the clearest examples to help understand this point is that of the mirror. In fact, the relative and the absolute condition can both be represented symbolically by a mirror, the former by the images reflected in the mirror and the latter by the mirror's intrinsic potentiality to reflect. The same holds for the state of the individual. What is the individual? It is the one who possesses the primordial state of consciousness, comparable to the nature of the mirror that is pure, clear, and limpid. This corresponds to the three conditions called "essence, nature, and energy." Just as a reflection arises from the mirror and in a certain sense is a quality of the mirror, all of our thoughts and all of the manifestations of our energy, both beautiful and ugly, are only our own reflection, a quality of our primordial state. If we are aware and are really in this state, everything becomes a quality of ours and there is no longer any separation into subject and object or any consideration of relative and absolute.

We have said that as individuals we are made up of our own primordial state as essence, nature, and energy. However, we should not think of these three aspects as if they were three separate objects: the original condition is one alone, and the fact that it is explained through three distinct concepts is only to help understand it. In reality we cannot define or distinguish "this is purity," "this is clarity," and "this is limpidity."

What is the essence? In order to discover the primordial state the reflection is needed, that in this case comprises the body, voice, and mind, and particularly the last of these three. In fact, it is from the mind that thoughts arise. If a thought arises while we are observing the mind, we must seek whence the thought originates, where it abides and, finally, where it disappears. However, the moment we recognize the thought it disappears and we find nothing at all: there is no origin, no abiding, and no place where it disappears. We find there is nothing, which is why the essence is said to be emptiness.

The concept of emptiness, or *śūnyatā*, is very widespread in Mahāyāna Buddhism, particularly in the Prajñāpāramitā tradition. However the fundamental point to understand is that emptiness is the true essence of material phenomena and not some abstract and separate entity. In fact, the same exercise of seeking the origin of thought can be applied to any object perceived by the senses. If we see a beautiful object and examine whence this "beauty" arises and where it disappears, we find nothing concrete: everything is at the same level; both subject and object are in essence empty. Just this is the ultimate condition of the individual.

What is clarity? If the essence is "emptiness" this does not mean that nothing exists. When we observe a thought and it disappears, immediately afterwards another thought arises, that might be: "I am seeking the origin of thought and I find nothing!" This too is a thought, is it not? It is a thought that thinks about the origin of thought. In this way many thoughts can arise continuously. Even though we may be convinced that their essence is emptiness, nevertheless they manifest ceaselessly. The same applies to our senses: all the objects we perceive are the ceaseless appearing of our karmic vision. This, then, is the nature of clarity.

What is energy, or the potentiality of energy? It is the active and uninterrupted function of the nature of our primordial state. In general, one talks of the "function of wisdom" in relation to the pure vision of an enlightened being and of the "function of the mind" in relation to the impure vision of saṃsāra. For example, we think something and then we follow this thought and enter into action. Or, while we are practicing, we transform ourselves into a deity with that deity's maṇḍala and pure dimension. All of this evinces the function of energy in the aspects of its continuity and its capacity to produce something. Through our energy there arise all the manifestations at the level of subject and object, that can be pure or impure, beautiful or ugly, etc. If we place a crystal in sunlight, we immediately see it radiate many iridescent rays. In this case, the crystal represents the state of the individual and the colors that manifest externally represent everything that we see and perceive through the senses. This "mode of manifestation" of energy, in which the reflection manifests externally, is called *tsal* in Tibetan. Impure vision tied to karma and to the material dimension and pure vision at the level of subject and object are both *tsal* manifestations of energy.

There is also a way in which energy manifests "internally," in the subject itself, in the same way that images are reflected in a mirror: this is called *rolpa*. For example, when we do a tantric practice and transform ourselves into the dimension of a deity with its maṇḍala, we are working with this kind of energy, because everything is taking place inside us. Obviously, in the first stages of the practice of transformation, it is very important to utilize the mind, concentration, etc., in order to achieve this function concretely. But at a certain point the pure dimension of the maṇḍala can manifest even without any effort on our part, and this occurs through *rolpa* energy.

The third way energy manifests is called *dang*, and represents somewhat the basic condition of energy, its potentiality to take on any form according to circumstances. The traditional example is that of a crystal placed on a cloth: the crystal will take on the color of the cloth even though in itself it is transparent and colorless.

Essence, nature and, energy are called the three "primordial wisdoms" because they represent the state of enlightenment in its entirety. The individual has these three aspects from the very beginning and continues to have them even upon the accomplishment of total enlightenment. One might think: "What then is the point of practicing, if we already have the same qualities as a Buddha? We can just stay in peace doing nothing!" Of course we can stay in peace doing nothing as long as we are not distracted, as long as we really find ourselves in this state. But if it is otherwise, it means we are slaves to dualism, conditioned by the object. In this case it is not enough to think that we have the essence, nature, and energy: conditioning by dualistic vision is precisely the obstacle that we need to overcome in order to allow the sun of the primordial state to shine again.

This is the reason why the path is necessary, that in its turn encompasses the three aspects of view, meditation, and behavior. In Dzogchen the "view," or perspective, does not address something external, it means simply observing oneself in order to discover one's true condition. Basically, it means discerning the dualistic conditioning undergone by the body, voice, and mind in order to overcome it through practice. In no way is the Dzogchen teaching intended to build a new cage in place of the one in which we already find ourselves; on the contrary, it serves as a key to open the door of the cage. In fact, it is not enough to discover we are trapped in the cage of dualism: we need to get out of it, and this is the purpose of "meditation."

As regards the second aspect, meditation, even though at the start it is necessary to utilize methods of concentration, breathing, etc., to calm the mind and foster a condition of stability, the true purpose of meditation is continuity of awareness, or presence of the primordial state. Here we should speak rather of contemplation, the essential point of which is pure instant presence, or *rigpa*. The Dzogchen practitioner seeks to understand this state of presence through diverse experiences: of emptiness, of clarity, of sensations of pleasure, and so on. Actually, the aim of the methods in the śūtras and the tantras is also solely to kindle experiences. The true path of the Dzogchen practitioner, however, is contemplation. In fact, it is only when we are in contemplation that all the tensions of body, voice, and mind are finally effortlessly released: until we discover and abide stably in this state, our experience of "relaxation" will be incomplete. Contemplation, as suggested above, can be tied to an experience of emptiness, of clarity, or of bliss, but its state is one alone: the instant presence of rigpa. There exist various methods to recognize, establish, and integrate this state in all the circumstances of everyday life tied to the three fundamental series of Dzogchen: Semde, Longde, and Mennagde.

"Behavior," the last of the three aspects of the path, concerns the attitude practitioners should have the moment they "come out" of a session of contemplation and undertake various activities. Its purpose is thus to achieve the total integration of contemplation with everyday life, overcoming any differentiation between meditation and non-meditation.

Let us now turn to the third and final aspect of the Dzogchen teaching, the fruit or "result" of practice: realization. We have already said that the primordial state contains in potentiality the manifestation of enlightenment. The sun, for example, naturally has light and rays, but when the sky is cloudy, we do not see them. The clouds in this case represent our obstacles that are a result of dualism and conditioning: when they are overcome, the state of self-perfection shines with all its manifestations of energy, without ever having been altered or improved. This is the characteristic principle of Dzogchen. Not understanding this may lead one to think that Dzogchen is the same as Zen or Ch'an. At heart, Zen, which without any doubt is a high and direct Buddhist teaching, is based on the principle of emptiness as explained in śūtras such as the *Prajñāpāramitā*. Even though in this regard, in substance it is no different from Dzogchen, the particularity of Dzogchen lies in the direct introduction to the primordial state not as "pure emptiness" but rather as endowed with all the aspects of the self-perfection of energy. It is through applying these that one attains realization.[162]

Concerning the fruit, there are the three kāyas, "bodies" or "dimensions": dharmakāya, saṃbhogakāya, and nirmāṇakāya. In no manner are the three kāyas levels of realization: there cannot be a dharmakāya without a nirmāṇakāya, or vice-versa. In order to understand their meaning we must return to the concepts of essence, nature, and energy. *Kāya* means "body," and thus the whole dimension, both material and immaterial, in which we find ourselves; *dharma* means existence. So dharmakāya is the total dimension of existence, without any exclusion. Thus it corresponds to the essence, the ineffable and immeasurable condition beyond all the concepts and limits of dualism.

Saṃbhoga means "wealth" or "enjoyments," so *saṃbhogakāya* means the "dimension of wealth." In this case wealth does not refer to something material but rather to the self-perfected qualities that manifest through the substance of the elements, that is, through color. In fact, when the elements take on the material state, they pass from the level of "color" to the solid level of the physical elements. In brief, everything that we consider as the pure dimension of the maṇḍala and of the deity pertains to the saṃbhogakāya, the source of the transmission of Tantra. This corresponds to the aspect of the "nature" of clarity of the primordial state.

Nirmāṇa means "manifestation" or "emanation" and corresponds to the aspect of uninterrupted energy. So *nirmāṇakāya* means the "dimension of manifestation." In fact, through energy, both pure vision and impure vision can manifest and both are deemed nirmāṇakāya dimensions. Pure vision transcends the material dimension and constitutes the essence of the elements, while impure vision corresponds to what is called "karmic vision," produced as the outcome of determined actions carried out in the past.

The word *nirmāṇakāya* can also refer to a realized individual, such as Śākyamuni Buddha, who takes on a physical form in order to transmit the teachings. In fact, it is only in the nirmāṇakāya dimension that the teachings can be uttered and transmitted at the level of subject and object. The saṃbhogakāya is that dimension in which the potentialities of sound, light, and rays (*sgra, 'od, zer*), the three fundamental sources of manifestation, appear as the pure vision of the maṇḍala, the origin of the tantric teachings. The books called "tantras," that contain the revelations of these manifestations, constitute the testimony of teachers who had direct contact with the saṃbhogakāya and only later put it in writing. As regards the Dzogchen teaching in particular, its tantras are said to arise directly from dharmakāya, symbolized by the primordial Buddha Samantabhadra depicted as a sky-blue Buddha, naked and unadorned: the original purity of the state of the individual.

4 The Eighty-four Chapters of the *Kunjed Gyalpo*

The title of the *Kunjed Gyalpo* is given in the Indian language and in Tibetan. When a tantra starts with the words *gyagar keddu*, which literally means "in the Indian language," sometimes this means Sanskrit and at other times it means the language of Oḍḍiyāna because it is very likely that at that time this country formed part of India. The original title is *Sarvadharma mahāsandhi bodhicitta kulayarāja*, translated into Tibetan as *Chö tamched dzogpa chenpo changchubkyi sem kunjed gyalpo*.

Sarvadharma mahāsandhi: *sarva* means all, everything; *dharma* in this case designates not the teaching, but existence, everything that exists. Thus *sarva dharma* indicates the totality of phenomena of existence. *Maha*, in Tibetan *chenpo*, means great, or total; *sandhi*[163] corresponds to the Tibetan *dzogpa*, meaning perfection or completeness: *mahāsandhi* or *dzogpa chenpo* means that everything is perfect or complete, nothing is lacking. Thus the expression *sarvadharma mahāsandhi* signifies that all existence is perfect, complete in all the aspects that we deem good or bad, of both transmigration in saṃsāra and of the liberation of nirvāṇa. In fact, the term "perfect" denotes that everything is included in it, but this should not be understood in the sense that all defects and negativities have been eliminated and only the positive kept. This is not what is meant. True Dzogpa Chenpo is not an object or a text: it is the state of consciousness possessed by each and every individual.

Bodhicitta: the sūtras speak at length about bodhicitta as a commitment motivated by compassion to help others. At the level of the relative condition, there are deemed to be two kinds of bodhicitta: bodhicitta of aspiration or intention and bodhicitta of action, and whoever keeps the bodhicitta commitment is called a Bodhisattva. However in Dzogchen, bodhicitta does not mean only the principle of compassion characteristic of the Bodhisattva path. Bodhicitta is the original state, the true condition as it is, immutable. In Tibetan it is called *changchubsem*. *Chang* means purified, or pure, clear and, limpid since the beginning, because there is nothing to purify. *Chub* means perfected, because even though one may think it is necessary to progress and to improve in order to achieve realization, the state of the individual has been perfect from the very beginning, there is nothing to perfect or to achieve that one does not already have. In general, *sem* means the mind, but in this case it refers to the state of consciousness, or "nature of mind." Distinguishing between the state of consciousness and the mind is like trying to separate a mirror from its reflection. Or, if we think of the sky, trying to distinguish the blue surface from the clouds that form on it. However, essentially, the true condition is indivisible: the reflection derives from the mirror, which is its sole base, and in the same way, the sky also includes clouds; the clouds themselves are sky. Thus, even though it is said that the mind is produced by dualism and its true condition, the state of consciousness, is beyond dualism, the nature of both is single and indivisible. This is the meaning of *sem* in the term *changchubsem*, bodhicitta. At times the texts speak of *nyingpo changchubkyi sem*, "bodhicitta of the essence," but this in like manner is a reference to the primordial state of consciousness, synonymous with *dzogpa chenpo*, "total perfection." *Gyüd* or tantra, which literally means "continuation," too refers to the state of consciousness, as does the term *Mahāmudrā* or "total symbol." In the sūtras, on the other hand, the expression *desheg nyingpo* or *sugatagarbha*, "essence of the enlightened ones," is widely used. The state of consciousness can be referred to in many ways, but in Dzogchen, and especially in the Semde series, one of the terms most frequently used is *bodhicitta*.

Kulayarāja, in Tibetan *Kunjed Gyalpo*, is the actual title, and the text clearly explains the principle comprised in this title. *Rāja*, or *gyalpo*, means "king" and *kulaya*, or *kunjed*, means the "creator," or "radiator" of all manifestation. Literally it could be rendered "all-creating king" or "creator king." But what does this actually mean? Always and solely it refers to the state of consciousness, regardless whether one calls it

Dzogpa Chenpo or bodhicitta. Kunjed Gyalpo thus denotes the primordial state of each individual. Why, then, is it called "creator"? Because all of saṃsāra and nirvāṇa, everything that we consider positive or negative, everything that we differentiate, defining it as good or bad, and so forth, can be compared to a reflection in a mirror. The state of consciousness, on the other hand, is like the condition of the mirror that remains clear and pure without changing. Thus all phenomena arise from the state of consciousness in the same way that reflections appear on the surface of a mirror: hence it is called *Kunjed Gyalpo*, "the all-creating king." This is the name of the tantra. Let us now move on to a brief analysis of the eighty-four chapters of which it is composed, dwelling only on the most important points.[164]

Chapter 1

The first chapter is introductory and explains how the revelation of this tantra took place. The primordial state, dharmakāya Samanta-bhadra, manifests as the teacher, and around him the purity of the five aggregates, of the five elements, and so on, appears as infinite Buddhas and Bodhisattvas in male and female form. Everything is a manifestation of the primordial state in the dimensions of dharmakāya, of saṃbhogakāya—in the various aspects connected with the five elements, and of nirmāṇakāya. Also present are yogins who are following the four paths of atiyoga, anuyoga, mahāyoga, and sattvayoga.

How does the tantra originate? It is as if there were a dialogue between dharmakāya, the state of consciousness symbolized by Samantabhadra (here called Kunjed Gyalpo) and saṃbhogakāya, represented by Vajrasattva. Here Vajrasattva, who asks the questions, is called Sattvavajra and is blue instead of white, as he is usually depicted. Since, basically, everything is a manifestation of the state of Samantabhadra, the dimension in which the tantra manifests is described as a great sphere or *thigle*: everything is one single sphere. The term *thigle* indicates the true nature or potentiality of emptiness, represented by a sphere because a sphere has no corners: the text frequently uses the expression "total sphere without corners" (*thig le chen po mtha' zur med*). In fact, "total sphere," or *thigle chenpo*, is a synonym of Dzogpa Chenpo. In short, what this really means is that the state of consciousness has no beginning or end and is free of limits, like an immense sphere.

Thus ends the first chapter, an introduction as is generally found at the beginning of every tantra to illustrate the environment and specific circumstances that give rise to the dialogue.

Chapter 2

The second chapter aims to explain the origin of manifestation, the source of pure vision and impure vision alike. All arises from Kunjed Gyalpo, the state of consciousness. The state of consciousness is composed of the three primordial wisdoms (*ye shes gsum ldan*): essence, nature, and energy. From the state of consciousness there radiate forth the five wisdoms, the true nature of the five passions: attachment, anger, pride, ignorance, and jealousy, or one can just as well say that from the five passions there arise the five wisdoms. The five elements too—space, air, fire, water, and earth—called "the five ornamental causes," arise as qualities of the energy of the state of consciousness.

The text often repeats the Tibetan word *nga*, which means "I," but it should always be understood to refer to the state of consciousness. Samantabhadra, the state of dharmakāya, has taken on the form of transmitter of the teaching. He says, "There is nobody apart from me who has created dualism," however, this does not mean that Samantabhadra has concretely done something, but rather that nothing exists apart from the state of the individual. Hence, usually it is said that the state of consciousness of each individual is the real center of the universe. The three dimensions (dharmakāya, saṃbhogakāya, nirmāṇakāya) too, are always and only the state of consciousness and do not exist apart from it. This holds for any pure manifestation, such as the vision of a maṇḍala or of a deity and also for any impure dimension: everything arises from the state of consciousness. So, when Samantabhadra Kunjed Gyalpo says: "Now I will explain my condition," this means he will clarify the condition of the state of consciousness. "I have three natures," he says finally, "and my fundamental essence is bodhicitta," explaining the meaning of the three syllables *chang chub sem* as was elucidated above.

Chapter 3

This chapter explains the place of origin or way of arising of existence, as the manifestation of the state of consciousness. Kunjed Gyalpo often tells Sattvavajra: "Engage your mind in hearing," that is, in sound. This is highly significant because sound is our main means of communication. A mantra, for example, only becomes effective when it is recited or chanted, because it is through sound that it is connected with a specific power. For us, moreover, living in the human dimension, any vision that appears before us, whether good or bad, is living energy manifesting externally. When there is a vision, there is also its energy, and it is thanks to the latter that we are able to see and perceive the other sense objects. But what is the means through which this energy is able to contact us? It is through sound. Living in sound means being connected with energy. This is the reason why the tantra frequently advises to "enter into sound."

Kunjed Gyalpo says, "Before I existed." What does this mean? It means before the state of consciousness. In general, one speaks of the origin, of the beginning of existence, but from which point of view? From the point of view of the condition of mind. In fact, if we want really to believe that there is a beginning, what could it be? The moment we enter into dualism. For example, when we meditate abiding in the condition of the state of consciousness, we can be in a calm state, free of thoughts (*gnas pa*). Then suddenly, a thought arises, like a fish jumping out of water; we follow it, and enter into dualism. This is the beginning. Obviously this is a "small" beginning, but it enables us to understand the true nature of the origin of existence: it is dualism. Whence, then, does this dualism arise? Always and only from the state of consciousness; there is no other origin. Thus, it is written that before the state of consciousness, there is nothing that can be identified by concepts or defined in any way.

Sattvavajra then poses an important question: "The three dimensions, dharmakāya, saṃbhogakāya, and nirmāṇakāya," which are a manifestation of realization, "arise from the state of consciousness, but is there a means for reaching this level?" That is, he is asking, Is there a way or path? "If there is no means, how does one get there? How do the three dimensions manifest? If there is a means, how does one proceed?" The state of consciousness replies: "There is no way to achieve the three dimensions, nor is there a path to tread in order to reach me," because otherwise there would remain the concept of a direction, of something to pursue outside. Instead, the true nature is the self-arising wisdom, so there is nothing objective.

Then the "five paths" are discussed, so called because they correspond to the five aggregates,[165] the five passions, and so on. The path that leads to the five self-arising wisdoms consists in the five passions: attachment, anger, pride, ignorance, and jealousy. We all have the five passions: when we know how to recognize their true condition, there is no other path to seek and to follow in order to realize oneself.

Sattvavajra then asks, "Why are the five paths called self-arising? Why are they wisdom?" Kunjed Gyalpo answers by explaining that self-arising means that they do not depend on cause and effect, and wisdom means that they are pure, uninterrupted clarity. As self-arising wisdom does not depend on cause and effect, there is no gradual course on which to progress, no path on which one progresses step by step: the path on which one does not progress and on which one does not tread: this is the true path!

The text then proceeds to explain the true condition of the passions and their correspondences with the three worlds of form, of formlessness, and of desire.[166] But what is the origin of the three worlds, what is their cause? They only appear when one is in dualism, and it is on dualism that they depend for their existence: in reality they are all manifestations of the state of consciousness and do not exist outside it.

Chapter 4

Chapter four explains why the terms *Kunjed Gyalpo* and *bodhicitta* are used to designate the state of consciousness, what other names are used to define it, and the meaning of each of these words. For example, it explains that another synonym is *dharmatā,* or "nature of existence," a term that does not refer only to the condition of external phenomena but also to the nature of the state of consciousness. Kunjed Gyalpo says, "If you conceive or understand my condition, my nature...." But, whose condition? The condition of the state of consciousness. Whoever knows its condition is able finally to understand the nature of all the teachers and at the same time to comprehend clearly the real meaning of all the teachings, from Hīnayāna up to the inner tantras and Dzogchen atiyoga. Knowing the condition of the state of consciousness is equivalent to knowing all dharmas, as if it were a universal key. However, to do this it is necessary to leave behind action and effort because these do not lead to knowledge: the true nature is self-perfection.

Chapter 5

In this chapter, Kunjed Gyalpo says, "Now I will explain my nature: it is not other than one." That is, not other than the single state of consciousness of the individual. "From it there arose the nine vehicles." In general, Buddhism talks of "three vehicles," of the śrāvakas, of the pratyekabuddhas, and of the Bodhisattvas. In the ancient tradition of Tibetan Buddhism, to these are added the "six vehicles" of Tantra: the three outer tantras: kriyā, ubhaya, and yoga, and the three inner tantras: mahāyoga, anuyoga, and atiyoga. "All is unified or perfected in

Dzogpa Chenpo, bodhicitta." The conclusion of all the teachings is Dzogpa Chenpo, the state of bodhicitta. "Where is this state? In the dimension of dharmatā," the true condition of the state of consciousness. This point is a bit difficult, but there are many explanations of this topic in other texts. "Where does it manifest, where does it become clear? In the sky—in the space of the pure presence of rigpa," meaning in the union of emptiness and clarity. "Where is it present? Both in the outer world, in the environment, and in the inner world, in beings." In short, it is omnipresent, but this should not be misconstrued as similar to the denotation of "omnipresence" as one of the attributes of God in Christianity. In this case "omnipresence" indicates that our outer world is our own creation, a karmic vision, an appearance tied to ignorance of the true condition. "What example can be given of the state of consciousness? The sky." However, even though an example can be helpful in order to understand the state, it can never furnish a perfect comparison. In fact: "However many analyses one can carries out with words, he who does not know my state will not meet me," that is, he will never enter the state of consciousness and, consequently, will never see the essence of the Dharma.

Chapter 6

This chapter discusses the single root. Kunjed Gyalpo says, "All dharmas conclude in Dzogpa Chenpo," and explains the meaning of the letter *A*, which represents emptiness and at the same time the essence of sound. Then he explains how karmic action arises. When the causes of the five passions and of the five aggregates are present, gradually one enters into dualistic vision and transmigrates in the six *lokas*, or dimensions of the diverse classes of beings.

Now there follows a point that is quite important to remember concerning the ways of realization based on the principle of cause and effect. All the sūtra teachings, for example, are based on the notion of the causality of karma. Karma is deemed important, whence derives the need to purify oneself, to accumulate good deeds, and so on. But all this remains at the outer level, very far from the true meaning of meditation. This is characteristic of the paths based on cause and effect, so Samantabhadra Kunjed Gyalpo's advice is not to communicate his words to those who follow or preserve these paths. Why so? Because persons who are heavily conditioned must ripen slowly. If one communicates the truth to them, all of a sudden they can get frightened and, consequently, stray far from the path. Since in terms of karmic vision, the law of the cause and effect, of actions, does exist, if such people were taught that the true condition is beyond cause and effect they might be overcome by doubts and turn against the teaching. Thereby they would block their progress and lose the opportunity to recognize the state of consciousness, thereby prolonging transmigration. So one must be careful about communicating these teachings.

The Mahāyāna talks at length about the two truths: the absolute truth is deemed something to accept, while the relative truth, all things considered, should be rejected. These analyses of the two truths may be necessary so long as one remains at the level of the mind, but when one transcends it and enters the state of consciousness, everything loses importance. That is why the text speaks of the single root, the state of consciousness: whatever one analyses, whether it is deemed good or bad, everything that exists has a single root in the state of consciousness.

Chapter 7

Chapter seven explains the principle of self-perfection: the fruit of enlightenment is already perfected and is not something to construct through effort because it has existed from the very beginning. This condition can be communicated in a more or less direct manner as befits the person to whom one is transmitting the teaching. In this regard, the text explains the meaning of two terms: *trangdön* and *ngedön*, the provisional meaning and the definitive meaning.

What does "provisional meaning" mean? If someone is heavily conditioned, with a very closed and limited outlook, then in order to communicate the teaching to that person, it is necessary to enter their attitude, take cognizance of their beliefs, and work on their level to enable them to "break through" their limitations. As long as the person remains confined within his or her "narrowness," everything the teacher communicates is the "provisional meaning." On overcoming their limits, understanding of the true nature dawns: this is the "definitive meaning." In general, in Buddhism all the explanations about karma, the law of cause and effect, etc., are deemed to pertain to the "provisional meaning." The real meaning corresponds to the explanation of the condition of the state of consciousness. This explains why Dzogpa Chenpo is the conclusion of all the teachings: *dzogpa* means perfection, and the various nuances of its meaning are explained in detail in the text.

Chapter 8

This chapter opens with an explanation of the essence, nature, and energy, which constitute the condition of the state of consciousness. It then goes on to discuss the ultimate concept of the outer tantras (kriyā, ubhaya, and yoga) and of the inner tantras (mahāyoga and anuyoga). These vehicles do not achieve the goal, they do not understand the true meaning. Each of them, in fact, has its own view or way of defining ultimate reality, of meditating, of keeping commitments, and so on. Here, however, the text explains that as from the beginning nothing concrete or objective exists, in the state of consciousness there is no view, no meditation, no commitments, etc.

The true meaning of "yoga" is to abide in the condition of the state of consciousness, however, this does not concur with the various techniques of visualization and concentration on the maṇḍala used in the various tantric series. In our text, the fundamental aims, but not the techniques, of the sundry series of tantras are summarized and explained in a simple way, enabling the reader to understand easily their essential meaning. On the other hand, if we seek to grasp the ultimate meaning of mahāyoga, for example, by directly studying its tantras, then we must devote a long time to reading them because many of the explanations found in these texts concern visualization of maṇḍalas, mantras, and so forth. Moreover, without a sound basic knowledge, we will not even be able to understand what they are talking about.

In Dzogchen, conversely, the condition of everything is bodhicitta: of the view, of the meditation, of the commitment, or samaya, etc., such that there is no need to generate another bodhicitta or to transform into bodhicitta something that already is bodhicitta. Knowledge of this condition is enough, so the text says that all the various aspects of tantric practice are without objective reality.

Chapter 9

Chapter nine explains the meaning of the vehicles based on the principle of cause and effect, that is, of those teachings tied more to the external, enabling the reader to understand that they are erroneous paths. For example, if we want to reach a certain destination and instead we arrive somewhere else, this means we have taken the wrong road: the text explains that likewise these vehicles are "wrong paths." This is by no means a censure of teachers of the vehicles of cause and effect based on karma; however, one can certainly assert that some of these paths display an imperfect understanding of the condition of the individual. Were this not the case, some teachers would not insist on the need for a gradual path that is the same for everybody, where ineluctably one has to proceed one step at a time.

In general, one speaks of the "ten natures" of Tantra as the fundamental means of realization. For example, first of all, there is the initiation, then the ritual, concentration on the maṇḍala, belief in the deity, and so on. However, these are refuted here, as one accedes directly to the state of consciousness. Kunjed Gyalpo says: "Seeking me through the ten natures is like wishing to walk in the sky and falling down to earth."

Chapter 10

Chapter ten, which discusses the perfection of the state of consciousness, brings up a very important point. A practitioner of Dzogchen must be aware of all the teachings (outer tantras, mahāyoga, anuyoga, etc.) and know how to apply them because Dzogchen is not a school or sect that imposes limits. Any method can prove useful as long as it is practiced in the spirit of Dzogchen. Each teaching has its "narrowness" that says you must do this, you must not do that. But this is not so in Dzogchen because the aim of this teaching is to liberate, and in this case this does not mean only from transmigration in saṃsāra, a topic that is much discussed. Liberation means helping one to emerge from one's "narrowness," to overcome one's limits, and any method can be used to achieve this aim. For example, a Dzogchen practitioner can practice the Vajrasattva purification method, visualizing Vajrasattva and reciting his mantra. But the Dzogchen tantras never speak of visualizing anything. Kunjed Gyalpo never says, "Visualize me!" or "Meditate on my form!" There is nothing to visualize. Visualizing and reciting mantras are methods characteristic of tantra, and it is important for the practitioner to be aware of this and to know how to apply these practices in an essential manner. Pronouncing the syllable *HŪṂ*, for example, one instantaneously finds oneself present in a pure dimension without needing meticulous visualization of the deity's various arms, the symbolic attributes in each of his or her hands, and so on, as is the case in the gradual meditation stages of tantra. The same applies to the offerings: whether or not one tenders offerings is not important, but if a practitioner deems it necessary, then he or she can offer material objects because neither is there any restriction on making offerings. Nevertheless, the offerings are always made in the

Dzogchen attitude and not in an ordinary way, without being conditioned by the concept of something exterior.

Chapter 11

Kunjed Gyalpo says, "I am the root of all dharmas. I am the nature of all dharmas, of all existence. Apart from my nature, nothing exists. The three dimensions, of dharmakāya, saṃbhogakāya, and nirmāṇakāya, are my nature. The realized ones, too, of the past, of the present, and of the future, are my nature." What does this mean? Whether we are considering a being that is already realized or one that has yet to achieve self-realization, they are both the same, they are the nature of the primordial state.

The state of consciousness is also the ultimate nature of the four yogas, of the path, of the three worlds, and constitutes the base of the five colors, of the five elements, and of the beings of the six lokas. All visions and all phenomena of the outer and inner world only exist as its nature: "I am the root of all existence," concludes Kunjed Gyalpo. Just as the sky is omnipresent, so everything that constitutes the existence of an individual, all that lies before us, is a manifestation of the state of consciousness. The body, voice, and mind are the source of existence of the individual, and the individual's final goal, too, consists in this same condition.

Chapter 12

The state of consciousness is the base of the *lungs*, of the teaching, of the scriptures, of the secret instructions, or *upadeśas*, of the tantras and their commentaries, and of the methods of kriyā, ubhaya, and so on. Despite all their divergences, the culmination of the various teachings too, resides in this state: the state of consciousness is the supreme teaching. Unless one achieves the level of Kunjed Gyalpo, one cannot overcome the condition of existence and of dualism. Many vehicles are discussed, but in reality there exists only one vehicle: the state of consciousness, and the *Kunjed Gyalpo* tantra is like the essence or fundamental epitome of all the teachings.

Chapter 13

This chapter explains that if a person meets a teaching like Dzogchen, this is the outcome of a precise cause of a previously established connection. Conversely, if a person is unsuitable or has not got a precise link, then, even if he or she is directly instructed about the nature of the state of consciousness, this would bear no fruit. Everything depends on the type of the person.

Chapter 14

Chapter fourteen explains the kind of person to whom one should transmit the teaching and the one from whom it should be kept hidden, just as a fitting vessel has to be found to keep a fine liqueur, otherwise it might spoil.

Chapter 15

Chapter fifteen has some verses that can only be understood by reading the secondary tantras. Among other things they explain that even were someone to sacrifice himself or herself for kalpas, i.e., for incalculable time cycles, they would not attain realization until they discovered their own state. There follows mention of one of the fundamental principles of the kriyā tantra, that of *trü* or "ritual ablution," which consists, for example, in sprinkling water over one's head while reciting a purification mantra. This rite is also performed during the conferral of an initiation. However, all of this is provisional until one enters the purity of the state of consciousness: no outer ablution exists that can purify the condition of the state.

The text goes on to discuss the principle of non-distraction, using the example of a horse tied by rope to a post: it can only turn close around it and cannot escape very far. In the same way, thought must be controlled through remembrance and presence.

Finally, another verse says that dharmakāya is one's own mind, uncorrected and unaltered, when one is in the natural condition. Not correcting the mind, there is nothing at all to do or to change: this is called the "unborn" state (*skye ba med pa*).

Chapter 16

In brief, this chapter contains advice given by Kunjed Gyalpo to Sattvavajra.

Chapter 17

Chapter seventeen talks of the relics of the Enlightened Ones. In general, it is said that at the moment of passing into nirvāṇa, Buddhas leave behind relics, for example in the form of small white or five-colored beads (*ring bsrel*) for the benefit of beings. Here the text explains their real meaning in relation to knowledge of the primordial state.

Chapter 18

In brief, this chapter asserts that the state of consciousness cannot be discovered or recognized by means of a quest.

Chapter 19

This chapter, too, which elucidates self-perfection, clearly affirms that there is nothing to seek.

Chapter 20

Chapter twenty explains that the state of consciousness is the root of all dharmas, the origin of all phenomena.

Chapter 21

This chapter explains why it is necessary to base oneself on definitions even though the true nature transcends words and explanations.

Chapter 22

This important chapter is one of the original sources of the practice of *tregchöd*. Dzogchen practice comprises two aspects: *tregchöd* and *thödgal*. Many teachers have written extensive explanations about *tregchöd*, which is the fundamental point whose origin can be found in tantras such as *Kunjed Gyalpo*.

Chapters 23, 24 & 25

These chapters are important, and above all they concern practice at the concrete level. Reading and reflecting on these chapters, practitioners who have understood the principle of Dzogchen will be able easily to grasp its meaning. In this way they become a true support for one's practice. However, an ordinary person, even a great scholar, would find it very difficult to understand them.

Chapter 26

Chapter twenty-six, which treats several topics, also discusses morality or *tsültrim*. In general, on taking monastic vows one has to comply with the Vinaya, and even though initially one may do it by imposition, gradually, by understanding their underlying reasons, one learns to obey the rules through awareness, that is, by comprehending the negative consequences of given actions. If a rule says not to kill animals, for example, one must understand that killing means causing another being to suffer, and, on the basis of this understanding, one abstains from committing such a deed. In this way the practitioner attains the level of self-discipline.

The same holds in regard to meditation. Tantra employs many techniques of visualization of cakras, channels, and so on in order to transform our condition. All of this remains at the dualistic level; however, by means of these methods we can gradually attain the state beyond dualism. Hence, here our text reiterates the importance of correctly understanding the final goal of all these practices and of not deeming them a kind of goal in themselves, otherwise one becomes like a thirsty man chasing a mirage of water in the desert.

The text goes on to discuss the five conditions "without an interval," proper to those who commit very grave deeds that cause immediate rebirth in the lower realms of existence without the "interval" of the bardo state: murdering one's parents, killing a Buddha, and so on.[167] Nevertheless, these deeds may be deemed "grave" so long as one remains, at the level of the mind, bound by the notion of acceptance and rejection. But the condition of the state of consciousness is pure from the very beginning and does not undergo any change, whether or not one commits a grave deed. On the basis of the Vinaya canons, we can be certain that one who commits one of the five most heinous crimes will go straight to hell when he or she dies. On the other hand, we would say that a monk who has observed his rules all of his life will have a good rebirth, as if the former were descending and the latter ascending. However, from the point of view of the state of consciousness, there is no difference between them because their condition is the same. Why, then, are they on two such different levels? Because both are conditioned by the mind, by the dualistic consideration that gives rise to the idea that rebirth in the higher states means "ascending" and in the lower states means "descending."

Which is the way to "ascend"? Performing good, virtuous deeds. But in terms of the state of consciousness, this is comparable to a reflection on the surface of a mirror. The only way to overcome obstacles is the path of wisdom, and in this regard, it is more important to practice one hour of meditation, cognizant of its true meaning, than to do prostrations for ten years. Why so? Doing prostrations is a means of physical purification that depends on one's intention. People who prostrate are convinced they need purification, they want to purify themselves, and it is precisely this intention that makes purification and the accumulation of virtue possible. Practitioners of meditation, conversely, know that the path of meditation can eliminate many obstacles, even in a relatively short time. In fact, realization follows upon total purification from obstacles. Returning to the evildoer and the virtuous monk in the example cited above, the moment understanding of the true meaning of meditation arises, both can accomplish realization in the same way. This is so because once one enters the true meaning of meditation, knowledge of the state of consciousness, then negative karmic deeds can easily be overcome without needing to resort to lengthy purification methods. That is why in Dzogchen it is said that realization does not depend on one's age, intelligence, or education but only on one's knowledge of the state of consciousness: this is the conclusion of the teaching.

Another important point often discussed is the state of "non-meditation" or *gom med*, literally "nothing to meditate." One might then ask, Why then does one need to meditate? "Non-meditation" means there is no object on which to meditate. If we visualize an external deity, or if we transform into the form of a deity, this means we are engaged in mental activity, in the imagination, which is always at the dualistic level. However, the final goal of meditation has nothing to do with this: "nothing to meditate" means not creating with the mind, not entering into activity, not correcting, leaving everything in the authentic condition as it is. If we pour muddy water into a glass and leave it for a while, we will see the muck settle at the bottom and the water become limpid. Likewise, when a thought arises, we do not block it, we do not enter into activity, we do nothing: we simply let it be. However *letting be* does not mean getting distracted: it is necessary to maintain presence without entering into activity. Can we say that someone remaining in this state is meditating or thinking of something? No, there is nothing on which to meditate, there is no color or form to imagine, there is no concept on which to fix one's attention. Were there one, it would no longer be true meditation. This is called *gom med*, and the highest level of practice in Mahāmudrā is defined in the same way, equivalent, in short, to tregchöd in Dzogchen.

Chapter 27

This chapter explains that the condition of existence, externally and internally, is not something concrete. All phenomena are our own manifestation.

Chapter 28

This chapter explains that the condition of the primordial state is immutable; it never changes. This means that nothing concrete or objective exists because *change* implies, first of all, that an entity exists that is subject to change. The true condition is said to be immutable like the sky because one cannot say of the sky: "Look, it starts here and ends there," it is beyond all limits. *ying*, a characteristic Dzogchen term, is also mentioned in this regard: it corresponds to the Sanskrit *dhātu*, "the fundamental condition." The sūtras generally use the term *chöying* or *dharmadhātu*, literally "the nature or condition of existence," as a kind of synonym of emptiness. However in Dzogchen, *ying* has two meanings: first, it refers to the general condition of space, which governs all. In fact, in order to exist, an object must be in space and have a "space" of its own. The second meaning presupposes a further division in two aspects called outer *ying* and inner *ying*. Outer *ying* can be explained as a reflection of inner *ying*, as if the condition of the state of consciousness were reflected outwards. So in this case *ying* should not be understood to mean space or the sky. This principle is particular to Dzogchen, it is not found in the sūtras or in the various series of tantras. In fact in all these other teachings *ying* always and only signifies space in the sense of the nature or condition of phenomena.

Chapter 29

This chapter concerns the meaning of the expression *sem naldu zhagpa*: *sem* is the condition of the state of consciousness; *naldu zhagpa* means letting be, without disturbing. The syllable *nal,* which means "authentic, natural condition," combined with the verb *jor,* meaning "possess," forms the Tibetan term *naljor* that renders the Sanskrit *yoga*. For example, if it meets no barrier, water flows freely; this is its authentic, characteristic condition. A stone, however, which is hard and solid, remains stationary where it is. Each element has its natural condition and its characteristic function. This original condition is called *nal* or *nalma*, and *naldu zhagpa* means leaving one's natural condition as it is. Possessing, or mastering, the authentic condition does not refer to something objective but instead to the subject, to the state of consciousness of the individual. This is the true meaning of the word *yoga*.

There follow some verses that are very important in order to understand the true meaning of tregchöd: *rang lü ma chö lha ma gom, mawai tsig tang ngag ma chö, tingdzin ma jed sem ma chö.*[168] *Rang lü ma chö* means "Do not correct your body." What does "correct your body" mean? Following instructions to assume a certain posture, for example the lotus position, in order to do breathing exercises, and so on. However, our text says not to correct but rather to relax. *Lha ma gom* means: "Do not meditate on the deity," do not think about, concentrate on, or visualize a deity.

Mawai tsig tang ngag ma cho means: "Do not correct your voice." Correcting the voice refers to two things: first, to reciting mantra or saying virtuous words instead of cursing or speaking arrogantly; second, to breathing and the circulation of prana, for example by using particular breath retentions (*kumbhaka*) or conducting the pranic force along determined energy courses of the subtle body. All of this entails "correcting" one's voice and breathing. *Tingdzin ma jed* means: "Do not concentrate or visualize," for example the channels, or cakras, or a syllable symbolizing the state of consciousness, etc.: one should not even do this. Why not? "Because if you correct," says Kunjed Gyalpo, "you will never reach the real condition. You need only discover what is, without correcting or seeking to construct something new. Unless you attain knowledge of the authentic condition you will never liberate yourself," forever remaining in the limited dualistic condition. In fact, the final phrase, *sem ma chö*, means: "Do not correct the mind!"

Chapter 30

Chapter thirty contains the root verses of the *Minub Gyaltsen*, or *Dorje Sempa Namkha Che*, "The Total Space of Vajrasattva," of which there exist a fundamental tantra of about twenty pages[169] and diverse secondary tantras. These are the verses that, according to tradition, Garab Dorje recited as a child when he was first brought before his grandfather, the king of Oḍḍiyāna. The story recounts that Garab Dorje, son of the princess of Oḍḍiyāna who had taken vows as a Buddhist nun, was miraculously conceived. When he was born, as well as feeling ashamed at having given birth, his mother was terrified at the idea of not being able to say who his father was. However, when the king saw the child and heard him recite the verses of the *Dorje Sempa Namkha Che*, he was so amazed that he named him Garab Dorje, "Vajra of Supreme Pleasure." At the age of seven or eight Garab Dorje asked his mother's permission to debate Buddhist philosophy with the court pandits. At first his mother tried to dissuade him, telling him, "You have not yet shed your milk teeth, how can you debate with sages?" But when the king granted his permission, Garab Dorje asked the pandits some questions about the true meaning beyond the principle of cause and effect that they were unable to answer. Those pandits, experts in the teachings based on cause and effect, were closed within and limited by their doctrinal convictions, but subsequently many became Garab Dorje's disciples.[170]

Chapter 31

This chapter contains the renowned "Six Vajra Verses," of which there is a tantra of about thirty pages.[171]

The first verse says *natsog rangzhin minyi kyang*. *Natsog* means diversity; *rangzhin*, nature; *minyi*, non-dual: the nature of diverse phenomena is non-dual. This means that both pure vision and impure vision are a manifestation of the energy of the primordial state. *Kyang*, the last syllable, means "but" and links with the second verse: *chashe nyiddu trö tang dral*. *Chashe* means a part, a single thing; *nyiddu*, in the real condition: even though in reality there is no duality, everything manifests separately. *Trö tang dral* means that it is not possible to define each individual manifestation, limiting it to one form, one color, and so on. This takes us beyond any definition, beyond all considerations and conceptual limits: this is the true meaning of dharmadhātu.

The third verse says *jizhinwa zhe mi tog kyang*. *Jizhinwa* denotes the true condition as it is; *mi tog* means not to conceptualize: the true condition cannot be defined, even by the expression "as it is." Even thinking "Now I understand, this is the way it is!" is a definition! *Jizhinwa* is the natural condition of self-perfection, but making it into a concept is like giving the name "No name" to someone without a name. As above, *kyang* is a link to the next verse: *nampar nangdzed kuntu zang*. *Nampar nangdzed* corresponds to the Sanskrit name Vairocana, one of the five saṃbhogakāya Buddhas, while *kuntu zang* corresponds to Samantabhadra, the state of dharmakāya. What this verse really means, however, is that although nothing can be confirmed or refuted, nevertheless what remains is not absolute emptiness: everything manifests at the relative level, and this itself is Samantabhadra, "always good," "good in all circumstances."

The fifth verse says *zinpe tsolwai ned pang te*. *Zinpe* means "completed," everything is already all right because the original condition is self-perfected, there is no need to construct anything. *Tsolwai ned pang* means overcoming the disease of effort, that is, remaining in the natural condition. Because were there still something to do, still effort of some kind, this would mean still being afflicted by this disease. Many teachers advise to "meditate without meditating," and this is the precise truth: there is nothing on which to meditate. However, this should not become an excuse for not doing anything: there is no concept to which to adhere, but we must not get distracted! The sixth and final verse is *lhungyi nepe zhagpa yin*: presence continues in a natural way and precisely this is meditation. This is the authentic principle of self-perfection, beyond being conditioned by a commitment or concept.[172]

Chapter 32

This short chapter has only four lines. The last two say *machö nyampai gyalpo tela ni, mitog chökui gongpa tela ne.*[173] *Machö* means not to correct; *nyampai gyalpo* is supreme equality: *mitog* means not thinking, not in the sense of blocking thought, but instead, simply not entering into mental activity, not creating thought nor correcting. This is the state of *chöku*, or dharmakāya. This chapter is one of the sources of tregchöd.

Chapter 33

This chapter discusses *ying* and the distinction between *sem*, the mind, and *yeshe*, wisdom. Returning to our example of the mirror: *sem*, or mind, corresponds to the reflection that appears on its surface, while *semnyid*, the nature of mind, corresponds to the condition of the mirror itself. But what does *yeshe*, wisdom, mean? If we consider dharmakāya to be the condition of the state of consciousness of a realized being, analogous to the mirror, then all the aspects tied to saṃbhogakāya and nirmāṇakāya, to the five wisdoms and the five Tathāgatas, and so on, must necessarily be part of the reflection. The reflection, in this case, is not conditioned by dualism but is instead a part, or a manifestation, of the purity of the primordial state. How is it possible to distinguish between a pure reflection and one conditioned by dualism? Pure reflection refers to a quality of the primordial state. Infinite wisdom and the qualities of dharmakāya, saṃbhogakāya, and nirmāṇakāya are not active, nor do they condition the three kāyas in any way. On the contrary, it is we who are conditioned by mind. It is crucial to understand this difference between mind and wisdom.

Chapter 34

Chapter thirty-four explains the true condition beyond *tagpa* and *chedpa*: *tagpa* means immortal or eternal, *chedpa* signifies the contrary, that there is nothing. The first viewpoint includes all definitions of "eternal," or "permanent" substance, some entity that always exists.

The second is the viewpoint typical of those who believe, as many assert, that after death nothing exists. However, the Dzogchen view transcends both limits, so it is said to be beyond *tagpa* and *chedpa*. There are also allusions to definitions characteristic of certain philosophical systems of ancient India.

Chapter 35

This chapter explains that Dzogchen is beyond cause and effect, starting from an analysis of eight arguments to be refuted, all subsequently treated in individual chapters.

Chapter 36

This chapter elucidates that the state of consciousness comprises body, voice, and mind, and that these form the base of everything that is created.

Chapter 37

Here the text explains that there is nothing on which to meditate by clearly analyzing the principles and goals of the various paths of realization. All of these paths are defined as *kolsa* and *drippa*: *kolsa* means "wrong way" like taking the wrong path at a crossroads; *drippa* denotes something that hinders or blocks, that is, something that obstructs a Dzogchen practitioner.

Chapter 38

This chapter, too, is very important in order to understand the various paths and to discover the defect inherent in being limited by the view characteristic of one's path.

Chapter 39

This chapter examines the ultimate meaning of certain fundamental aspects of the teaching: view, meditation, commitment, spiritual action, or *trinle*, and so on.

Chapter 40

This chapter resumes the explanation of the nature of bodhicitta and contains an interesting question asked as if it were posed by mind itself to the state of consciousness: "If the state of consciousness or bodhicitta has been pure and enlightened from the beginning, and thus there is nothing else to do, this means that all beings are already enlightened. Why, then, do beings transmigrate?" This question aims to clarify the condition of the state of consciousness in relation to dualism. Kunjed Gyalpo's answer elucidates the true meaning.

Chapter 41

This chapter explains the principle of the "same essence" (*ngo bo gcig*) and is also very useful for gaining deeper knowledge of prana and of external energy linked to the five elements. Moreover, as regards tregchöd it is important to understand what the functions of energy are. In fact, people not only have their own energy but are also surrounded by external energy.

Chapter 42

Here the discussion of topics treated in previous chapters is resumed: in short, it asserts that bodhicitta is the base and origin of everything.

Chapter 43

This chapter illustrates the true significance of the teacher. The teacher is the person who explains and clarifies the condition of the state of consciousness. However, if one considers him or her someone "outside" who shows something to the disciple, this would not correspond to the ultimate meaning. It is rather a case of reawakening or of rediscovering the truth for oneself. Teacher and disciple are not two different things: there is no dualism between them. The teacher is not outside, but instead manifests inside, from the very condition of the state of consciousness. Teachers cannot discover the truth for us: their role is only to give us the means that enable us to understand. What is the purpose of Dzogchen? To awaken, to liberate. A Dzogchen teacher does not say, "You must change. First, you did things that way, now you must do them this way! First you were in that narrow dimension, now come into this one!" The point is not to change something. Dzogchen simply says, "Get out of your cage and stay free! Wake up!" But how can one awaken? Certainly, teachers cannot pick up a stick and force someone to act in a certain way. Rather, they can tell disciples: "You must gain understanding. Try to understand!" such that at a certain point the individual finally awakens and perceives his or her nature. However, this understanding arises from within oneself, not from the teacher. That is why it is said that, fundamentally, teacher and disciple are one and the same: they are a manifestation of the state of consciousness of the individual. One must avoid turning the teaching and the tantras into dogma, limiting them with assertions such as: "Samantabhadra said this! Garab Dorje said that!" This is utterly meaningless because the teaching concerns only us, our condition. This is the point that we need to discover, and if we succeed, we discover our true condition!

Chapter 44

In short, this chapter states that Dzogpa Chenpo does not depend on whether a person is more or less learned, intelligent, important, and so on, but only on whether one discovers and understands the real meaning in oneself.

Chapter 45

This chapter deals at length with *tawa*, the view of Dzogchen. In fact, without understanding *tawa*, at most there can arise a kind of "faith" in the teaching, and if one remains conditioned by faith, this means that there is not yet true conviction. But Dzogchen practitioners must not be conditioned by anything, not even by the teaching, the practice, rituals, beliefs, and so on: they must only discover the real condition, just as it is. Discovery does not mean letting oneself be conditioned, but rather emerging from one's limits, like a little bird that finally comes out of its cage and starts flying wherever it wishes. Perhaps as soon as it gets out of its cage, the bird does not know how to fly, and being accustomed to living in the cage, it will be afraid. It is somewhat the same for us, but even though it is not so easy, the truth is we have to get out! If we do not how to do it, it means we are heavily conditioned, that we always try to understand the real meaning relying on something, on assertions such as: "This text says such and such." But the texts have got nothing to do with it, leave them in peace! For example, some people defend their point of view saying, "Our tradition affirms this," but tradition has nothing to do with it at all, leave it in peace! A true teacher will say: "Come out, without delay! Like a bird out of its cage: look what happens. If you don't manage, if you fear danger, go back inside your cage for a while and then, gradually, train yourself to come out!"

Chapter 46

This chapter concerns *samaya*, commitment, one of the ten main topics of the tantras: on receiving an initiation there is always a specific commitment to observe. There are many kinds of samayas: in the mahāyoga, for example, there are fourteen main ones. As all deeds are done through the body, voice, and mind, the samayas, too, must be complied with on the basis of these three aspects. However, in Dzogchen the principle is different. When, in daily life, one remains in the natural state, abiding in awareness and presence, there are no rules to observe, there is nothing specific one has to do: it is enough not to get distracted, remaining in present awareness. Our text talks of the principle of "samayaless samaya" because there is not the limiting consideration of having to perform a particular action. In Dzogchen, commitment is not something one has to uphold with effort because the nature of the state of consciousness is the unborn, beyond all limitations: this is its condition, and real samaya simply consists in the presence of this knowledge.

Dzogchen talks of four characteristic samayas: (1) *medpa,* or absence—as all is empty from the beginning there is nothing to confirm; (2) *chalwa,* or omnipresence—this is clarity that manifests; (3) *chigpu,* or single—the state of the individual as pure, non-dual presence; (4) *lhundrub,* or self-perfected. In short, this means that the state of consciousness of each individual is the center of the universe. The condition of each person is like the sun beyond the clouds. Even though at times the clouds obscure the sun so that we cannot see it, the quality of the sun always exists and never changes. That is why the state is said to be *lhundrub,* self-perfected from the origin. A realized being may seem different from us, but the only difference is that he or she has overcome the obstacle of the clouds and lives where the sun shines. So, we must recognize and have these four samayas, whose gist is that as practitioners we should never get distracted—this is our only real commitment!

On taking vows, a monk must obey them as his rules of life until he reaches the level of self-discipline. In a certain sense, he is conditioned by the Vinaya rules. Conversely, in Dzogchen there is no need to impose any rules that condition the individual because any rules devised by man derive from a dualistic consideration of reality. If we have awareness, there is no need of outer rules, which is why there is said to be no commitment to observe. Obviously, as long as one remains undistracted in the condition of the state of consciousness, there is no need of anything else, but if this is not the case, then self-control of the three doors is necessary.

The outer tantras, too, have very many rules. The kriyā tantras, for example, attach great importance to cleanliness (rather like the Brahmins in India do), to ritual purification by mantras, and so on. All of these are relative means, and undeniably, they do occasion a certain benefit. In mahāyoga and anuyoga too, and clearly also in the higher tantras, there are rules, but they are somewhat the opposite of those of the kriyā tantra. In general, that which in the sūtras and outer tantras has to be given up becomes that which in the inner or higher tantras has to be accepted and utilized. Thus if kriyā tantra practitioners are introduced to the mahāyoga practices they may find it difficult to understand why they should do everything that until then they have had to eschew. In fact, in kriyā tantras the main means consists in preparing oneself to receive the deity's wisdom, but in mahāyoga one discovers that this is not the ultimate path.

In the sūtras, for example, the body is defined as "that which undergoes suffering" and in consequence, is not regarded as important. In the higher tantras, conversely, the body is called *dorjei lü*, "vajra body," because it is the physical support of all the maṇḍalas of the deities. Consequently, the three doors of body, voice, and mind are called the "three vajras," and it is on this principle that the rules are founded. In the sūtras and the kriyā tantra alike, one of the fundamental means of physical purification is fasting, whereas in the mahāyoga, fasting is a violation of one of the fourteen main vows: to respect the body inasmuch as it is one of the three vajras. It is for this reason that the *gaṇapūjā*[174] is practiced: eating and drinking becomes a rite during which, instead of making external offerings, one makes offerings to the deities visualized inside the physical body.

While in the kriyā tantras it is important to have a shrine with a sacred image or statue to which one offers flowers, light, etc., the principle in mahāyoga consists in recognizing oneself as the true nature of the three vajras. In this case, instead of offering something on the shrine, it is the practitioner who eats, but with awareness, recognizing the inner maṇḍala as the true condition of the body.

In fact, on the accomplishment of realization, the five aggregates and the five elements manifest as the five Tathāgatas and their consorts. However, one should not think immediately of the Buddha of the east, the Buddha of the north, etc., as if these were different entities residing in wonderful pure dimensions. In reality, it is we who have the five aggregates, the five passions, and so on; when only their pure aspect manifests, these are said to be the corresponding five Tathāgatas, five wisdoms, etc. The iconographic representation of the five Buddhas, based on the royal garb of ancient Indian princes, laden with jewels and ornaments that symbolize the "richness" of the essence of the elements of the saṃbhogakāya, only serves to give an idea of the saṃbhogakāya. The five Buddhas with their five specific colors have meaning only inasmuch as they correspond to the principle of the five directions of the maṇḍala: blue at the center, white to the east, yellow to the south, red to the west, and green to the north. The purpose of these depictions is thus only to help the practitioner to visualize a particular form better, and this is probably the origin of the iconography of the five Tathāgatas. However, as in the outer tantras, the deity is seen as a realized being from whom one needs to receive wisdom, the depictions of the five Buddhas have become the object of reverence in temples.

Returning to the five passions, in the sūtras they are called the five poisons, something to avoid, to reject. Nevertheless, "rejecting" the five passions still implies dualism, a limitation—accepting the positive and refuting the negative—and this is by no means the way to overcome the dualistic condition. Conversely, the higher tantras understand that poison can be used and transformed into medicine to transmute our impure vision into pure vision. To this end, one applies visualization and concentration on the form of the deity, the pure dimension of the maṇḍala, and so on. But in the Dzogchen view, is it correct to do this "transformation"? Dzogchen does not stop even at this concept, instead adopting the principle of self-liberation. The transformation of the poison of the passions into wisdom requires the dualistic consideration of "poison" on one side and "wisdom" on the other. It is as if we were "playing" at transforming something. As the dualism remains, this cannot be the ultimate solution. According to the principle of self-liberation, without necessarily maintaining the dualistic notion of "poison" and "wisdom," the practitioner perceives passions and wisdom on a par. Whichever passion arises, the practitioner remains in the natural condition, without creating or judging. This is the fundamental point of self-liberation, the final aim of Dzogchen.

In the *Kunjed Gyalpo*, basically, all rules are automatically negated. However, this does not mean that they are worthless; obviously, they are valid at the relative level. The point is, if we want to discover our true condition, it is important to identify our goal from the very beginning.

Chapter 47

This chapter explains the principle "beyond *trinle,*" or beyond the capacity for spiritual action. Tibetan has two terms to render the Sanskrit "karma," *le* and *trinle. Le* means action based on cause and effect that produces transmigration; *trinle* on the other hand, mainly denotes action based on the power obtained through a tantric practice. Regarding *trinle,* there are ordinary actions and higher action, corresponding respectively to ordinary and higher *siddhis,* or attainments. The higher attainment is total realization, while the ordinary attainments are the four actions tied to the four cardinal points of the maṇḍala and to the four colors. The color white in the east direction corresponds to Buddha Akṣobhya and to *shiwa,* action of "pacifying." Yellow in the south corresponds to Buddha Ratnasaṃbhava and to *gyepa,* action of "enriching"; red in the west corresponds to Buddha Amitabha and to *wang,* action of "conquering"; dark green in the north corresponds to Buddha Amoghasiddhi and to *tragpo,* or "fierce" action. This last category contains all the magic rites of "elimination" which can be used to overcome certain types of hindrances. In short, all four actions can be useful until the attainment of total realization. However, at times practitioners get stuck on secondary aspects, and once they obtain certain powers, such as those tied to the fourth action, they block their own progress and diverge from the fundamental aim. A practitioner may realize the specific power of only one of these four actions, as this does not automatically include the other three: thus it is a limited attainment. On the other hand, whoever attains total realization no longer has any need to practice the diverse actions to obtain their power, just like someone who climbs to the top of a very high mountain can enjoy a comprehensive view without needing to visit all the various sites.

Practice in the Mahāyāna sūtra, for example, consists in the six *pāramitās,* or perfections: generosity, morality, patience, diligence, concentration, and wisdom. Furthermore, the process of spiritual evolution follows the gradual course of the "five paths." The first is the "path of accumulation," or *tsoglam,* subdivided in its turn in "lower," "median," and "higher." The second is the "path of application," or *jorlam,* subdivided in its turn in four levels. The third is the "path of seeing," or *thonglam,* followed by the "path of meditation" or *gomlam,* and finally the "path of no more learning," or *miloblam* (also called the "path of obtainment"). All of this is closely connected with the partition of progress in ten *bhūmis,* or levels of realization. Thus, the principle of the gradual path is to improve and to "build" something positive a bit at a time, through self-sacrifice and acts of generosity, through complying with morality, and so on. In fact, according to the path of the Bodhisattva, realization is the result of a gradual process of improvement. As this path lacks the direct introduction to knowledge of the primordial state, the only means that remains is gradual improvement.

In the kriyā and ubhaya tantras, the fundamental principle of the practice consists of the "wisdom deity" and the "commitment deity." "Wisdom deity" denotes an Enlightened One, such as Avalokiteśvara, while the "commitment deity" is the practitioner who visualizes himself or herself in that deity's form. Thus, the wisdom deity is the means of empowering the commitment deity. In the yoga tantra in particular, greater emphasis is laid on the unification of the two forms, and the term used is *tamnye nyimed,* or non-duality between wisdom deity and commitment deity.

In Tibetan, wisdom is *yeshe,* a word composed of two syllables, *ye,* which means "origin," and *she,* "consciousness" or "knowledge": so, "primordial knowledge." Another term frequently used is *rangjung yeshe,* where *rangjung* means "self-arising," that is, a natural quality of the state of knowledge. So we see that the sūtras and outer tantras deem it necessary to progress gradually in order to increase wisdom: wisdom, in this case, becomes something to "build" by means of action. However, were this possible, one could not speak of "self-arising" wisdom as a natural quality, because it would be a state that is not always present.

If one follows a concept or an idea during one's meditation, this means one is correcting. Correcting means entering into action with an object to think about: in this case one is not in the condition of the primordial state and one can no longer speak of self-arising wisdom.

Chapter 48

Here recurs a very common Tibetan expression: *phunsumtsog,* also used in the spoken language to mean "perfect," "excellent." The etymology of the word is somewhat difficult to explain: *phun* means "aggregate," or "group," *sum* means "three," and *tsog* means "together," thus it means "three things together." This term is also found in ancient texts, and the fact that it contains the term "three" is very probably connected to the meaning this number assumes in the Dzogchen teaching. In fact, the number three symbolizes the three "doors" or fundamental aspects of existence: body, voice, and mind. At a deeper level, related to our nature, there are the three aspects of essence, nature, and energy. Finally, as regards realization there is the manifestation of the three dimensions or kāyas: dharmakāya, saṃbhogakāya, and nirmāṇakāya. As can be seen at the base there is always the number three.

The same applies in Tibetan medicine, where the first thing explained is that the three categories of illness: of wind, of bile, and of phlegm, derive from the three fundamental passions: attachment, anger, and ignorance, where the last one denotes lack of clarity or a condition of sleepiness.

Chapter 49

This chapter explains that the *bhūmi*s, or levels to surmount, do not exist because the true condition is beyond the concept itself of "levels." As we have seen, the Mahāyāna posits five paths and ten *bhūmi*s, or levels of realization of the Bodhisattva. In this case the accomplishment of enlightenment corresponds to the tenth *bhūmi*, and until this level is achieved, there is not total realization. Some series of tantras add three more *bhūmi*s and reckon there are thirteen levels of realization: in this case, only the thirteenth *bhūmi* corresponds to enlightenment. Other series of tantras consider that there are sixteen *bhūmi*s up to total realization. But how does Dzogchen explain this? The *Kunjed Gyalpo* says there are no *bhūmi*s because once we have properly understood what realization is, then everything depends on knowing or living in this condition: it is merely a matter of ripening. Once we have discovered the sun, the only thing that remains is to overcome the obstacle of the clouds. But just as clouds sometimes disappear slowly, and at other times all together all at once, there can be no limits to the levels of realization: one can traverse thousands of *bhūmi*s or none at all. Fundamentally, there are no *bhūmi*s, no levels in the condition of the "sun," so, in general, one says *dzogpa chenpo sa chigpa*, total perfection is the single *bhūmi*, and it depends on knowing or not knowing, having or not having knowledge of the primordial state. This is the first and sole *bhūmi*.

Chapter 50

This chapter describes self-arising wisdom, *rangjung yeshe*, a synonym of bodhicitta, explaining that its condition is beyond hindrances, rather like saying that the sun has never known clouds. The clouds stand before us, yet the true condition of the primordial state has never been hindered. Wisdom is knowledge which has existed from the beginning and has never changed, hence it is called "self-arising." It is completely wrong to deem it an object or to believe that it can come from outside.

In this chapter we find the various expressions generally used to explain and define the state of consciousness: bodhicitta, dharmadhātu, condition of space, self-arising wisdom, dharmakāya, saṃbhogakāya, nirmāṇakāya, three vajras, omniscience, *nampa thamched* (totality of forms), three wisdoms, four wisdoms, five wisdoms, and so on. Each tradition has coined a term based on its own view, but for the state of consciousness nothing changes: its condition always remains as it is.

Chapter 51

This chapter explains that there is no path to traverse or to tread. Here too, the fundamental point is being present and not, for example, devoting two hours a day to meditation while losing oneself in distraction the rest of the time.

Chapter 52

This chapter is about the principle "beyond desire." In fact, usually we live at the mercy of desire on the one hand and of worry on the other. For example, to think: "I want to practice for my realization in order not to suffer any more!" is a desire. Instead to wonder: "If I don't practice whatever will happen to me?" means being prey to worry. In this way we only create problems, so we must overcome both desire for liberation and worry about transmigration.

In this regard, the text discusses the *pagchag* (*vāsanā*) or "karmic traces," attachments that have remained latent, like traces: just as a bottle that has contained perfume continues to exude the scent even after having been emptied and washed, so do these karmic traces remain. In the same way, in our life many kinds of traces may manifest, especially in our dreams in the early part of the night.

Chapter 53

This chapter discusses the "unmoved" condition and says that all phenomena abide in it, that is, in the original condition where no movement has ever occurred. But then, whence does dualism arise? The only example possible is again that of the mirror and the reflection. If the reflection moves, this does not mean that the mirror must also do the same. For the mirror, nothing ever changes, as it has no intentions and never undergoes change. If the mirror reflects an exquisite deity, it feels no pleasure, if it reflects something terrible, it feels no displeasure. Because it has never "moved," it has never entered into movement: its condition has the quality of reflecting, and the reflection manifests through the dualistic principle of interdependence. Any definition, of being or not being, any philosophical analysis one elaborates, concerns the reflection and takes place within the sphere of the reflection and never in the condition of the mirror.

Chapter 54

This chapter explains the diverse ways of introducing self-arising wisdom: analyzing its meaning, clarifying its authentic condition, and so on. It also mentions the minor, or secondary, tantras that explain certain topics in depth. The *Kunjed Gyalpo* is a fundamental tantra, but if we come across a concept in it that is not explained in great depth, then it becomes necessary to refer to a minor tantra.

Chapter 55

This chapter explains that all dharmas are nothing other than the essence of bodhicitta. The base of sundry phenomena is bodhicitta and these sundry phenomena are all equal.

Chapters 56 & 57

These are the concluding chapters of the root tantra (the first part) of the *Kunjed Gyalpo*. The first part (the root tantra) was translated by Vairocana probably soon after his return to Tibet from Oḍḍiyāna. In particular, the first texts translated by Vairocana when he returned from Oḍḍiyāna are known as "the first five translations," and originally they formed part of the *Kunjed Gyalpo*. According to some sources, he translated the second and third parts on his return from exile to Tibet through the intercession of Vimalamitra.

The story is told that some of the king's ministers accused Vairocana of promulgating "heretical" teachings that did not concur with the Buddhist law of cause and effect. Others accused him of mixing Buddhism with Bön. In any case, the king discovered a plot hatched by his ministers to assassinate Vairocana and arranged instead to banish the great translator, to whom he was very devoted, to a remote area in east Tibet, a kingdom called Gyalmo Tsawarong. Vairocana remained in exile for many years and started teaching Dzogchen, in particular to Yudra Nyingpo, prince of the kingdom, who according to tradition was the reincarnation of the translator Legdrub, Vairocana's companion on their voyage to India who had died during his return journey. Yudra Nyingpo attended Vairocana for several years and became expert in Dzogchen.

In the meantime, King Trisong Deutsen had invited the great pandit Vimalamitra, another exceptional Dzogchen teacher, from India. On arriving in Tibet, he found out that the Dzogchen teaching had not been promulgated and also heard about the exile that had befallen Vairocana, whom he had met in India, and he started to teach the gradual sūtra path, adhering to the traditional system of Śāntarakṣita. Vairocana heard about Vimalamitra's arrival in central Tibet and decided to send Yudra Nyingpo to him with a message. Vimalamitra was teaching at Samye, and Yudra Nyingpo, who was dressed like a simple beggar pilgrim, was afraid to introduce himself directly to the guards and ministers surrounding the teacher in order to deliver Vairocana's secret message. So he decided to employ a strategy, and during a pause in the teaching, he left a note on the desk in front of the teacher's seat: "Walking like a crow, one doesn't get far. One won't get enlightened through the childish teaching of the śrāvakas." When Vimalamitra returned to his seat to resume the teaching he read the note and immediately asked who had written it. When Yudra Nyingpo stepped forward, Vimalamitra stated his surprise about the contents of the note because at that time, everybody in Tibet followed the sūtra system. So he questioned him and discovered that he was a disciple of Vairocana. From that moment, Vimalamitra started teaching Dzogchen Semde. Moreover, he appealed to the king and ministers, vouching for the authenticity of Vairocana's teachings, and finally succeeded in obtaining his return from exile. On his return, Vairocana translated the remaining chapters of the *Kunjed Gyalpo* and other important Semde texts.[175]

Chapter 58

This chapter, which opens the second part of the *Kunjed Gyalpo*, discusses the "unborn" or *kyewa medpa*, also very important in the Mādhyamaka sūtra tradition. In fact, one of the most famous texts by Nāgārjuna starts with these very words. The principle of "birthless" or "unborn" necessarily also implies that of "unceasing" and this is one of the fundamental concepts of Dzogchen Semde. Furthermore, the "Song of the Vajra" starts with the line: "Never having been born, it cannot cease."[176]

Here the text explains that, unless one understands the meaning of "unborn" right from the beginning, then one cannot achieve or even conceive of the condition of the primordial state. In Dzogchen there is wide use of the word *kadag*: *ka* is the first consonant of the Tibetan alphabet, corresponding to the western or Sanskrit *A*, and signifies "the beginning"; *dag* means "pure." "Pure from the beginning" is a synonym of śūnyatā, or emptiness, the real meaning of which is that nothing concrete exists.

Chapter 59

This chapter concerns *tawa*, a term that can be rendered as "view," "point of view," "theoretical opinion," and so on. It is often coupled with the word *gom*, that means "meditation" or "practice." But what is there to practice? What one has understood of the view, because, in order to practice, it is necessary to comprehend *tawa* correctly. Here the text says that in the true view there is neither a subject that looks nor an object as reference point: there is nothing whatever to confirm.

Chapter 60

This chapter is about commitment, or samaya, a point that has already been discussed above. Here, as in all the second part, there often recurs the term *togpa*, which can be rendered as "real understanding" or "real knowledge." *Tawa* refers to the intuitive understanding of one's nature, while *togpa* means actually entering the state of knowledge. In order to enable people to understand *tawa*, the teacher explains and introduces knowledge in various ways. When the disciples have understood and their understanding becomes something that cannot be erased, this is *togpa*. Also regarding the commitment, all the relative instructions about what must or must not be done, and all their underlying reasons, pertain to the sphere of the view. A practitioner who has truly understood and does not find any commitment in particular to take on has reached the level of *togpa* "beyond commitment."

Chapter 61

This chapter, too, clarifies commitment in relation to the three aspects of body, voice, and mind: it is necessary to go beyond the concept of the "three doors."

Chapter 62

This chapter regards the principle "beyond visualization, or creation, of the maṇḍala." The general function of the maṇḍala has already been explained: the transformation of our vision on the basis of the fact that we have impure dualistic vision. Because for us, the concept of "impure vision" exists, in order to eliminate attachment to our concrete vision, we visualize the maṇḍala and concentrate on "pure vision." This is the principle of transformation. So the main aim is not only to "transform" but also to overcome attachment. For example, if we see a mountain, we believe it is something concrete existing in front of us. However, it is necessary to overcome this belief in the concreteness of the mountain because this is the basis of dualism and of attachment. How? Imagining or visualizing that the mountain is no longer such, but is instead, for example, made of clouds, will change its "status" in our mind. Proceeding resolutely in this way, at a certain point we will be in a position really to see clouds in place of the mountain, because the mind has this capacity. All this serves to enable us to discover that the mountain is not something concrete and objective, that instead it pertains to the subject. Thus, the purpose of transformation and visualization of the maṇḍala is to understand the true condition of phenomena.

In conclusion, the practice of the maṇḍala has two main aims: first, to engage in transformation to overcome attachment, second, to transform impure vision into pure vision. But whence does impure vision arise? What is its origin? Our dualism, our attachments, our hindrances. When these are absent there is "pure vision." Nevertheless, as regards the true condition of the state of consciousness, not even these concepts can be taken into consideration, because both pure vision and impure vision remain at the dualistic level and do not constitute the ultimate meaning. This does not imply that such a "provisional" view is without value or that it must be refuted: it is always useful to bear in mind the principle of the two truths, absolute and relative. However, from the position of the absolute view, not even creating pure vision is positive.

Chapter 63

This chapter explains the principle "beyond initiation." In this regard, first of all it is important to understand the true meaning of initiation, or empowerment. Usually, on admittance to tantric practice, one receives an initiation, the purpose of which, in a certain sense, is to give one the possibility of ripening. In fact, in tantra there are many methods of visualization and of recitation of mantras, etc., however to be able to apply them, it is necessary first to receive the initiation and transmission of the mantra from a teacher. By and large, in kriyā tantra the initiations are not so elaborate as in the higher tantras, nevertheless they are still indispensable, like a kind of permission in order to be able to apply the various phases of the ritual. Without the permission, the practice does not give results.

For example, if we learn a mantra straight from a book and recite it without having received the transmission of the sound, even if we follow to the letter the written instructions, our practice will be futile, because the power of the mantra resides in sound. There are many ways of conferring the transmission of the sound: in most cases it is sufficient for the teacher to pronounce the mantra while the disciple listens carefully, but this is not always the case. At times, it is indispensable that the mantra be transmitted on a certain day of the week, let's say on Monday, or even on a Monday which falls during the time of a particular constellation called *Gyal*, an astrological conjunction that occurs at most two or three times a year. In other cases, the determinant factor may be the place: a mantra may have to be transmitted on a mountain, say, facing north where the sun does not shine; or, for example, in a place where there is a spring of a river running north. Furthermore, some kinds of mantras must be transmitted at particular times of the day, and so on. As can be seen, there are many external factors involved because we are discussing the transmission of a power linked to the energy of sound.

Even though in the higher tantras the initiations are very elaborate and tied to factors such as breathing, posture, visualization of the maṇḍala, etc., the true meaning of initiation is to introduce, or to enable understanding of, the condition of the primordial state. So in mahāyoga and anuyoga, everything follows a ritual scheme in which sundry symbols are used.

In Dzogchen, on the other hand, the most important thing is understanding the principle, the function, and the true meaning of initiation. Whether knowledge is transmitted through a formal initiation as in mahāyoga or anuyoga or the nature of the primordial state is directly introduced as in Dzogchen, the goal is always to enable the recipient to understand the true condition of the state of consciousness. Thus the term used in Dzogchen is "introduction" rather than initiation: in fact we can only claim to have received the final initiation the moment we really understand the state of knowledge introduced by the teacher. A person may have received countless tantric initiations over a period of many years, but unless he or she has been introduced to the true meaning of Dzogchen, then in fact he or she has not yet received the true initiation. This is not to deny the value of ritual initiation, as evidently a person can benefit from the power of the mantra, mudrās, and visualization even without having understood the true meaning: the initiation will reduce their hindrances, but it will not enable them to achieve the final goal.

There are many people who are always hunting after initiations. As soon as they hear that some Lama is giving an initiation, they hurry to receive it, and maybe the day after, they rush to some other Lama to receive another. There is nothing wrong with all this, but it is a real pity that these people do not engage a little more in trying to understand the true meaning of initiation. On discovering it, there is no longer any need to seek further initiations: there are many means and practices that are more effective for overcoming hindrances and dualism, because problems are not resolved from the outside. Thus the *Kunjed Gyalpo* says that the true initiation is knowledge of the state of consciousness: right from the start we try to attain this level without thinking that there is something to receive from outside.

Chapter 64

We have already discussed the difference between *tawa* and *togpa*. This chapter concerns the *togpa* of the path: on the path there is no succession of stages to tread, there is no concept of "first stage," "second stage," and so on.

Chapter 65

This chapter explains *togpa* in relation to the *bhūmi*s, or levels of realization and repeats the celebrated expression *dzogpa chenpo sa chigpa*: total perfection is the single level that is knowledge of this condition.

Chapter 66

Chapter sixty-six, which is about behavior, can be epitomized in the phrase *chödpa lang dor med pa*. *Chödpa* is behavior, *lang dor med pa* means "without accepting or rejecting," beyond this dualism, because in the true condition of the state of consciousness there is no accepting or rejecting anything. However, it is important to distinguish between the absolute condition and the relative one. When it says that the behavior is not accepting or rejecting anything, that it is without desire or worry, and so on, this simply means one must not be conditioned from outside. Obviously, in order to live our lives it is necessary to perform deeds that involve accepting and rejecting. If we are hungry, then we have to accept food. However, we should not let ourselves be conditioned by the outside and instead should base ourselves on the principle of awareness. In this case, one can talk of *chödpa rangdrol* or "self-liberation of behavior": the individual becomes the center of existence and is no longer conditioned by anything.

Chapter 67

This chapter talks about wisdom, particularly in reference to practice. In general, two modes of practice are described, called *rejog* and *nyamjog*. By and large, *rejog* can be rendered "changing level." If a thought arises which disturbs us, we do not get rid of it. Instead, we notice that this thought is worrying or disturbing us and pursue it a little, observing it: in this way we bring it to the level of presence of awareness, as if we were watching a film, noticing everything that happens without falling into indifference. The aim, evidently, is not the investigation of where the thought ends up, but the achievement of the state of presence and awareness. So from the first moment a thought arises, we must not remain indifferent. For example, we might think: "This evening I want to eat that special dish I had yesterday," after which quite easily the thought could arise: "But I wonder if there is any left or if it's all been eaten?" However, even if we "allow" ourselves to be transported by the thought a bit, this must always be done with awareness, governed by presence.

Nyamjog, on the other hand, means that any thought, good or bad, that arises, whatever disturbing factor occurs, we do not judge it but instead remain, in that very instant, in its own condition: in this way we allow it to disappear by itself. So in this case we do not undertake to observe what is happening: if a thought arises, we leave it instantaneously in the authentic condition. In this way the thought disappears, just like a wave that rises to the surface of the sea and is immediately absorbed back into it. This is the fundamental difference between *rejog* and *nyamjog*, but why is it necessary to practice *rejog*? The principle of the practice of self-liberation is based on *nyamjog*, and true practitioners apply it much more than *rejog*. Nevertheless, the practice of *rejog* is necessary for those people who do not have sufficient clarity, or who are unable precisely to find the level of presence of awareness. For example, if someone makes us angry, we can respond in different ways to our anger: we can reject it, as in the path of renunciation typical of the sūtras, or transform it on the basis of the characteristic principle of the tantra, and so on. In our case we "let" ourselves get angry, but we do not enter into the anger as if we were compelled or conditioned by the emotion. We do not block it, nor do we let it disappear by instantaneously finding ourselves in its own condition, like in the principle of self-liberation or *nyamjog*. So, we let ourselves get angry and observe how far we go, how we react, but always with awareness: this is called *rejog*. This way of practicing is quite useful in life, because in this manner one can learn to be in control of any action one carries out. To give another example, at times a child can irritate his or her parents terribly, but it is unlikely that they will really get angry with their child: rather they will show anger so the child can understand his or her mistake. This is somewhat similar to the practice called *rejog*, because it is based on the principle of awareness.

Chapter 68

This chapter explains the nature of self-perfection, which can be encapsulated in the expression *lhundrub tsaldu medpa*: self-perfection is not something that can be sought. This point concerns in particular the achievement of realization, whose fundamental principle is to leave behind desires and worry, hope and fear. In *Chöd*[177] practice the verses that express the commitment of altruistic aspiration for enlightenment say: "In order to become aware of the true condition, I commit myself beyond hope and fear."[178] Both the desire and hope to achieve enlightenment and the worry and fear of not succeeding must be transcended.

Chapter 69

This chapter concludes the second part of the *Kunjed Gyalpo*. Basically, the first part concerns *tawa*, to enable one to understand the principle of the Dzogchen teaching, while the second part focuses on *togpa*, or knowledge, the level at which the practitioner actually comprehends and experiences the true condition.

Chapter 70

Chapter seventy, which opens the third and last part of the tantra, deals in particular with the aspect of *gompa* or meditation. In this regard it says that "there is something to meditate on and there is nothing to meditate on." What does this mean? "There is something to meditate on" from the relative view, for example using our vision to visualize the maṇḍala, although in any case it is necessary to be aware of the final aim one is trying to achieve. Likewise, if we feel the need to engage in a practice such as *tummo*, which involves a complicated series of visualizations of cakras, channels, etc., then we need to know what its aim is. So in these cases, one cannot say that there is nothing to meditate on because the meditation practice constitutes the express means to accomplish determined results. However, in reality "there is nothing to meditate on" because the absolute condition cannot be generated or produced through dualism. It is necessary to overcome dualism, and in this view there really is nothing on which to meditate.

Usually the practice of Buddhist meditation starts with *shiné*, or "calm state" (*śamatha*), subsequently proceeding to *lhagthong*, or "clear seeing" (*vipaśyanā*). To achieve the state of shiné, which can be compared to a calm sea, one applies concentration with or without an object. So the principle underlying all of these practices is that of remaining in a condition of neither creating thoughts nor blocking them if they arise. Focusing on a candle flame can be a useful way to concentrate attention, but one must not think about the flame one is focusing on: thinking about it means creating thoughts. It is necessary to continue without thinking of anything and without leaving the point of focus, which serves to hold the attention. In this way, whatever thoughts arise, whether good or bad, are left alone in their own condition and this fosters the experience of *nepa*, the calm state, a space without thoughts like a sea without waves, not stirred by the wind. When thoughts arise again, they are like waves: if we do not pursue them, they abate and disappear by themselves, followed by another space without thoughts. To give an example, the calm state can be compared to the surface of a lake, while arising thoughts are like the fish that occasionally jump and emerge from the water. So the calm state and the movement of thoughts, or *gyuwa*, continuously alternate. This is generally termed *shiné*.

Lhagthong usually means the arising of particular experiences tied to real understanding. In fact, many practitioners judge lhagthong mainly on the basis of the experiences of bliss, of emptiness, and of clarity. By practicing, one can have many experiences and sensations, all of which to a certain extent comprise the base of lhagthong. However true lhagthong, especially in Dzogchen, is the blooming of clarity, and this only takes place upon actually achieving knowledge of the state of consciousness. Before this level one cannot talk of real lhagthong because one is still relying on experiences and sensations. A practitioner can feel very happy, can feel indescribable joy, but basically remains conditioned by sensations tied to the body and its energy.

However, Dzogchen, as mentioned above, says that there is only the single level of total perfection. In this case, then, one cannot say that shiné reaches to a certain point and then, after that, lhagthong starts. Likewise, it is not necessary to retreat to an isolated place in order to find the calm state of shiné and only subsequently carry on to "taste" the sensation of lhagthong as if it were a different level. Because, in conclusion, shiné and lhagthong are at the same level, just like the calm state and the movement of thought. When we see clouds, we think: "Here are some clouds covering the sky," because we are convinced that the sky stretches behind the clouds. But in fact, sky and clouds are the same thing: what is sky is also cloud, what is cloud is also sky, it is only their way of appearing different that makes us call one sky and the other cloud. It is the same here. Whether one calls it shiné or lhagthong, the true condition always remains the same: shiné is lhagthong and lhagthong is shiné. And in any case, their final goal must concur with knowledge of the state of consciousness.

Chapter 71

This chapter explains the principle of *tagong yermed*: the inseparability of view and state of consciousness. *Tagong* is made up of *ta* and *gong*: *tawa*, the view, has already been explained, while *gongpa* means the state of knowledge by which the practitioner lives, so *tawa* and *gongpa* cannot be separated, they are the same thing. This occurs when one really attains the level of practice of Dzogchen. Understanding *tawa* but not actually being in the condition that has been introduced cannot at all be called *tagong yermed*.

Chapter 72

This chapter by and large continues the explanation of this fundamental issue.

Chapter 73

Here the text explains the way to remain continuously in the state of consciousness. Different methods are explained that concern the practice of tregchöd, the meaning of which cannot easily be explained in a few words.

Chapter 74

This chapter, too, explains practice, and is almost an introduction to knowledge of the state of consciousness. Usually those with intellectual tendencies are keen to read as many commentaries and explanations as they can. However, for a true practitioner, a few words can be enough, like the pages of this chapter, in order to understand the fundamental meaning.

Chapters 75, 76, 77, 78, 79 & 80

All these chapters explain the essence of the path and the diverse modes of practicing continuity of the state. It is useful to remember that on the practice of the *Kunjed Gyalpo* the great teacher Longchenpa has written a marvellous guide that also quotes the most relevant passages.[179]

Chapter 81

This chapter states that the *Kunjed Gyalpo* is like a key to all the tantras, in particular the Semde.

Chapter 82

This chapter describes Sattvavajra's eulogy of Kunjed Gyalpo.

Chapter 83

This chapter, as is customary in all tantras, describes the qualities of the disciples who are suitable to receive the teaching of *Kunjed Gyalpo*, describing those who should receive its transmission and those who should not.

Chapter 84

The last chapter mentions other names of this tantra, such as *Tawai Melong*, "Mirror of the View." Thus concludes the *Kunjed Gyalpo*, translated by Śrī Siṃha and Vairocana.

It is very likely that the original *Kunjed Gyalpo* was in the language of Oḍḍiyāna and that only subsequently was it translated into Sanskrit. The original version has never been found because the Sanskrit texts pertaining to the first promulgation of Buddhism in Tibet were preserved at Samye Monastery, which burnt down twice. Other important libraries, such as the one at Sakya, are not so old and thus do not contain such ancient texts.

In conclusion, anyone interested in the Dzogchen teaching cannot but study a text such as the *Kunjed Gyalpo*, because the Semde series is the indispensable base for knowledge of the primordial state, corresponding to the first statement by Garab Dorje: "Directly discover your own state."

PART THREE

The *Kunjed Gyalpo* Excerpts in Translation

A NOTE ON THE TRANSLATION METHOD

For the larger part the *Kunjed Gyalpo* is written in seven or nine-syllable verse, as is the case with almost all the classical Sanskrit texts translated into Tibetan. This entails the use of particles and repetitions that do not actually add anything meaningful to the text. Wishing to make the text as easy to read and as accessible as possible, I have chosen a prose translation instead of a strictly literal one. For example, a paragraph that repeats several times "the manifestation of me, the supreme source" I have rendered as "my manifestation." On the other hand, in other cases I have had to resort to paraphrases and additions [marked in square brackets] in order to disclose the true meaning of the text. Be that as it may, in the case of texts such as the *Kunjed Gyalpo* translation is impossible without an interpretation based on existing commentaries and on explanations by teachers of the lineage, in this case Chögyal Namkhai Norbu. Conversely, producing a "scientific" translation can only expose one to the danger of completely misconstruing the original message of the text.

I have limited to the bare minimum the use of Tibetan terms, rendering some of the most frequently recurring technical terms with diverse expressions according to the context. Some of them are listed below.

chos (*dharma*): being, existence, reality, phenomena

chos nyid (*dharmatā*): ultimate nature; natural, real, or fundamental condition; fundamental reality

chos dbyings (*dharmadhātu*), *chos nyid dbyings*: ultimate dimension of phenomena, of essential reality

mnyam pa, *mnyam pa nyid*: condition or state of equality, of equanimity

ji bzhin ba, *ji bzhin nyid*: natural or authentic condition or state, lit. "as it is"

snying po: fundamental, ultimate essence/substance

de bzhin nyid (*tathatā*): essential, fundamental, natural condition/state; authentic nature; lit. "that thing as it is"

rnal ma: natural, fundamental or authentic condition or state

dbyings: fundamental, ultimate dimension

Another problem concerns the term *byed* (literally "make," "create") and the expressions based on the past forms of this verb, *byas* and *ma byas* (practically synonymous with *bkod pa*). On the basis of the principle of universal manifestation clearly explained by Chögyal Namkhai Norbu in the preface and in his oral commentary, in many cases I have used the verb "manifest" rather than "create." Likewise *sems*, usually translated as "mind," has been often rendered by the term "consciousness," especially in the first part of the tantra that explains the principle of primordial manifestation. In any case, almost throughout the *Kunjed Gyalpo* the word *sems* is to be taken as an abbreviation of *byang chub sems* (*bodhicitta*), rendered "pure and total consciousness." A passage from the text (184.4: *sems zhes bya ba'i nges pa bstan pa ni/ rgyu rkyen med pa'i rang byung ye shes te/ ma 'gags kun la dbang po sgo lngar gsal*) explains that "the true meaning of the word *sems* refers to self-arising wisdom, free of causes and conditions, which manifests in everything ceaselessly as the clarity of the sense doors."

For my translation I have mainly used the mTshams brag edition; however, I have also referred to three other available editions: the first found in the *Nyingma Gyüd Bum*, published by Dilgo Khyentse, the second contained in the *Nyingma Kama* and the third in the Peking *Kangyur* (see bibliography). At times there are significant discrepancies between the various versions. However, for reasons of space and time, as well as of the difficulty of the text itself, I have not redacted a critical edition of the text and have confined myself to indicating the major divergences in footnotes: my apologies for this to Tibetologists and scholars. The end of every passage translated is marked by dots in square brackets, and the location of the passages indicated at the end of each chapter of the text. For example, 2.2-6.6; 6.7-7.7 denotes that the first passage starts on page 2, line 2 and ends on page 6, line 6, while the second passage starts on page 6, line 7 and ends on page 7, line 7, of the mTshams brag edition. I have been unable to resolve all the problems of translation and hope to have the opportunity in the future to correct any errors that may have been made.

5 The Root Tantra

I. THE TEACHINGS ON PRIMORDIAL MANIFESTATION

In the supreme abode of Akaniṣṭha, in the sky of the ultimate nature of phenomena, in the space of the fundamental dimension, in the abode of the nature of mind, in the divine palace of unhindered wisdom, there manifested the assemblies of disciples of Kunjed Gyalpo's essence, nature, energy, and wisdom. The assembly of the dharmakāya were the audience of his essence. The assembly of the earth element of the saṃbhogakāya were the audience of his nature, the assembly of the water element of the saṃbhogakāya were the audience of his nature, the assembly of the fire element of the saṃbhogakāya were the audience of his nature, the assembly of the air element of the saṃbhogakāya were the audience of his nature, the assembly of the space element of the saṃbhogakāya were the audience of his nature. The assembly of the nirmāṇakāya were the audience of the energy of his wisdom, consisting of the beings of the world of desire, of the world of form and of the formless world. Also present were the assemblies of those who, through the four kinds of yogas, abide in his essence: the practitioners of atiyoga, of anuyoga, of mahāyoga, and of sattvayoga, inseparable from the fundamental condition of essence, nature, and energy, and the assembly of those who have realized his essence: the Buddhas of the past who abide in the primordial state, the Buddhas of the present who carry out actions in order to communicate it, and the Buddhas of the future who will arise from this same state. All were inseparable from his essence.

Then, in order to empower all the disciples and to enable them to recognize his essence, the supreme source, pure and total consciousness, dissolved them into the nature of his Mind[180] and made self-arising wisdom appear clearly to all of them. Then, in order for all of them to enter into the state of the ultimate nature, he re-absorbed all of them and concentrated them into an immense single sphere, wherein they all remained.

Sattvavajra manifested forth from this immense natural sphere. Full of joy, with devotion he presented himself before the supreme source, pure and total consciousness. [...]

Sattvavajra asked: Teacher of teachers, supreme source! Is the teacher the ineffable sphere? Are all the assemblies of disciples the ineffable sphere? Are all the teachings the ineffable sphere? Are the diverse epochs and places the ineffable sphere? If all and every thing has the nature of the sphere, who could ever be the "teacher of teachers"? What reason could there ever be for the appearance of disciples? What teaching could ever be transmitted? And can epochs and places ever be one single thing?

Then the supreme source, pure and total consciousness, answered: Great being, concentrate on the sound, I will explain the true meaning to you! I, the supreme source, the ultimate nature of mind, am the fundamental substance of all phenomena, the ineffable essence that from the very beginning is a sphere: "sphere" precisely indicates that which has always transcended concepts. The teachers, the teachings, the assemblies of disciples, the epochs, and the places arise from me and remain the primordial sphere, for my nature is the sphere.

[*1. The introductory chapter*, 2.2–6.6; 6.7–7.7]

[Sattvavajra asked:] Teacher of teachers, supreme source, I too am among your disciples, but what is the meaning of my manifestation? Why am I here? I beseech you, please explain this to me!

Then the supreme source, pure and total consciousness, explained that all phenomena arise from his essence, nature, and energy. From his single, total, self-arising wisdom manifest the five great wisdoms: the self-arising wisdom of anger, the self-arising wisdom of attachment, the self-arising wisdom of ignorance, the self-arising wisdom of jealousy, and the self-arising wisdom of pride. These five natural wisdoms give birth to the ornamental causes of the five great [elements][181] and this gives birth to the three worlds subject to destruction. [...]

[Sattvavajra asked:] Teacher of teachers, supreme source, the five wisdoms that give rise to the five elements arise from your single state of self-arising wisdom. But, why does your wisdom manifest in these five aspects?

The supreme source, pure and total consciousness, explained: Listen, great being, to the reason. I, the supreme source, am the sole maker, and no other agent exists in the world. The nature of phenomena is created through me, the three teachers manifest from me and the three classes of disciples arise from me. The very manifestation of existence itself depends on me. I will explain my nature to you, Sattvavajra.

[2. *The chapter that discloses the manifestation of the ultimate nature*, 8.2–8.7; 9.6–10.4]

Then the supreme source, pure and total consciousness, explained that he himself is the primordial womb whence all phenomena originate: Great being, concentrate on the sense of hearing! Through sound, understand the meaning! I am the supreme source, I am pure and total consciousness that is all-accomplishing. Before I existed, there was not the fundamental substance whence all phenomena originate. Before I existed, there was not the supreme source whence everything springs forth. Had I not existed, no teacher would ever have appeared. Without me, no teaching or assembly of disciples would ever have appeared. Sattvavajra, have no doubts! You yourself, great being, are an emanation of my nature.

Then Sattvavajra asked: O supreme source, pure and total consciousness, you are the primordial totality! As the teacher, the teachings, the disciples, and all the rest have arisen from you, you are the source of all phenomena. But, is there only one teacher or are there many? Is there only one disciple or are there many?

The supreme source, pure and total consciousness, continued thus: Self-arising wisdom is the single true teacher of all, yet my essence manifests in three aspects, and thus there arise the three categories of teachings. I am the oneness of the fundamental condition, and precisely this is the reality of all phenomena: there is only me, pure and total consciousness. The teachers of the three dimensions, who are my emanations, teach their disciples three kinds of teachings. Manifesting my single nature, I evince that instead my essence is one alone: thus for me, the source, there exists only one category of disciple. However, for the teachers of the three dimensions, my emanations, there are three distinct categories of disciples.

[3. *The chapter that discloses how the origin arose*. 10.7–12.5]

I am self-arising wisdom that has existed from the beginning. I am the fundamental substance of all phenomena that has existed from the beginning. I am the supreme source of everything, pure and total consciousness. Sattvavajra, understand the meaning of my names! Understand them, and you will understand the totality of phenomena without exception.

[I am self-arising wisdom that has existed from the beginning:][182] "I" means the essence, the fundamental substance of all phenomena. "Wisdom" refers to the fact that, being uninterrupted and unhindered, [this nature] clearly discloses all phenomena. Its being "self-arising" means that, as it is free of causes and conditions, it transcends all effort. I am called "pure and total consciousness," and "from the beginning" means that I have existed from the first moment.

[I am the fundamental substance of all phenomena:] The real condition, what is called the "fundamental substance," is the womb whence all phenomena arise. In fact, the teachers, the teachings, the disciples, the places, and the epochs manifest from the essence of pure and total consciousness. "Of all phenomena" means that all the teachers are the real condition of existence, and the same holds for all the teachings, disciples, places, and epochs. Nothing exists that is not this essential reality.

[I am the supreme source of everything, pure and total consciousness:] As I am the essence of mind, the fundamental substance, I am the source of all phenomena. "Supreme" refers to self-arising wisdom, the supreme maker that gives rise to the creation of all the phenomena of existence. "Source" refers to the "creator": since the teachers, the teachings, the disciples, the places, and the epochs manifest from self-arising wisdom that has existed from the beginning, it itself is the only maker. "Of everything" refers to the totality of phenomena. But what are these? All the teachers, teachings, disciples, places, and epochs. "Pure" means that pure and total consciousness, the true essence, is self-arising and has always been completely pure: consequently, all that manifests from the supreme source keeps its purity whole in the condition of Samantabhadra. "Total" means that self-arising wisdom, the true essence, permeates and pervades the whole animate and inanimate universe, all circumstances and forms of existence, the Buddhas of the three times, the three worlds, the six classes of beings, and all possible situations. "Consciousness" means that self-arising wisdom, the true essence, dominates and clearly perceives all the phenomena of the animate and inanimate universe. This self-arising fundamental substance, not produced by causes and conditions, governs all things and gives life to all things.

Listen, great being! When you understand my essence you will also understand all the teachers and all the teachings. You will perceive the minds of the disciples and recognize the fundamental oneness of all places and all epochs. As I am existence in all of its entirety, perceiving my essence you will understand the totality of all phenomena and overcome all actions and efforts, realizing the natural perfection in which there exists no effort whatever.

[4. *The chapter that explains his names,* 15.3–17.6]

Listen, great being! I will explain my nature to you. Though only one, it nevertheless manifests in two aspects. It gives rise to the nine ways of realization, yet its end is total perfection. Its being is pure and total consciousness, and its abode is the dimension of essential reality. It shines in the sky of pure instantaneous presence, it pervades all habitats and forms of life, it gives rise to the whole animate and inanimate world. It has no material characteristic that can be shown, is it not an object that can be seen, nor can it be explained in words. This fundamental substance, not produced by causes, transcends all definitions based on concepts. If you really want to understand this state, take the sky as the example, the ultimate, unoriginated nature as the meaning and the uninterrupted nature of mind as the sign. Being like the sky, the ultimate nature is denoted by the example of the sky. As it cannot become an object, it is denoted as something that cannot be objectified. As it cannot be expressed in words, it is made known by saying that it transcends definitions. This is the nature of that which cannot be objectified. This concise explanation serves to clarify the fundamental essence. Through this explanation understand my state and enable others, too, to understand it! Whoever does not understand me in this way cannot meet me, however many words might be used. That person will move away from me and will cast a veil over me, unable to perceive the ultimate essence of reality.

[5. *The chapter that explains the true meaning,* 18.1–19.2]

Then Sattvavajra asked: Teacher of teachers, supreme source! If all phenomena are your nature, what is the reason for the manifestation of the teacher, the teaching, and the disciples? And what is the meaning of the "perfect conditions" [for teaching]?

The supreme source, pure and total consciousness, answered thus: Great being, listen! All phenomena manifest in perfect conditions, because I myself am the nature of perfection: I will disclose it to you! As my nature transcends concepts and cannot be divided into parts, the ultimate dimension of phenomena manifests from me, and therein abides only the pure and total condition. As my nature is unhindered and all-pervading, it is the celestial abode of wisdom in luminous space: therein abides only self-arising wisdom. As I am the substance whence everything arises, the five great elements, the three worlds and the six classes of beings are only my body, my voice, and my mind: I myself create my own nature. Thus, the Buddhas of the three times and the beings of the three worlds are only my own nature. As I have no origin and I transcend all concepts, my essence abides nowhere and is beyond all the objects of experience. It does not appear visibly and is beyond all the objects of meditation. [...]

Do not make my teaching known to those who follow the vehicles based on cause and effect! If you do, by affirming the law of cause and effect of positive and negative deeds, they would cover my true condition with conjectures, and for a long time they would lose any possibility of meeting me. I am the teacher, pure and total consciousness, whence everything manifests. Pure and total consciousness is the supreme source, it has created the Buddhas of the three times, from it have arisen the beings of the three worlds and the whole animate and inanimate universe. [...]

Pure and total consciousness has created everything and has not created anything. It has created everything because it has created its own nature, pure and total. It has not created anything because within it there exists no need to create. When my nature is not understood and the phenomena that manifest from me become the object of judgement, desire and attachment give rise to the creation of concrete vision that is impermanent and destined to vanish like a magical apparition, and one becomes like a blind man who does not know what is happening. [...]

The root of all phenomena is pure and total consciousness, the source. All that appears is my nature. All that manifests is my magical display. All sounds and words express only my meaning. From the very beginning, the pure dimensions, the wisdoms and qualities of the Buddhas, the karmic inclinations and bodies of beings, all the things that exist in the animate and inanimate universe, are the nature of pure and total consciousness.

[6. *The chapter on the single root*, 20.1–21.1; 21.6–22.2; 22.5–22.7; 25.5–25.7]

Listen, great being! Consciousness is the nature of the authentic condition. Although it transcends form, the bliss of the authentic non-dual condition contains all forms within itself. Like space, from the beginning it is beyond conceptual limits, it cannot become an object and cannot even be conceived of in terms of "one." Pure and total consciousness is not subject to quantity and cannot be depicted in any way. However, for the phenomena created by consciousness, multiplicity arises. What is created by consciousness? From the natural condition of consciousness are created the animate and inanimate world, Buddhas and sentient beings. In this way there appears the manifestation of the five elements, of the six classes of beings, and of the two types of emanations of the dimension of form [saṃbhogakāya and nirmāṇakāya] that act for their benefit. All of this manifests from the nature of consciousness as multiplicity. [...]

I am primordial self-perfection. I am the essence of the state of self-perfection of all the Buddhas. I am the nature of the potentiality of energy, and I teach that the nature of consciousness is the source of all. [...]

To those attracted by oneness, I teach that the ineffable essence is one alone. As all phenomena are contained in the single [essence], I teach that the condition of pure and total consciousness, the true nature of mind, is the source of all. Whereas, to those attracted by multiplicity, I teach the infinite variety that manifests from me: it too is my nature. One is my essence. Two is my manifestation, the multiplicity of created phenomena. Numbers start from one and two, but their end cannot be determined. The ineffable is the ultimate nature of existence: this ineffable essence is the one. One is the supreme source, pure and total consciousness. The phenomena of creation are duality. [...]

There is nothing [in this nature] that is not perfect. One is perfect, two is perfect, everything is perfect. All actions are easy because they are already accomplished and perfect. "One is perfect" signifies perfection in pure and total consciousness. "Two is perfect" signifies perfection in the manifestation of consciousness. "Everything is perfect" signifies perfection in completeness. Thanks to this teaching on the perfection of the one, you can enter in the state of enlightenment. Thanks to the meaning of the perfection in duality, you can understand that everything that appears is the perfect manifestation of consciousness. Thanks to the meaning of the perfection in totality, everything can become perfection. Those who remain in this condition beyond action, whether in a body that is human or divine, abide in the state of enlightenment, in the ultimate nature of reality. When they help other beings, this is easily and effortlessly accomplished.

[7. *The chapter that epitomizes multiplicity*, 26.3–26.7; 27.3–27.4; 27.5–28.2; 30.2–30.6]

Great being, listen! This pure and total consciousness, which is the essence of the universe, is the authentic condition of all phenomena, a spontaneous, natural state that has been present from the beginning. However, this fundamental condition that transcends action is understood in four different ways [by practitioners] of the four yogas: sattvayoga, mahāyoga, anuyoga, and atiyoga.

Practitioners of sattvayoga take into consideration the sense faculties and their objects, which, empowered through the five factors of realization[183] and the four miraculous actions[184] are perceived as the two deities (of wisdom and of commitment).[185] Thus they do not understand the authentic, fundamental condition: may they recognize the unaltered natural state!

Practitioners of mahāyoga understand the authentic condition beyond action in this way: in the original maṇḍala of their pure mind there is the maṇḍala of the deity [that can manifest only] as the effect of a cause. Thus they have to complete all the phases of the practice on the basis of the four "approaches and accomplishments,"[186] only then do they realize the self-perfection of the totality of their state, endowed with the functions of radiation and re-absorption.[187] Thus they do not understand the authentic, fundamental condition: may they recognize the unaltered natural state!

Practitioners of anuyoga understand the authentic condition beyond action in this way: the dimension of emptiness is the cause of the fundamental condition, while total wisdom is its effect. As this implies that a single essence is perceived through the dualism of cause and effect, in this view they do not understand the authentic condition beyond cause and effect: may they then recognize the unaltered natural state!

Practitioners of Dzogchen atiyoga understand the authentic condition beyond action in this way: pure and total consciousness is the universal essence. Leaving it as it is without correcting it means being in the authentic state. From the beginning there is no idea of having to meditate on a view. From the beginning there is no idea of having to maintain a commitment. From the beginning there is no idea of having to acquire the capacity for spiritual action. Leaving everything as it is, one is in the authentic state.

The views of the four yogas are each further subdivided into four categories.[188] The four subdivisions of sattvayoga are: not conceptualizing the sense faculties and their objects represents sattvayoga; the factors of realization, the empowering flow, and the miraculous actions represent mahāyoga; practicing the four mudrās[189] represents anuyoga; the view according to which neither the wisdom deity nor the commitment deity have self-nature constitutes the sattvayoga practitioners' understanding of the state of atiyoga. Nevertheless, they do not apprehend the authentic condition beyond acceptance and rejection.

The four subdivisions of mahāyoga are: the three initial contemplations[190] represent sattvayoga; deeming the wisdom deity as the purity of one's own mind corresponds to mahāyoga; the perfection accomplished by means of the "four approaches and accomplishments" corresponds to anuyoga; the view according to which everything is the totality of one's state corresponds to atiyoga. Nevertheless, [these practitioners] do not apprehend the authentic condition beyond effort.

The four subdivisions of anuyoga are: recognition of the pure nature of the real condition, without needing to visualize oneself in the form of the deity in a gradual manner, corresponds to sattvayoga; perfecting the maṇḍala basing oneself solely on the fundamental essence, without relying on [the union of] method and prajñā, of "male and female,"[191] corresponds to the knowledge of mahāyoga; the experience of the real condition of "appearance and absence of self-nature" corresponds to anuyoga; the view according to which the dimension of emptiness is the fundamental cause of all the phenomena of existence, while wisdom is its effect, corresponds to atiyoga. Nevertheless, [these practitioners] do not apprehend the authentic condition beyond cause and effect.

The four subdivisions of atiyoga are: pure and total consciousness beyond acceptance and rejection corresponds to sattvayoga; pure and total consciousness beyond effort and practicing corresponds to mahāyoga; pure and total consciousness beyond cause and effect corresponds to anuyoga; the condition of existence that transcends being and non being, affirming and negating, this is what corresponds to atiyoga!

Sattvayoga, mahāyoga, and anuyoga do not really have knowledge of self-arising wisdom. For this reason they believe there is a path to tread and levels of realization to achieve, together with a precise commitment to keep and a view on which to meditate. In consequence, their view and behavior are not effective in inducing familiarity [with the true condition]. Conversely, from the very beginning the view and behavior of atiyoga [is based on the understanding that everything] is a manifestation of the [supreme] source, thus it does not presuppose the need to tread a path or to achieve levels of realization, to keep a commitment or to meditate on a view.

In fact, if everything arises from pure and total consciousness, then pure and total consciousness has no need of a path to tread to reach itself. If all the levels of realization are only pure and total consciousness, then pure and total consciousness has no need to practice in order to achieve them. If the true meaning of all the commitments is only pure and total consciousness, then pure and total consciousness has no need to "keep" itself. If the true meaning of all the meditations is only pure and total consciousness, then pure and total consciousness has no need to meditate on itself. If the aim of all the views is pure and total consciousness, then pure and total consciousness has no need to aim for itself. Thus the view and behavior of atiyoga, which do not imply effort, really induce familiarity with self-arising wisdom. It is the path to innermost acquaintance with me, the supreme source, and does not form part of the field of experience of the vehicles based on cause and effect.

[*8. The chapter that explains how all views about the ultimate nature have arisen from it*, 32.5–36.4]

Then the supreme source, pure and total consciousness, explained that the vehicles based on cause and effect err by following a gradual path and consequently they constitute a deviation and a hindrance in terms of total perfection.

Listen, great being! Just this nature of pure and total consciousness is the ultimate essence of all that exists. Never having been born, it is totally pure and unhindered; as it cannot be achieved by treading a path, it has no deviations; spontaneously perfect from the beginning, it cannot be the outcome of a quest. Yet by conceiving this single pure and total consciousness, the universal essence, in terms of multiplicity, deviations and hindrances arise. Treading a path to reach what cannot be reached by treading causes deviation; seeking to understand conceptually that which cannot become an object [of thought] causes the hindrances that obstruct understanding.

Even though in the fundamental condition all is equal, [the Bodhisattvas] deem that practicing the ten pāramitās enables one to realize the ten bhūmis[192] because they think that by acting on a cause, one can benefit from its fruit in the future. In this way they deviate and remain hindered for three more kalpas.

[Practitioners of kriyā] deem the outer world, the inner world, and thoughts to be the three purities[193] and engage in the factors of realization and in the miraculous actions. But even though in this way they keep their vows and commitments perfectly, they deviate and remain hindered for seven more lives.

[Practitioners of ubhaya,] whose behavior corresponds to the cause and whose view corresponds to the effect, deem view and behavior as two separate things. In this way they deviate from the non-dual state and remain hindered for three more lives.

[Practitioners of yoga,] by adhering to behavior of acceptance and rejection in relation to the single essence, lose sight of oneness and enter into dualistic vision. In this way they deviate and remain hindered until they free themselves of accepting and rejecting.

[Practitioners of mahāyoga,] by meditating on the single self-arising condition as if it had three characteristics,[194] deviate from the state that transcends effort.

[Practitioners of anuyoga,] by not understanding that the natural condition is the ultimate essence of all the phenomena of the animate and inanimate world, conceive the dimension of emptiness and wisdom in terms of cause and effect.[195] As this amounts to affirming a cause that does not exist and, conversely, negating an effect that does exist, they remain hindered until they achieve the certainty that transcends affirming and negating.

These, then, [in summary] are the six ways of seeking to obtain a fruit it is believed one does not [already] possess: basing oneself on the two truths; engaging in the three purities; separating view and behavior; engaging in behavior entailing acceptance and rejection; meditating on the three [characteristic] phases; apprehending the dimension of emptiness and wisdom in terms of cause and effect. [...]

Pure and total consciousness is like space. In the true condition of the nature of mind, similar to space, there is no view on which to meditate nor commitment to observe, there is no capacity for spiritual action to obtain nor wisdom to develop, there are no levels of realization to cultivate nor path to tread, there is no consideration of a subtle substance[196] nor of a duality to be re-integrated as unity, there is no final teaching apart from pure and total consciousness. Being [the true nature] beyond affirmation and negation, there is no secret teaching that can compare with it. This is the view of total perfection, pure and total consciousness.

Followers of the vehicles based on cause and effect who aspire to see me and apprehend my essence seek me by means of the "ten natures." But inevitably they fail, like someone who tries to walk in the sky and falls down to earth. I will explain my true essence to you: as it transcends any sphere of experience, in my regard there is no view on which to meditate. Likewise, none of the "ten natures" enable one to realize the true aim. Do not think the opposite! Seeking to understand me by means of concepts, one finds nothing at all to "see." So do not make me the object of your view, leave me in the natural condition! As there has never been any separation in the ineffable unborn state, there is no need to observe vows and commitments. As the fundamental essence is spontaneously perfect from the beginning, there is no use in striving in practice to obtain it. As self-arising wisdom can never be hindered, there is no use in seeking to make clearer the wisdom of pure presence. As all is already at my level, there are no levels of realization to cultivate and to tread. As I pervade all of existence in its entirety, there is no path that can lead to me. As I always transcend the dualism of subject and object, there is nothing to define as "subtle substance." As my form is present in everything, duality has never existed. As I am primordial self-arising wisdom, there is nobody else who can confirm me. As I am the essence of universal enlightenment, there is no other secret instruction.

As I transcend all affirmations and negations, I am beyond all phenomena. As no object exists that is not myself, I am beyond meditating on a view. As there is nothing to keep apart from myself, I am beyond a commitment to observe. As there is nothing to seek other than myself, I am beyond obtaining the capacity for spiritual action. As no place exists outside myself, I am beyond a level of realization to surpass. As I have never encountered obstacles, I am beyond [everything] as self-arising wisdom. As I am the ultimate unborn nature, I am beyond [everything] as the [true] subtle ultimate nature. As there is no place to go outside myself, I am beyond treading paths. As everything manifests from myself, I that am the essence of enlightenment, I am the original non-duality [that is] beyond [everything] In order to establish definitive knowledge of self-arising wisdom, I am beyond [everything] as direct and total understanding of the scriptures. As no phenomena exist apart from myself, I that manifest everything, am beyond everything.

In reality, "hindrance" means not understanding me. "Deviation" means seeking something other than me. Hindrances can be of two kinds: karmic and conceptual. The inability to understand me is karmic hindrance; the inability to discern me is conceptual hindrance. As all the phenomena of the animate and inanimate world are the nature of fundamental pure and total consciousness, not apprehending and not discerning me are the two kinds of hindrances; seeking something and striving to obtain it constitute deviation.

[9. *The chapter on the elimination of the defects related to deviations and hindrances*, 36.5–38.3; 38.5–38.7; 40.2–42.4]

Listen, great being! I am called "the perfect condition" because everything is contained in me. I am called "the source" because the teacher, teaching, and disciples arise from my three natures. First of all, I will explain the perfect condition of the teacher. From my self-arising wisdom there arise the three natures that manifest as the teachers of the three dimensions: the dimension of the essence [dharmakāya], the dimension of the wealth of qualities [saṃbhogakāya] and the dimension of manifestation [nirmāṇakāya]. This is the nature of the three dimensions: the nature of dharmakāya is the unborn that transcends subject and object; the nature of saṃbhogakāya is the perfect enjoyment of everything one could wish; the nature of nirmāṇakāya is the capacity to emanate oneself in any form necessary to transmit the teaching.

The teaching of the teachers of the three dimensions is comprised in three categories: outer, inner, and secret. The teaching of the dharmakāya teacher discloses the nature of the three secrets: from the pure condition of original reality there manifest the three natures of secret creation, of secret completion, and of secret total perfection, called "secret" because they do not enter within all people's fields of experience.

"Secret creation" [of mahāyoga] consists in secretly generating the three contemplative phases that it is believed one does not [already] possess.

In the "secret completion" [of anuyoga], prajñā [discriminating wisdom] is not the result of the three contemplations: all the phenomena of existence are the ultimate essence of prajñā that arises from inner contemplation. As from the beginning, one's pure mind is the deity, one deems that all the sense faculties of the "vajra body" are already the totality of one's state,[197] beyond the separation of view and behavior, of accepting and rejecting. This is secret inner perfection.

In the "secret total perfection" [of atiyoga] all the phenomena that appear to perception are not transformed into pure and total consciousness by means of the three contemplations. They are not perfected by reciting the seed syllable of the deity. I, the source, am total perfection because there is nothing in me that is not perfect. My three natures are the three aspects of pure and total consciousness of total perfection. This is secret total perfection. This is the end of the explanation on the teachings of the dharmakāya teacher.

Now I will explain the teachings of the saṃbhogakāya teacher, which comprehend the three outer series of action.

[In kriyā] the conceptual series of ritual action, first of all one meditates on the three purities of the outer world, of the inner world, and of thoughts through contemplation of the non-discursive state. One starts the practice at a propitious hour, taking into account the positions of the constellations and planets. Then, engaging in the factors of realization and the miraculous actions, one tenders the offerings complying with the principle of the three purities, regarding oneself as a servant and the wisdom deity as the lord. One aspires in this way to obtain the spiritual powers of the Body, Voice, and Mind [of the deity,] that one does not apprehend one already possesses.

[In the ubhaya series,] even though it is explained that both the absolute and the relative are illusory, one separates view from behavior and seeks to achieve the single aim on the basis of this dualism. However, by seeking to realize that which has no concrete existence by means of behavior based on the concept of "concreteness," one becomes like a hungry she-wolf that stretches out unsupported into the void.

In the outer secret [yoga] series based on accepting and rejecting, everything is empowered in the wisdom deity through non-discursive contemplation, [the methods for receiving] the empowering flow and the miraculous actions. Then, tendering the outer, inner, and secret offerings one receives the [power of the] Body, Voice, and Mind [of the deity] and of the four mudrās, hoping in this way to obtain the desired siddhis. However, this contemplation based on the hope of obtaining the state that transcends attachment does not provide the means for realization, as it surely implies acceptance and rejection in terms of view and behavior. This ends the explanation on the teachings of the saṃbhogakāya teacher.

Now I will explain the teachings of the nirmāṇakāya teacher, the three series of the śrāvakas, of the pratyekas, and of the Mahāyāna sūtras, called "outer" or "of the outer characteristics." The five sense objects, which are my nature, manifest as the nature of the five primordial wisdoms, and in this way there arise the three passions: attachment, anger, and ignorance. The eighty-four thousand Dharma methods have been taught as the antidote to subdue these passions. In fact, when the five sense objects appear, it is precisely from forms, sounds, smells, tastes, and tangible objects that attachment, anger, and ignorance arise. The antidote to vanquish them consists in the three sections of the scriptures. To overcome attachment, the twenty-one thousand series of the *Vinayapiṭaka* were taught; to overcome ignorance, the twenty-one thousand series of the *Sūtrapiṭaka* were taught; to overcome anger, the twenty-one thousand series of the *Abhidharmapiṭaka* were taught; to overcome all three poisons in equal measure, the twenty-one thousand series of the *Tripiṭaka* were taught. Thus, even though one speaks of eighty-four thousand methods, they were transmitted only as the antidote to subdue the three poisons. In fact, the three analytic causal vehicles contain the three sections of Vinaya, Sūtra, and Abhidharma. [...]

Now I will explain the three kinds of disciples of the teachers of the three dimensions. Listen, great being: this is the retinue of the dharmakāya teacher. All beings, which have originated from me, form the retinue of the dharmakāya, which is my essence. All the Buddhas and sentient beings, everything that exists in the animate and inanimate world, without exclusion, form the retinue of the dharmakāya teacher.

Listen, great being, now I will explain the retinue of the saṃbhogakāya teacher. All those who have gone beyond the level of the four practices based on aspiration,[198] and who tread the bhūmis starting from the first, "The Joyous," to the tenth, "The Cloud of Dharma," form the retinue of the saṃbhogakāya teacher.

Now I will explain the retinue of the nirmāṇakāya teacher. When the disciples of the four schools—*mutegpa*, *murthugpa*, *gyangphenpa*, and *chalwa*[199]—who are far from the path that leads to complete enlightenment, are empowered by the compassionate energy that befits their capacity, they take four kinds of ordination: bhikṣu, bhikṣunī, upāsaka, and upāsikā. They form the retinue of the nirmāṇakāya teacher.

Listen, great being, now I will explain the specific places of the teachers of the three dimensions that have arisen from me. The place of the dharmakāya teacher is the "Akaniṣṭha palace" as the ultimate dimension of phenomena: this is the "ultimate Akaniṣṭha." The place of the saṃbhogakāya teacher is the celestial Akaniṣṭha abode made of luminous layers: this is called the Akaniṣṭha "place."[200] The place of the nirmāṇakāya teacher is "Vulture Peak," abode of the seven Buddhas and of Śākyamuni; however, it can be any other place of emanation of compassionate energy.

[*10. The chapter on the manifestation of perfect conditions*, 43.4–47.2; 47.7–49.2]

II. THE TEACHINGS THAT DISCLOSE THE TRUE NATURE

I am the essence of all phenomena; nothing exists that is not my essence. The teachers of the three dimensions are my essence. The Buddhas of the three times are my essence. The Bodhisattvas are my essence. The four types of yogins are my essence. The three worlds, of desire, of form, and without form, too, are my manifestation. The five great elements are my essence. The six classes of beings are my essence. Everything inanimate is my essence. Everything that lives is my essence. All the habitats and the beings living therein are my essence. Nothing exists that is not my essence because I am the universal root: there is nothing that is not contained in me. The unborn, the wonder of birth, and the manifestation of energy are the three aspects of the three teachers: this is their condition.

As the three times, past, present, and future, abide exclusively in me, all the Buddhas are in the same condition: this too is my essence. As I transcend the dualism of subject and object, like space I am all-pervading, and I constitute the fundamental substance of all phenomena: my essence is pure and total consciousness. I, that am the source, abide in the single state, and in this same authentic condition the practitioners of the "four yogas" find knowledge: this is my essence.

All that manifests from my Body, my Voice, and my Mind springs from my essence, is re-absorbed in it, and is nothing other than my essence: thus the three worlds are my essence.

My essence has five aspects whence there manifest the five natures: space, air, water, earth, and fire. They are my essence.

From the manifestation of my energy there arise the five self-arising wisdoms: even though they appear as the six classes of beings, they too are my essence. From my essence the whole animate and inanimate universe manifests: there is no phenomenon that does not arise from me.

[*11. The chapter that shows that the sole root of all phenomena is Kunjed Gyalpo bodhicitta,* 55.1–56.6]

I, the supreme source, pure and total consciousness, am called "the peak of all the vehicles." All the hundreds of thousands of teachings of the Vinaya, of the Abhidharma, of the sūtras, and of the different classes of tantras, all the secret methods of creation and completion transmitted by the teachers of the three dimensions, my emanations, are all based on effort. They aim at me, I that transcend effort; however, by engaging in effort they do not succeed in seeing me. Thus I am considered the peak of the teachings.

I, the supreme source, pure and total consciousness, am called the core of all the vehicles. In reality the three vehicles led by the three teachers are nothing other than the single vehicle of the real meaning: the universal vehicle that is the level of pure and total consciousness. It is the core of all the vehicles of realization.

Dispelling the darkness of ignorance, I kindle the light of great wisdom. In fact, not knowing that all the phenomena of existence are precisely the natural condition of enlightenment, beings become enfolded in the thick darkness of erroneous conceptions. Showing them that everything that exists springs from the supreme source, pure and total consciousness, I enable them to recognize this condition. In this way, dispelling the darkness of discriminating concepts and judgements, I kindle the light of great self-arising wisdom; thus, I am called the one who dispels the darkness of ignorance and kindles the light.

Listen, great being! Rending the net of conceptual thought, I break the chain of the passions.

Followers of the vehicles based on cause and effect [hold diverse views about the nature] of existence. [The śrāvakas] deem it poison and form the concept of "renunciation." [The Bodhisattvas] deem it an object of mental attachment and develop the principle of non-attachment based on the two truths. [Kriyā practitioners] deem it something that needs to be purified, and through the three purities, the empowerments, and the miraculous actions they conceive the notion of [the deity as] lord and [the practitioner as] servant. [Followers of mahāyoga, even though they] deem the nature of mind as pure, they hold the belief that it has to be realized through the four "approaches and accomplishments." Rending concepts that presuppose the existence of something other than me, I, the supreme source, pure and total consciousness, break the chain of the passions that issue from discriminating thoughts.

Listen, great being! Realize my nature, the supreme source that is pure and total consciousness. Teach that all the phenomena of existence are only myself! If you transmit my teaching, all your disciples will realize my nature and will become this very nature. At that point there will no longer be any need to relinquish or reject anything or to strive to progress on the basis of the two truths. There will be no need to observe the rules of cleanliness, to empower oneself through the three purities or to strive to generate the three contemplations in order to obtain a result. As all is already accomplished in me, I that am the source, all is in a state of absolute equality: I that am equality have no need to enter into action to produce another "equality."

[12. *The chapter that demonstrates the true nature of the teachings*, 58.2–60.5]

On seeing that their mind is the fundamental condition, all the beings of the three worlds will no longer remain at the level where enlightenment is merely a word but instead will immediately attain the supreme yoga. [Conversely,] however much [the true meaning] is disclosed to them, the unfortunate ones who do not have appropriate karma will not understand, just like someone who, wishing to obtain a precious jewel, cleans a piece of wood in vain. For fortunate practitioners of the supreme yoga who have appropriate karma, there are no view, no commitment, no spiritual action, no level, no path, no generation of altruistic commitment, no meditation on cause and effect, no *sādhana*, no antidotes. They see that neither the absolute nor the relative exists and in this way they understand the fundamental condition of mind. This is the great necessity [of this teaching].

[13. *The chapter that explains the nature of mind*, 64.3–64.7]

If my nature were to be compassionately displayed to the beings of the three worlds who have originated from me, the teaching of the three teachers would not exist, and consequently, all the phenomena that manifest from me could no longer be called "the perfect conditions." Thus I, the supreme source, disclose my nature, displaying it to myself. I, the source, do not transmit my teaching to the disciples of the teachers that manifest from me. As I am the source and the supreme yoga, my nature must be displayed [to those who understand in this way].

[14. *The chapter that exacts secrecy towards the unsuitable*, 66.2–66.6]

From the very beginning, the real condition of one's mind and of all the phenomena that manifest to perception are one single thing, so do not espouse thoughts in this regard that are those of followers of the vehicles based on cause and effect. On examining the fundamental condition of one's mind, one finds only the nature of enlightenment; nevertheless, some people apply the term "relative" to that which appears and "absolute" to that which does not, or they affirm that the relative and absolute inseparably are the single truth. However, no "real" truth exists, and the very fact of deeming something "real" betokens illusion.

The desire for happiness is the disease of attachment; one can be happy only when free of desires. Realization is not achieved by striving for it; it arises spontaneously when one abides in the natural state without seeking anything. So remain in the natural state without seeking, without concepts! Even though the name "enlightenment" is used for the real nature, this does not mean that "enlightenment" concretely exists. If someone believes the opposite, [let them go ahead and try to find] enlightenment: apart from the dimension of fundamental reality, they will find nothing at all. So, instead of aiming for enlightenment, one has to understand the nature of one's mind beyond action. On examining one's mind, one finds nothing, yet at the same time there is clarity that is ever present. It does not manifest concretely, yet its essence is all pervading: this is the way its nature presents itself.

Followers of the vehicles of cause and effect do not believe this, so they negate, they block, they engage and empower themselves using sundry diverse methods, deviating from the natural actionless condition of their own minds. Just like a person who leaves something at home and then goes out looking for it far away, they neglect the happiness of non-action and undertake the commitment of effort: there is no disease worse than this.

Undistracted concentration is the rope binding one to the pole of the notion of a subject:[201] for what has always existed there is no possibility whatever of distraction. The misleading method of aspiring after undistracted concentration is the provisional teaching for followers of the vehicles of cause and effect, [whereas conversely] the fact that one cannot be distracted from the original condition destroys all the antidotes based on effort.

When my teaching is disclosed to disciples of the teachers of cause and effect, they obstinately assert that a result must issue from a cause, and consequently in order to achieve enlightenment they wish to abide in a state of "concentration." However in this way they forsake the natural unaltered condition.

The authentic unaltered state is the true essence of all, and no enlightenment exists apart from this natural condition. "Enlightenment" is merely a name indicating what is called the "natural condition," one's own mind: just this very mind, unaltered, is dharmakāya. What has never been altered is also what has never been born, and the true "unborn" cannot be sought or realized through effort. That which transcends action is not realized through seeking and commitment. [...]

Listen, great being! My essence manifests as the state of enlightenment of the "five greatnesses" [*che ba lnga*] in the following manner.

My nature, the fundamental condition that gives rise to the appearance of the animate and inanimate world, directly manifests everywhere. Without needing to carry out any action, it is the original state of enlightenment. Without needing to strive in one's practice, it is a "quality" that has always been present.[202] This is the ["greatness" of the] direct manifestation of enlightenment.

The manifestation of my essence is the innermost core of everything and is thus its ultimate substance. Without needing to carry out any action, it is the original state of enlightenment. Without needing to strive in one's practice, it is a "quality" that has always been present. This is the "greatness" of enlightenment in the totality of one's state.

The manifestation of the unborn condition that transcends the limits of concepts, that has always been beyond the consideration of subject and object, is the ultimate dimension of phenomena. Without needing to carry out any action, it is the original state of enlightenment. Without needing to strive in one's practice, it is a "quality" that has always been present. This is the "greatness" of enlightenment in the ultimate dimension of phenomena.

That which I really teach is disclosed through the example, meaning, and sign [of experience]. The meaning of the real condition is indicated with the example of the sky and attested by the experience of pure and total consciousness. So, to afford certainty to those afflicted by doubt, the nature of enlightenment is attested through example, meaning, and sign [of experience]. [This is the "greatness" of enlightenment that proves its own nature.]

Even though it is manifest to all, the condition of my nature, just as it is, is not perceived. [This is the meaning of *teshinnyid,* or "that itself just as it is":] *te* means the true nature; *shin* means that this nature cannot be altered; *nyid* refers to the ultimate essence. In the natural condition, "just as it is," it is senseless to affirm the existence of the Buddhas of the three times and to refute that of the beings of the three worlds. As no concept or judgement whatever is at all possible, I teach the "greatness" of the absolute nonexistence of enlightenment.

[15. *The chapter on the manifestation of the three natures,* 71.7–73.6; 75.3–76.5]

As I, the source, am perfectly realized from the beginning, do not teach that it is necessary to act! If you teach your disciples that they need to act, they will be afflicted by the disease of effort, they will not allow the self-arising wisdom to manifest and will fall into the defect of wanting to correct pure and total consciousness and to alter the fundamental condition. All of these defects will conceal the natural qualities. When the truth is dissembled by the deception of falsehood, it is useless to strive to realize what transcends action. Sattva, understand me, I that am the source! Throughout all of time, all phenomena that have arisen from me are the natural condition of self-arising wisdom.

[16. *The chapter of advice to Sattvavajra,* 77.3–77.7]

Listen, great being! The Buddhas of the three times revere my remains and my relics, continually observing their mind. The benefits of this are that, attaining inseparability, all phenomena will be empowered as the supreme source.

[17. *The chapter on relics,* 79.2–79.3]

Listen, great being! All that exists in the animate and inanimate world manifests as my nature, is pure in the ultimate dimension of phenomena, and emanates in manifold forms in order to teach. The various manifestations of the three dimensions transmit the teachings of the three vehicles and in this way they satisfy those who base themselves on cause and effect. However, once there is no longer dependence on a past object one no longer strives to work with the cause and no longer yearns for the fruit. This state beyond desire vouchsafes the spontaneous realization of self-perfection: there is no purpose in creating what already exists from the beginning.

As all phenomena are the natural immovable condition, there is no sense in wanting to achieve this "natural condition." As all phenomena are naturally and spontaneously perfect, none of the realized Buddhas of the three times has ever said it is necessary to rely on effort in order to achieve something. The way of meditating that presupposes a "quest for something" does not vouchsafe realization, on the contrary, it becomes the greatest affliction for contemplation. [...]

Great being, listen! The teaching that asserts that it is possible to achieve self-realization by seeking something outside is transmitted to followers of the vehicles based on cause and effect. For followers of the vehicles of cause and effect the "real condition of existence" derives from the dualistic consideration of an "existence" separate from its "real condition" whereby existence finds itself compelled to seek its own "existence" without being able to find it.

[18. *The chapter that demonstrates that realization cannot be achieved by seeking it*, 79.4–80.2; 80.4–80.5]

Listen, great being! From my pure and total nature there manifest the three dimensions, effortlessly and spontaneously perfect, that are the core of all the Enlightened Ones. My unaltered essence manifests as the dharmakāya dimension, my unaltered nature manifests as the saṃbhogakāya dimension, and my energy is revealed as the nirmāṇakāya dimension. These three dimensions are not the result of a quest or effort.

Listen, great being! The three dimensions are contained in me, the source. The essence, nature, and energy of any phenomenon that exists are the fundamental condition of my three dimensions. Apart from me and my fundamental condition, there is nobody to praise as "enlightened" or to disparage as "sentient being": the fundamental condition is the equality of the non-conceptual state.

Nothing other than this exists; none of the Buddhas have ever received a higher teaching than this from me, the source. Aside from this condition of equality beyond concepts, I myself, the supreme source whence everything arises, have absolutely nothing whatever to display to myself.

[19. *The chapter on self-perfection that transcends seeking*, 81.2–81.7]

I am the core of all that exists. I am the seed of all that exists. I am the cause of all that exists. I am the trunk of all that exists. I am the foundation of all that exists. I am the root of existence. I am "the core" because I contain all phenomena. I am "the seed" because I give birth to everything. I am "the cause" because all comes forth from me. I am "the trunk" because the ramifications of every event sprout from me. I am "the foundation" because all abides in me. I am called "the root" because I am everything.

Listen, great Sattvavajra! It is said, but only so as to put it into words, that the three dimesions spring forth from the unaltered three natures of me, the supreme source and pure and total consciousness. In reality, even though the three dimensions manifest, they are not something other than my fundamental condition.

I, the source, pure and total consciousness, am beyond birth and the dualism of subject and object: this is called the unborn "dharmakāya." But in reality dharmakāya is merely a name, it is not something other than the natural condition.

When I, the source, pure and total consciousness, manifest my nature, this is called saṃbhogakāya, but this too is merely a name: in reality saṃbhogakāya is not something other than the natural condition.

When I, the source, pure and total consciousness, manifest my energy potentiality, from the unaltered condition of this energy is said to issue the nirmāṇakāya, but this too is merely a name: in reality nirmāṇakāya is not something other than the natural condition. [...]

I am the primordial source, pure and total consciousness. All that manifests from me, too, is pure and total consciousness. "Pure" because my essence is completely pure from the beginning; "total" because I have always pervaded everything; "consciousness" because my essence, being clarity, has always been consciousness.

[20. *The chapter that demonstrates how all phenomena originate from Kunjed Gyalpo bodhicitta*, 82.2–83.3; 84.1–84.2]

III. THE TEACHINGS BEYOND CAUSE AND EFFECT

Listen, great Sattvavajra! I am the supreme source of all that exists. I am the mother and father of the teachers of the three dimensions. I am the forebear of all the Buddhas of the three times. [...]

I, the supreme source, am pure and total consciousness. Pure and total consciousness is total primordial perfection. Total perfection from the beginning transcends cause and effect. [...]

The true nature of consciousness cannot be expressed in words, however, as unless it is explained it does not disclose itself; it is indicated by saying that it is not something visible or that can be represented. Were this not the case, people would not understand their own mind and would continue to act by striving. Thus it is said to be "beyond explanation."

[21. *The chapter that explains the reasons*, 84.6–84.7; 85.3–85.4; 86.4–86.5]

Then, in order to grant the possibility of keeping the mind in its natural condition, the supreme source, pure and total consciousness, taught this fundamental *lung*, the origin of the teachings beyond action:[203]

Listen, Great Sattvavajra! Just like space, the state of non-action cannot be localized. The path of Dharma of absence of thought, without abode or support, derives from a subtle desire tied to intention. However, such conceptual meditation does not at all touch dharmakāya because self-arising wisdom is the absence of thought naturally present in everything.

Thus, self-arising wisdom is the true non-discursive state, the natural condition present in everything. It does not get attached to the notion of non-action as if it were an object, nor does it need antidotes in order to be corrected.

Even if one were to seek the fundamental essence through [the twelve links of] interdependence,[204] the non-discursive state has no form, thus one accedes to it only by remaining without concepts. As the essence manifests naturally, only this can be dharmakāya.

It is beyond all the possible parts or divisions of the atom. From this non-conceptualizable state, the wisdom of qualities spontaneously arises: this is the essence of total openness in which the discursive state is directly present. Whoever enters this pure path achieves supreme equality.

As this state is unchanging and not subject to transformation, there is no room for attachment. Likewise, as no object exists, there is no room for the mind. Those who get stuck in the desire for a concrete achievement always meditate on a cause, but the state of equality does not derive from the pleasure of attachment to such meditation.

As the single dimension [of pure and total consciousness] is all-pervading, there is nothing to add. As [self-arising wisdom] is without limits, there is nothing to take away from the ultimate dimension of phenomena.

The manifestation of the ultimate nature does not give rise to any special exaltation: everything naturally abides in the state of total wisdom. There is no marvellous object to see: the [nature] cannot be seen or heard and transcends all definitions.

What is deemed "Dharma" and what is deemed "non-Dharma" are always joined: an absolute reality to be considered a higher dimension does not exist. Judging the path of enlightenment in terms of illusion and non-illusion one achieves nothing. Self-arising wisdom transcends the limits of words. In the condition of primordial expansion of the totality of one's state thoughts arise as if they were a shadow. It is not non-exisent insofar as this non-existence has a core that manifests. It is not empty insofar as this emptiness has its own dimension. When one remembers the nature of the sky, even without wishing for it, one obtains the happiness beyond action and already present from the beginning. It is not an object to conceptualize, but from [this condition] wisdom manifests. Some sages of the past, fixing their minds with attachment [to their object of meditation], have been caught up in the torments of effort and engagement. Omniscience arises only when one enters the path of the essence; when one conceptualizes the condition "as it is," meditation becomes conceptual.

Desiring bliss is the disease of attachment: unless one cures it with the efficacious medicine of unmovable equanimity, then even the causes of rebirth in the higher states get stained by the passions.

The perilous disease of those who adopt as their path what is not a path, drives them to want to reach a goal, just like deer pursuing a mirage. However they will never find their goal, not even by seeking it throughout the three worlds. In fact, even though in this way one might reach the level of one of the ten bhūmis, the essence of enlightenment remains hindered.[205]

Instantaneous wisdom beyond all thoughts is like a precious jewel that comes from all the teachers. It cannot be objectified and without needing to change, by its very nature, it completely satisfies all wishes. Examining it, one does not find anything, but leaving it as it is it is the source of all qualities. It does not appear visibly yet it displays itself in all the aspects of manifestation. Whoever is able to teach without the dualism of self and other is a precious treasure because he or she teaches selflessly and compassionately the universal object of realization.

It does not move from within, yet there is nothing to seek within. It is not an object to which to get attached or on which to fix one's aspiration. In the state beyond entering and leaving there is no need to act [intentionally] for the benefit of beings through selflessness and compassion: everything takes place naturally.

Wishing for happiness, one moves away from it because happiness is already present, and seeking it is like happiness seeking itself. Not recognizing the essence of enlightenment, one aims for an outer object to confirm. However, following this direction one does not see enlightenment.

As in reality no "enlightenment" exists [as a separate phenomenon], nor does its name exist; displaying enlightenment and designating it with this name are errors. Hoping to achieve enlightenment from outside is the wrong path. [In the true nature] no form, not even an atom, exists of all phenomena that appear. It is already perfect, beyond attachment, serene, immaterial, and not confined in a form: the nature of the great nectar cannot be grasped by concepts.

Immense, great, total existence, antidote for those who adhere to the lesser vehicles!

However one should not get stuck on the concept of "great" because [the nature] transcends the concepts of great and small. The words of the scriptures and their commentaries tied to concepts are like the drawings of a conjurer. The darkness of the wisdom of entering and leaving [does not] allow the birth [of true wisdom]. This is the supreme vehicle.

This nature, which leaves everything and holds everything, is beyond desire and grasping. It does not give birth to even a grain of complacency. Like a garuḍa in flight, it has no worries; it is not afraid of losing anything nor does it wish to accept anything.

That which from the beginning is like the ocean, gives life to the variety of phenomena. Qualities are infinite as space and have no specific place whence they spring forth. As soon as [one understands] the essence of enlightenment, supreme contemplation manifests. Vision becomes like a vast sea, and the non-discursive state as immense as the sky. The sphere of experience of Samantabhadra is unborn and unchanging.

The twelve causal links [of interdependence] are explanations created for the benefit of the deluded: let the wise know this! Even though the six classes of beings appear, they are nothing but the primordial path! If enjoyments are anointed by compassion, in any object of pleasure one enjoys the essence of enlightenment. Butchers, prostitutes, those guilty of the five most heinous crimes, outcasts, the underprivileged: all are utterly the substance of existence and nothing other than total bliss.

All phenomena being such, this is the true nature of existence. Thinking that reality can seek itself, that the sky can seek itself or that an "outer" reality can exist is as useless as attempting to put out fire with fire.

This essence of the non-discursive state is not hidden in anybody's mind. For those who experience the essence of enlightenment beyond action, it becomes naturally present in all circumstances.

[22. *The chapter on the state beyond concepts*: *The Great Garuḍa in Flight*, 87.2–91.6]

Listen, great being! As all that appears to perception is one's pure and total consciousness, there is no object of the view. As all is in the non-discursive state, all is equality. This is the state of the sky, and this is named "yoga" [knowledge of the authentic condition].

When objects of the five senses are perceived in their natural clarity, without judging, they too are the state of the sky: the yogin abides in this condition.

When one tries to examine the absolute state by means of words and letters and then recognizes that the absolute cannot at all be examined in this manner, one remains in the natural condition of the non-discursive state: this too is the state of the sky.

Like the sky, this reality, that cannot become the object of thought, has existed since the beginning.

[23. *The chapter that discloses the state of the sky, the view free of reference point*, 92.1–92.4]

These are the modes of being of Samantabhadra, the nature of mind. In his being pure and total consciousness, he is the ultimate essence of all phenomena: whoever realizes this, is the supreme source. The supreme source does not change, thus it is said to be "unchanging."

In his being the dharmakāya dimension, he transcends all objects tied to the dualism of subject and object. That which is beyond subject and object does not change.

In his being the saṃbhogakāya dimension, he has the five sense enjoyments and consequently is the perfect condition that fulfils all wishes.

In his being the nirmāṇakāya dimension, he takes on any form necessary to communicate with beings, and consequently, he is the perfect condition of necessary factors, unchanging in the three times.

All phenomena are like the sky, and the characteristic feature of the sky is its natural condition. This is also the natural condition of the three dimensions: everything abides in this nature.

No phenomena manifesting to perception can be altered from their authentic state.

Nobody in the past who has set out on the path has reached the destination by persisting in seeking and striving. Nobody who has undertaken action has ever achieved the fruit. Nobody has achieved self-realization by practicing with effort. Nothing can be altered from the natural condition, all abides therein.

[24. *The chapter on the unchanging condition of perfection beyond action,* 92.6–93.6]

Listen! The pure and total consciousness of each being of the three worlds without exclusion is the true teacher. For those who, after hundreds and thousands of kalpas, have not understood that their own mind is the teacher, I, the supreme source, manifest as the teacher of their mind: listen to this teaching!

From pure and total consciousness, that is the universal cause, I, the supreme source, emanate the five elements, the nature of mind. Thus there arise the five teachers of pure and total consciousness. The dimension is saṃbhogakāya, the teaching is transmitted through one's nature; what is disclosed is one's true essence.

The saṃbhogakāya teacher does not judge the fundamental state and does not communicate something external to be conceptualized. The five teachers of pure and total consciousness teach the true nature of reality.

The primordial wisdom of pure and total consciousness manifests as the teacher in the form of the earth element and does not teach through words and letters: it communicates its own nature directly. Without judging in terms of self and others, it discloses the non-discursive state of equanimity. On understanding it, the beings of the three worlds become equal to the Buddhas and effortlessly realize that reality which had been the object of their efforts.

The primordial wisdom of pure and total consciousness manifests as the teacher in the form of the water element and does not teach through words and letters: it communicates its own nature directly. Without judging in terms of self and others, it discloses the non-discursive state of equanimity. On understanding it, the beings of the three worlds become equal to the Buddhas and effortlessly realize that reality which had been the object of their efforts.

The primordial wisdom of pure and total consciousness manifests as the teacher in the form of the fire element and does not teach through words and letters: it communicates its own nature directly. Without judging in terms of self and others, it discloses the non-discursive state of equanimity. On understanding it, the beings of the three worlds become equal to the Buddhas and effortlessly realize that reality which had been the object of their efforts.

The primordial wisdom of pure and total consciousness manifests as the teacher in the form of the air element and does not teach through words and letters: it communicates its own nature directly. Without judging in terms of self and others, it discloses the non-discursive state of equanimity. On understanding it, the beings of the three worlds become equal to the Buddhas and effortlessly realize that reality which was the object of their efforts.

The primordial wisdom of pure and total consciousness manifests as the teacher in the form of the space element and does not teach by means of words and letters: it communicates its own nature directly. Without judging on the basis the dualism of self and others it discloses the inseparable state.

These teachers that manifest to all beings of the three worlds teach through their nature: due to them may everybody realize understanding!

Listen! As all of you are created by me, you beings of the three worlds are my children, equal to me, the supreme source. You are me, inseparable from me, so I manifest to you and through the five teachers of my natures I teach the single state of the five essences [of the elements]. I am the single state, I, the supreme source: you too are, you must become certain of this!

Listen, beings of the three worlds! If I did not exist, neither would you exist. If you did not exist, the five teachers would not manifest and the teaching of the non-discursive state would not be transmitted.

[25. *The chapter that demonstrates that one's own mind is the teacher*, 93.7–96.3]

Listen, great being! Pure and total consciousness, which transcends thought and explanation, is the lamp of all the teachers, and thus it is supremely praised. Being the essence of the teaching, it is equal to Mañjuśrī. It transcends action, it is spontaneously perfect, natural bliss.

It is the basis of morality and of all the infinite behaviors that lead to the path of liberation. It is the universal path, the mother of all the enlightened ones. If it did not exist, there would be no path, so I am the supreme path to liberation.

The universal path is subtle and difficult to understand, non-discursive and beyond concepts. It cannot be localized or objectified, it cannot be delimited by concepts, and it transcends all thoughts. Words do not fathom it, nor does it fall within the field of sense experience of form and color. Difficult to display and to examine, there is nothing concrete at all that can be defined.

Some ascetics of the past, afflicted with the disease of attachment to meditation and believing they had to base themselves on the limited words of their teachers, followed concepts, like deer pursuing a mirage. But the real path cannot be pointed out with words. I too would fall into error if I attempted to point out reality.

Pure and impure are indivisible, indissolubly conjoined. The darkness of wisdom that does not distinguish any form and the lamp of clarity that illuminates everything without hindrance are both beyond thought. The naturally quiescent condition is the supreme contemplation.

"Really seeing" means seeing there is nothing to see: this is called "the eye of omniscience."

"Recognizing spacious nature beyond center and border" means abiding in supreme equality beyond acceptance and rejection.

The mind and its karmic tendencies are indissolubly integrated.

All phenomena that appear and become the object of our concepts are merely our ornament, so we must neither reject nor relinquish them. Without judging, we can enjoy them!

[Even though one has performed] negative deeds censured by all such as the five passions and the five crimes without interval, on entering the path of purity, one obtains supreme equality and not even women, etc., need be given up.

Those who put their faith in the logic of history and its meaning and who engage in limited conduct that is the outcome of stabilizing the three contemplations deviate from the teachings beyond effort, so they remain deluded. Self-perfection beyond action abides in spontaneous happiness.

The essence of great self-arising wisdom is without commotion or change and transcends all definitions.

The nectar of natural perfection eliminates all the suffering of effort. Perfection that transcends action is a natural condition.

Listen, great being! As all phenomena are the nature of pure and total consciousness, which is the immense sphere, there is nothing to radiate or to unify, there is neither birth nor cessation: without blocking anything, this is the natural condition.

Like the sky, the essence of this non-discursive state has always existed beyond all words and thoughts.

[26. *The chapter that demonstrates that perfection beyond action is not something on which to meditate: Pure Gold in Ore*, 96.5–98.6]

Listen, great being! I will teach you that, being my manifestation from the beginning, all phenomena are the pure dimension of emptiness.

The outer and inner world, all is the dimension of emptiness of primordial being. In this sphere of original purity there is no duality of Buddhas and sentient beings. How could it ever be improved by using the antidotes of a path?

It cannot become the object of effort or intention: it is the primordial reality of self-perfection that transcends action. All concepts and judgements are the purity of the dimension of non-dual emptiness. How could this dimension ever be deceived by the infantile behavior of followers of concepts?

The bliss of non-duality is available to all beings, and even the wrong paths based on analysis are not something other than this universal path. Apprehending its equality, one becomes lord of the Enlightened Ones.

Thinking in terms of I and mine is the erroneous path of the mutegpas. Misguided by the ignorant, followers of this conceptual path will never reach their goal nor achieve understanding. In fact, if existence seeks existence is there anything to be found?

By following the words of these teachers who are devoid of qualities and are like monkeys, one certainly ends up on a path conditioned by concepts.

So, just like the mineral that separates gold from ore, a true teacher is a precious treasure worthy of being bought at any price.

[27. *The chapter that discloses the dimension of purity of non-action: The Great Potency*, 991.–100.1]

Listen, great being! My nature never changes from its dimension of emptiness. My wisdom is unchanging like the sky. My being is naturally unchanging. My mind is the unchanging essence of all that exists. [...]

Listen, great being! As the universal base does not change in its dimension of emptiness, this dimension cannot at all be transformed.

The teachers of the three dimensions who seek to transform this emptiness teach their disciples to meditate to find the calm state: this is what is called the "provisional teaching."

Likewise, the sky does not change: were the sky to seek to become "the sky" it could never succeed. The nature of being does not change: were being to seek to become its own nature, it could never succeed. The nature of mind does not change: were the nature of mind to seek to realize itself it could not succeed. Meditation that seeks to transform that which cannot change presupposes hope in some future time: as it is based on desire and depends on time it becomes a desperate meditation and is utterly not what I mean by the "definitive teaching."

[28. *The chapter that demonstrates that unchanging perfection beyond action cannot be found by seeking it*, 100.2–100.3; 102.1–102.5]

Listen, great being! I am the supreme source, pure and total consciousness. All phenomena are me myself, and from the beginning all is in the authentic condition of my nature. [...]

Listen! As I am in the authentic condition, all phenomena self-liberate in the fundamental nature. Without needing to alter anything, the teacher self-liberates in the fundamental nature. Without needing to alter anything, the teaching self-liberates in the fundamental nature. Without needing to alter anything, the retinue of disciples, too, self-liberates in the fundamental nature.

Listen! As all self-liberates there is no need to correct the body posture or to visualize a deity. There is no need to correct the voice or speech. There is no need to correct the mind through meditation. By correcting oneself, it is not possible to find the authentic condition, and without finding the authentic condition, one cannot self-liberate. In this way, one does not achieve the state of equality of the fundamental nature.

Listen, great being, to what I am explaining to you! From the beginning, pure and total consciousness, the supreme source, abides in the authentic all-transcending condition; however, the various traditions with their views are not able to relax in it.

Total perfection, the source of all, has always been the authentic condition, but when the śrāvakas and the pratyekabuddhas hear about it, convinced that the mind is the cause of the poisons, they try to refute it and block it. With this view they are not able to relax in the authentic condition, and they continue in this way for infinite kalpas.

When practitioners of the Mahāyāna sūtras hear about total perfection, as they do not understand that their own mind is the fundamental nature, they are not able to relax in the authentic condition. In this way they continue training and progressing for three kalpas.

When [yoga] practitioners hear about total perfection, as they do not understand that the nature of all the phenomena of existence is the same fundamental nature of their own mind, they are not able to relax in the authentic condition. In this way they continue empowering themselves through the factors of realization and miraculous actions for seven lives.

When mahāyoga practitioners hear about total perfection, as they are convinced that the true nature is subject to cause and effect, they seek to realize by means of effort that which exists from the beginning. In this way, as they are not able to relax in the authentic condition, for two thousand six hundred years they continue practicing to attain the level of the three contemplations.

When anuyoga practitioners hear about total perfection, as they define the primordial state in terms of cause and effect, they are not able to relax in the authentic condition. Working with the cause, that is the pure dimension of emptiness of phenomena, they realize its effect: the pure maṇḍala of wisdom. For one whole life they continue practicing in this way without interruption.

When atiyoga practitioners hear about total perfection, they find themselves on the level of primordial enlightenment, and in this way, without acting, they achieve total bliss. Without need for effort in their practice they achieve enlightenment.

Human beings and deities have different capacities. Some are more inclined to training and gradual progress, while others have the capacity for instantaneous understanding. Thus what is most necessary is taught in congruence with the various capacities.

Atiyoga is total perfection [and this is its literal meaning]: *a* means being in the authentic condition, the fundamental nature that has never had a beginning; *ti* means that this nature is self-perfected, without needing to rely on a quest; *yoga* refers to the supreme yoga[206] of total perfection. Speaking about this condition in terms of cause and effect does not conform with knowledge of total perfection.

Speaking dualistically of absolute truth and relative truth derives merely from the notion of wanting to add or remove something [to or from the fundamental nature]: in this way one does not discern non-duality. The knowledge of the Buddhas of the three times does not entail duality because it is the recognition of the single authentic condition.

[29. *The chapter on relaxation in the authentic state*, 102.7–103.1; 103.6–105.7]

Listen, Sattvavajra! I will show you your own nature. You are me, the source. I am and have always been pure and total consciousness. What is pure and total consciousness?

> The total space of Vajrasattva
> Is the vast dimension of being in which all is always good
> [Samantabhadra].
> As it is the perfect universal path that liberates all,
> It is beyond birth, cessation, or being thought.
>
> As it is loving kindness that realizes the true meaning,
> It does not strive to exercise great compassion.
> As it is the total state, it does not need to praise
> The deepest and most supreme qualities.
>
> All phenomena are the unchanging natural condition:
> Letting it be without acting, it self-liberates.
> Spontaneously arising wisdom should not be sought:
> In liberating itself, it also shows the path of liberation.
>
> The five elements are the Buddha
> Abiding in the nature of all beings.
> Even if one entertains wrong concepts
> Liberation arises from within oneself and not from outside.
>
> Total wisdom is difficult to find:
> It is realized through prajñā and method.
> However, even though said in this way, it seems to depend on
> something.
> True bliss arises from within oneself.
>
> The great miracle is not difficult:
> From subtle understanding of the authentic condition
> All the qualities and capacities
> Immediately arise in oneself.
>
> Meditation is letting be without seeking
> The ultimate nature that never discloses itself visibly.
> Hoping to find it as something other,
> It will never be obtained.
>
> This ultimate nature, which is so secret,
> Cannot be received through the sense of hearing.
> Likewise there is nothing
> That can be expressed by speech.

Beings' suffering is pure and total consciousness
Which, pervading everything, manifests in form:
Without ever moving,
It abides in all equanimously like infinite space.

That which is the equality of all distinctions
Is designated as "karma."
However, were it really under the sway of karma,
Self-arising wisdom would not exist.

The first cause is the Vajra, as are the secondary conditions:
Never having been born, it cannot be destroyed.
The essence of enlightenment that has existed from the beginning
Is not disclosed through the effort of thought.

Meditative stability of supreme quality
Does not involve the thought of meditative stability.
Without applying thought and without needing to purify,
Wisdom arises from discursive thought itself.

Coining the expression "access to something subtle,"
Some seek the path by isolating the mind,
Maintaining emptiness in a silent place:
But on examination, this is conceptual meditation.

Coining the terms "cause and effect,"
Some believe that by eliminating both virtues and negativities
They can release themselves from this world:
However this merely shows great complacency in accepting and rejecting.

Attachment and non-attachment are only words
As is something in between, like an echo.
Happiness and suffering have the same cause:
This was said by Vajrasattva, lord of beings.

Attachment, anger, and ignorance
Derive from the path of total enlightenment.
The five objects of enjoyment, too,
Are said to be the ornaments of the ultimate dimension.

The thought of space is unborn,
That thought itself is like space.
Without attachment, without intention like space
One's own benefit manifests like space.

Equality beyond thought is dharmakāya
Which, like the moon's reflection in water, cannot be grasped.
Through the manifestation of the energy of Samantabhadra
It displays the depth of the vowels [*āli*] and consonants [*kāli*].

With *A* and *Ta* that embellish,
All phenomena manifesting as *Pa*
And all the sphere of experience in the world
Are the deep Voice of the Buddha.

Marvellous! The sphere of experience of the Buddhas
Is not something that is found by seeking it.
Like the six sense objects, it is not an object:
Thus [those who seek it] are like a blind man trying to grasp the sky.

The path of purification that proceeds from level to level
Does not concur with the teaching of non-action.
Were there really a path to tread,
Then, just like the bounds of the sky, one would never reach one's destination.

So, the authentic condition being thus,
Precisely because it displays itself in its real nature, it can be understood.
As it is the very essence,
All arises from it: marvellous!

Time past and time present
Abide in the total state of the authentic condition:
Its path, too, is thus,
This is its very nature.

The universal path in harmony with that [nature]
Manifests as the moon and its support.
As it is the absolute equality of everything,
Having a partial view of it, one does not realize it.

Present pleasure and future pleasure
Are what is directly experienced and its consequence:
As they entail the defect of a limited aspect
One should not get stuck on them.

The three times are equal, without any difference.
There is no past or future; everything has existed since the beginning.
As all is one, being pervaded by dharmakāya,
The supreme qualities exist in nature.

Being reborn in the three dimensions of existence,
All is just a name and a magical illusion;
Even the supreme birth of a universal emperor
Is a magical illusion and only a dimension to purify.

Those whose engagement depends on time
Do not see it manifest in time:

For one who engages in desire without having overcome it
The example of emptiness is valid.

It is one, totally beyond form.
The path of yoga is like a bird's flight across the sky.
In the unborn and unarisen essence
Wherever are all the dharmas that are supposed to exist?

Outer and inner are [one thing]: the outer itself is the inner.
Not even the tiniest aspect of the deep condition can be understood.
Existence is only a name and is caused by an erroneous view;
In this manner one remains separate from the equality of contemplation.

Here the outer and inner commitments
Abide in the nature of the aggregates and of the sense spheres.
As the three times have never been separate from the true condition,
There is no need to use the word "commitment."

Being unperturbed, it is the symbol of the Body.
Being immoveable, it is wisdom.
Not grasping anything, it is free of I.
Not rejecting anything, it is equality that transcends words.

In any possible circumstance
All beings that transmigrate and enjoy arise solely from this state.
The king of equality has never spoken
Of male and female.

Here there is nothing whatsoever to realize
By means of resolute, wrathful conduct,
However some say that by possessing *A* and *Pa*
The happiness of the magical illusion manifests.

As the ultimate nature cannot be defined in any of its aspects,
It appears on the basis of the manner in which one observes it.
Delighting in effort, wishing it to manifest,
Is a great hindrance and a defect.

All the secondary methods of realization,
In which one meditates on the various attributes, are like the reflection of the moon in water.
Even if one attains a detached state free of defilements,
Meditating in this way is like the affairs of ordinary folk.

Even though by visualizing oneself as great Heruka
With the maṇḍala of wrathful attributes
One can realize the letter,

Nirvāṇa is not discovered in this manner.

Just as one crops the top of the palm tree,
Just as one burns a seed,
To confront the power of passions
These secondary meditation methods are taught.

All the hundreds and thousands of methods
Give birth to their characteristic flower,
But as [the true nature] is free of characteristics,
It does not manifest from these abodes.

Fortunate are the yogins
Who abide in this ineffable state:
Not discriminating between self and others,
They delight in self-perfection as magical illusion.

Without anything excluded, it is perfectly complete.
It is unchanging and always remains whole,
Boundless like space:
Existence does not depend on anything else.

The bliss of the state of self-perfection
Derives solely from the instantaneous presence of the natural power
Of incomparable wisdom:
Existence does not derive from anything else.

Easy and difficult, difficult because it is easy:
Not manifesting visibly, it is all-pervading.
But not even Vajrasattva can name it,
Saying: "Here it is!"

This marvellous and extraordinary manifestation of energy,
Like space, transcends action.
From that ignorance that does not conceptualize anything
It immediately arises within oneself.

This is the sole path for all,
That naturally abides in all beings.
But for ignorant people, deluded because they are conditioned by dualism,
The example of the doctor finding the medicine is valid.

Bliss lies in understanding,
This itself is the pure dimension of the world.
When light gathers in a limited aggregation
Then the four main directions, the intermediate ones and above and below appear.

From the undefinable colors of the rainbow
There manifest all the variety of the [five] families.

In the same manner, the entire animate and inanimate world
Originates from the five elements.

Not bound by the definitions
Of past, present, and future
And understanding what is unborn and unceasing,
The three times become the total state.

Being equal in everything, there is nothing to arrange in a gradual manner.
Being oneness, there is nothing to offer in a limited direction.
Even if one prepares the ornaments of the gaṇapūjā
As they already naturally exist, there is nothing to arrange.

Being self-perfected, there is nothing to offer.
Being pure from the beginning, it is already nectar.
There is nothing in particular
Of the twelve sense bases to visualize.

Mind, the benefactor of the offerings,
Manifests everything through the power of the gaze:
The siddhi that derives from seeing
Is perfect equanimous contemplation.

Keeping this state for an instant is union,
Being satisfied is commitment.
Performing the dance steps of method
One offers the union of non-duality.

Letting go without grasping is the torma [ritual cake].
Transcending action, all the activities are already consummated.
As disturbing beings naturally recede due to non-conceptual wisdom
Remaining in equanimous contemplation without speaking is the supreme mantra.

Making offerings to the teacher, performing generosity
And all the other similar meritorious deeds:
If they are done without the power of non-attachment and of imperturbability,
They become a great fetter.

Thus acting in any way hinders
The obtainment of the true meaning of the scriptures.
By conceptualizing the true condition
One can never attain it.

[*30. The chapter on the nature of Vajrasattva, the victory banner that does not wane*: *The Total Space of Vajrasattva*,[207] 106.2–113.1]

IV. THE TEACHINGS ON PERFECTION BEYOND ACTION

Listen great being!

> The nature of the variety of phenomena is non-dual
> Yet each phenomenon is beyond the limits of the mind.
> The authentic condition "as it is" does not become a concept
> Yet it manifests totally in form, always good.
> All being already perfect, overcome the sickness of effort
> And remain naturally in self-perfection: this is contemplation.

[31. *The chapter of the six vajra verses*: *The Cuckoo of Presence*, 113.3–113.5]

Listen, great being! Understand the real meaning thus!

> All that appears is one in the fundamental condition:
> Let nobody correct it!
> In this supreme unaltered equality
> Abides the state of knowledge of non-discursive dharmakāya.

[32. *The chapter of the four verses of knowledge*, 113.6–113.7]

Listen, great being, king of pure presence! The true teaching of the absolute meaning cannot be comprehended nor shown [through concepts]. It cannot be defined, it cannot become an object of fixation, it cannot be thought: it concerns a nature that transcends thought. [This nature] cannot be meditated on and cannot be the object of thought. It does not know desire and does not conceive the idea of having to accept the fruit [of realization].

Those who abide in this natural non-discursive state reach enlightenment without embarking on a path; without exercising the mind, they obtain self-arising wisdom; without striving, they spontaneously achieve the capacity for spiritual action; without keeping a commitment, they naturally maintain purity.

[In this state] the senses and their objects manifest as the clarity of the fundamental condition, Buddhas and sentient beings are no longer seen as a duality, and everything is perceived as unity in the fundamental condition.

The fundamental nature knows neither unity nor multiplicity: could the essence, which has never been born and has never manifested, ever become the object of definition?

Listen, great being, king of pure presence! All the Buddhas and sentient beings, the whole universe and the forms of life inhabiting it, are my nature, beyond any concept of affirmation or negation.

My nature is one in the fundamental condition, and that which is taught by the teachers of the three dimensions serves only to lead all beings, in an indirect manner, to this single reality.

[33. *The chapter that demonstrates the definitive and provisional teachings,* 116.6–117.5]

My essence is like the sky. My meaning is fundamental reality. My nature is pure and total consciousness.

Listen! I have no hindrances, and I transcend concepts: the sky beyond concepts is the dharmakāya dimension.

I am the non-discursive state beyond accepting and rejecting: being like the sky means not accepting or rejecting. Just as the sky never accepts nor rejects anything, Samantabhadra does not know the dualism of accepting and rejecting. Contained within me is the essence that never accepts nor rejects anything.

Listen, great being! Like the sky, I was never born. Just as the sky has never been born, Vajrasattva never had a beginning. Contained within me is the unborn essence. [...]

If you understand the source, pure and total consciousness, you will apprehend that its self-arising nature transcends the limits of both eternalism and nihilism. Being unborn and beyond the dualism of subject and object, it transcends the limit of a material, eternal substance. Being uninterrupted, self-arising wisdom, it transcends the limit of nothingness and nihilism. [This is the true meaning of the word muteg]: *Mu* refers to the dimension of emptiness of phenomena, *teg* means the understanding of this. Those who discern a duality between Buddhas and sentient beings do not see the source that is pure and total consciousness.

[34. *The chapter that concentrates the essence of knowledge,* 118.5–119.1; 121.4–121.7]

Listen, great being! My essence is difficult [to understand]. Its view and behavior do not concur with those of the five vehicles taught by the three teachers on eight issues: access, view, commitment, spiritual capacity, path, level of realization, primordial wisdom, and ultimate nature.

Access occurs on the basis of the principle of effortlessness. The view is disclosed without needing to meditate. The commitment is kept without needing to observe it. The capacity for spiritual action is acquired without striving. The path is not something to tread gradually. There is no level to achieve through training. Wisdom is a non-conceptual state that cannot at all be produced in any way. The ultimate nature is the authentic condition that cannot be altered.

Listen, great being! If this is taught to followers of the vehicles based on cause and effect, they would deem it impossible. In fact, they believe that as the world is founded on cause and effect, everything must be tied to this principle. They believe that in order to achieve the effect, the Buddhas of the three worlds, it is necessary to act on the cause, the beings of the three worlds. Meditating on the view as the cause, they believe they can achieve the effect. However this manner of meditation does not enable realization of the fruit.

As all is the authentic, natural condition, seeking to alter or correct this condition is a deed as grave as dissembling the truth! View, meditation, commitment, etc., all the instructions that entail effort serve only as a guide to knowledge for those who need to eliminate the distractions of the sense objects and to retreat to a solitary place in order to attain the non-discursive state of equanimity.

[35. *The chapter that demonstrates the system of total perfection*, 122.2–123.3]

Listen, great being! Understand my nature! I am the nature of pure and total consciousness: pure and total consciousness is the supreme source. The nature of the supreme source is the state of the Body, Voice, and Mind. There is nothing that does not originate from the Body, Voice, and Mind. The Buddhas of the three times are created from the Body, Voice, and Mind. The body, voice, and mind of the beings of the three worlds too are created from the Body, Voice, and Mind of the supreme source.

Everything contained in the outer and inner universe is created from my Body, Voice, and Mind in the nature of the authentic, unalterable condition. [...]

Listen, great being! This is the nature of my Body, of my Voice and of my Mind.

My Body is the fundamental nature that manifests as the marvellous energy of Samantabhadra.

My Voice is the manifestation of the sounds and words that bring about understanding of the fundamental nature.

My Mind is uninterrupted self-arising wisdom that becomes the teacher's lamp of wisdom to show unmistakably the fundamental nature.

Listen, great being! Understand well! Everything that appears and exists, the whole animate and inanimate world, is nothing other than the nature of my Body: in this way my essence is directly communicated! Great Sattvavajra, you too, teach this to those who do not understand!

Listen, great being! All the sound of the five elements: earth, water, fire, air, and space, and everything uttered by the beings of the six lokas, are nothing other than my Voice: in this way the teaching is communicated through speech! Great Sattvavajra, you too, teach this to those who do not understand!

Listen, great being! All [thoughts tied to] the six classes of beings and to the five elements are the equanimity of the non-discursive state, the fundamental nature, unborn and unceasing, beyond thought: my Mind. Sattvavajra, you too teach this to others! Unless you do so, it will be very difficult to understand my nature.

[36. *The chapter that demonstrates that all is contained in the Body, Voice, and Mind*, 123.5–124.1; 124.2–125.3]

Then the supreme source, pure and total consciousness, explained that the nature of total perfection is not something on which one needs to meditate.

Listen, great Sattvavajra! I am the universal aim to which everybody aspires: those at the level of Vidyādhara, the Bodhisattvas at the sundry levels of realization and all the beings of the three worlds who are ready [for knowledge]. So, understand that my nature is fundamental reality, pure and total consciousness, and that it is not something on which to meditate!

Even though my nature is fundamental reality that transcends meditation, the teachers of the three dimensions teach cause and effect in order to conform to the principle of causality that governs the world. They explain that an effect must necessarily manifest from a cause, and to this end they teach diverse meditation methods.

Even though the fundamental nature, pure and total consciousness, is one alone, [the śrāvakas and pratyekabuddhas] speak of the four noble truths concerning suffering and its origin. Affirming that the origin of suffering is the cause of rebirth in the three lower states, they forsake the fundamental nature that is pure and total consciousness. Thus, not understanding the fundamental nature, they forsake it.

Even though the fundamental nature is pure and total consciousness, [the Bodhisattvas] speak of the two truths: absolute and relative, and on this basis they apply the ten pāramitās, starting with generosity and morality, to tread gradually the ten levels of realization. Thus, not understanding the fundamental nature, they remain at the level of training.

Even though the fundamental nature is pure and total consciousness, [followers of the kriyā] speak of the propitious moment, selected on the basis of planets and constellations, for starting to practice the five factors of realization and the four miraculous actions. In this manner they empower the whole of existence and meditate on it in the form of the deity. Thus, however, they do not understand the true nature of their own minds which is beyond meditating.

Even though the single fundamental nature is pure and total consciousness, [followers of mahāyoga] apply the three contemplations and the five rituals[208] in order to fulfil the four "approaches and accomplishments" and to transform their vajra body, which is already naturally pure, into the form of the deity and to realize its simultaneous "appearance and insubstantiality." Through commitment and effort they try to transform their mind into the deity and in consequence they do not see the true nature of mind, which is beyond action.

One's fundamental nature is pure and total consciousness, and I, the supreme source, teacher of teachers, do not teach the teachers of the three dimensions to meditate in order to alter the mind, because the true nature of mind has always been self-liberation. Striving to meditate amounts to forsaking the true nature of mind.

Listen, great being! If you want to realize the nature of your mind, which is possible only by not having desires, you must not intentionally seek to "find" the non-discursive state of equanimity.

Remain naturally, without accepting or rejecting. Remain spontaneously in the state free of commotion. The mind is precisely the natural condition, and all phenomena exist only in this very condition: do not seek to alter it! Do not strive to attain something other than this nature! As this is the very essence, do not seek anything else! Even if the Buddhas were to try, they would not find anything.

As all is already perfect, now there is no need to do anything. As all is already realized, now there is no need to act. Remain in equanimity, without judging or thinking!

Listen, great being! Not even the Buddhas of the past found anything outside their own minds. They never altered the natural condition; they never meditated visualizing conceptually: abiding in the non-discursive state they realized their own mind. The Buddhas of the present, too, and those to come in the future, achieve self-realization through the non-discursive state of equanimity.

[37. *The chapter of the essential teaching on the state beyond meditation*, 126.5–128.7]

Followers of the sutric tradition of the Bodhisattvas aspire to the level of realization called "total light," and judging and analyzing the two truths, they assert that the true nature of phenomena is emptiness, like space. The total bliss of atiyoga is pure and total consciousness, beyond judging and analyzing. That which transcends judging and analyzing is hindered by the sutric tradition: judging and analyzing total perfection means falling into the misleading deviation of the followers of the sūtras.

Followers of kriyā aspire to the level of "vajra holder" and, having entered the path of the three purities, they remain with the consideration of a pure subject and pure object. The total bliss of atiyoga is pure and total consciousness, beyond subject and object. That which transcends subject and object is hindered by kriyā: conceiving total perfection in terms of subject and object means falling into the misleading deviation of the followers of kriyā.

Followers of ubhaya base themselves on the kriyā principle as regards conduct and on the yoga principle as regards practice. However, as they do not succeed in integrating view and behavior, they do not understand the meaning of non-duality. The total bliss of atiyoga is pure and total non-dual consciousness. That which is non-dual is hindered by ubhaya: conceiving total perfection in dualistic terms means falling into the misleading deviation of the followers of ubhaya.

Followers of yoga aspire after realization of the "dense array" and having entered the path "with characteristics" and "without characteristics,"[209] they mainly practice the four mudrās. Consequently, they do not succeed in applying the principle of "not accepting nor rejecting." The total bliss of atiyoga is pure and total consciousness, beyond accepting and rejecting. That which transcends accepting and rejecting is hindered by yoga: an attitude of acceptance and rejection in relation to total perfection means falling into the misleading deviation of the followers of yoga.

Followers of mahāyoga aspire after realization of Vajradhara and, having entered the path of method and of prajñā, they apply the four phases of approach and accomplishment in the pure maṇḍala of their own mind. The total bliss of atiyoga is pure and total consciousness, beyond effort. That which transcends effort is hindered by mahāyoga: striving to attain total perfection through effort means falling into the misleading deviation of the followers of mahāyoga.

Followers of anuyoga aspire after the level of "indivisible" realization and, having entered the path of the dimension of emptiness and primordial wisdom, they understand that the cause of all phenomena is the pure dimension of emptiness, while their fruit is the maṇḍala of wisdom. The total bliss of atiyoga is pure and total consciousness, beyond cause and effect. That which transcends cause and effect is hindered by anuyoga: conceiving total perfection in terms of cause and effect means falling into the misleading deviation of the followers of anuyoga. These, then, are the deviations and hindrances regarding view and behavior.

Listen, great being! The view and behavior of total perfection is not like that of practices based on cause and effect. The view and behavior of pure and total consciousness is like the sky: the sky is beyond thoughts and analysis. Whoever tries to reason and analyze will never achieve enlightenment that is like the sky: the arising of judgement and analysis denotes deviation and hindrance.

Whoever applies the view and behavior that are like the sky in terms of subject and object will never realize the sky of enlightenment: the arising of subject and object is deviation and hindrance.

Some separate view from behavior, but just as the sky cannot be divided, so also pure and total consciousness cannot be reduced to duality. Those who divide will never realize the sky of enlightenment: separating view and behavior constitutes deviation and hindrance.

Pure and total consciousness is like the sky, and the sky is beyond accepting and rejecting. Those who accept and reject will never realize the sky of enlightenment: the dualism of acceptance and rejection constitutes deviation and hindrance.

Pure and total consciousness is like the sky, and the sky is beyond effort. Those who practice with effort will never realize the sky of enlightenment: practicing with effort constitutes deviation and hindrance. Pure and total consciousness is like the sky, and the sky is beyond cause and effect. Those who conceive it in terms of cause and effect will never realize the sky of enlightenment: conceiving a cause and an effect constitutes deviation and hindrance.

Listen, great being! All phenomena are the nature of the sky: the sky is without substance, the sky transcends all examples, the sky is beyond all measure. This is the way to understand the true meaning of all phenomena!

Listen, great being, and understand! Every vehicle has its view, but the true view cannot pertain to anything external: pure and total consciousness, which is the fundamental nature, cannot become the object of a view. Thus, conceiving a view is a mistake.

Every vehicle has its commitment to keep, like an escort along the path to enlightenment. However, as pure and total consciousness is beyond subject and object, there is nothing external to keep: thus there is no commitment to observe.

Every vehicle has its capacity for spiritual action, like a helper along the path to enlightenment. However, as pure and total consciousness is self-perfected, there is no need to obtain a spiritual capacity. That which is already perfect is not realized through action.

Every vehicle has its level of realization, like a base, or support, along the path to enlightenment. However, as all the Buddhas of the three times, the teachers of the three dimensions, the beings of the three worlds, and all things that exist in the animate and inanimate world abide at the level of total perfection, pure and total consciousness, there is no need to train oneself to progress along the levels of realization.

Every vehicle has its conception of an "ultimate nature": the ultimate nature of total perfection is pure and total consciousness. As beyond it nothing exists, all the teachings contemplated in the other vehicles are pure and total consciousness. Fixing dualistically on the "ultimate nature" constitutes a mistake.

The self-arising wisdom of total perfection does not conceptualize an object: without judging, without moving, it is primordial wisdom!

[*38. The chapter that indicates the deviations and hindrances related to view and behavior*, 129.3–133.2]

Listen, great being! I am the supreme source, pure and total consciousness, thus I am the fundamental essence of everything. The teachers of the three dimensions, the Buddhas of the three times, the Vidyādharas and Bodhisattvas, all the beings of the three worlds and all that exists in the animate and inanimate world have arisen from me. In what way?

From the condition of non-discursive equanimity there arises the dharmakāya that has no origin. From the condition of one's nature arises the saṃbhogakāya of perfect enjoyment of the senses. From the total state of enlightenment of energy there arises the nirmāṇakāya that acts for the benefit of beings.

The Buddhas of the past attained enlightenment by understanding the non-discursive state of the nature of mind, self-arising wisdom, and still now they abide in this non-discursive state. The Buddhas of the present, too, act for the good of beings through the non-discursive state of the nature of mind, self-arising wisdom. In the same way, the Buddhas to come in the future will certainly benefit beings by teaching the non-discursive state of self-arising wisdom, the total state of enlightenment.

When the Vidyādharas and [Bodhisattvas] on the various levels of realization observe this pure and total self-arising consciousness and see nothing, right in that moment they encounter the essence of their mind!

As the self-arising wisdom of all beings of the three worlds cannot at all be blocked, that which is [ordinarily] perceived in the clarity of sense objects is unaltered pure and total consciousness: this is the true essence!

Among all things existing in the animate and inanimate universe, there is not one single thing that has not been created by me, nor is there a cause that does not derive from me. Thus I am the essence of all, and nothing surpasses me. I am superior to the three dimensions, to the Buddhas of the three times, to the Vidyādharas, to the Bodhisattvas, to the beings of the three worlds, to the whole animate and inanimate universe, because I am the maker of all. Before there was any other teaching I, that am the source, pure and total consciousness, disclosed the teaching of pure and total consciousness.

[39. *The chapter on the fundamental essence of the Victorious Ones*, 133.4–135.1]

Sattvavajra asked: Teacher, Supreme Source! If your teaching is pure and total consciousness, and this itself is the state of enlightenment, are the beings of the three worlds not already enlightened? Why, in that case, do they transmigrate in the three worlds? Then the supreme source, pure and total consciousness, said:

Listen, great being! All the phenomena that spring forth from pure and total consciousness are a manifestation of the fundamental nature. This nature is single in its essence, yet it manifests in the five [sense] objects.

When desire and aversion arise, [śrāvakas] deem [the five sense objects] to be the cause of the passions and of suffering. Consequently, they try to eliminate them, even though precisely these five natural objects are self-arising wisdom. Thus, being unable to eliminate them in less than three kalpas, they continue to transmigrate in the three worlds.

When the five objects of the single, natural condition manifest, due to desire and aversion [pratyekabuddhas] deem them to be the cause of saṃsāra. Consequently, they try to eliminate them, even though in reality precisely these are self-arising wisdom. Thus, unsuccessful for many kalpas, they continue to transmigrate in the three worlds.

When the five objects of the single, natural condition manifest, due to desire and aversion, [Bodhisattvas] deem them the abode of attachment. Consequently, they try to purify them, even though in reality precisely these are self-arising wisdom. Thus, unable to purify them in less than one long kalpa, they continue to transmigrate in the three worlds.

When the five objects of the single, natural condition manifest, due to desire and aversion [followers of kriyā] deem they have to be empowered by means of spiritual energy. Consequently, they empower the outer and the inner to make them pure, and likewise they purify the five natural objects even though in reality precisely these are self-arising wisdom. However, being unable to empower them in less than seven lives, they continue to transmigrate in the three worlds.

When the five objects of the single, natural condition manifest from pure and total consciousness, due to desire and aversion [followers of yoga] deem them the cause of the higher and lower states. Consequently, they act in terms of acceptance and rejection as regards the fundamental nature. But, as self-arising wisdom cannot reject itself, however obstinately they try, they continue to transmigrate in the three worlds.

When the five objects of the single, natural condition manifest from pure and total consciousness, due to desire and aversion [followers of mahāyoga] recognize that the five objects are the Body, Voice, and Mind, and so they try to realize them by practicing. However, as they try to attain that which already naturally exists, due to their striving, they continue to transmigrate.

So, great being, beyond pure and total consciousness, no "self-arising wisdom" exists. Beyond saṃsāra, no nirvāṇa exists. Beyond the subject who is the experiencer of existence, no "ultimate nature" exists.

All is one in the natural condition, just as it is, so seeking to alter it is a mistake! [This is the meaning of *teshinnyid,* or "that very thing just as it is:] *te* means "authentic"; *shin* means that it cannot be altered; *nyid* denotes its natural characteristic. Do not alter the natural condition! If you do, you alter pure and total consciousness. Whoever alters pure and total consciousness realizes the very essence of saṃsāra.

[40. *The chapter that shows the nature of bodhicitta,* 136.4–139.2]

V. THE TEACHINGS THAT ESTABLISH KNOWLEDGE

I am the lamp of the teachers, pure and total consciousness. I am the fundamental essence of all the Buddhas of the three times. I am the mother and father of the beings of the three worlds. I am the final cause of all that exists in the animate and inanimate universe. There is nothing that has not originated from me.

As I abide nowhere yet penetrate all, from the beginning I am the Buddhas of the three times. As my condition is equanimous and transcends thought, I am the primordial dharmakāya Buddha, the non-discursive state of equality. As my nature manifests as total enjoyment, I am the primordial saṃbhogakāya Buddha, perfect enjoyment. As I manifest as self-arising wisdom, I am the primordial nirmāṇakāya Buddha, the potentiality of energy. Thus I am the fundamental essence of the Buddhas of the three times. My primordial wisdom manifests as pure and total consciousness. The five self-arising wisdoms are the mind of the six classes of beings. Therefore I am the father and mother of all the beings of the three worlds. All of the universe and its living beings, the animate and inanimate world are my essence manifested as the earth element: as my manifestation exists from the beginning, [the earth element] is the Buddha. As everything unifies in my non-dual state, I am the water element. As it gathers everything, the nature of mind is the water element. As I spread equally and everywhere my heat, I am the fire element. As it abides equally in everything, the fire element is the Buddha. I am without material obstructions and my nature is movement: in this way the air element manifests as the Buddha. I am unhindered and all-encompassing clarity: therefore what is called "space" is the Buddha.

[41. *The chapter on the single essence*, 139.4–140.5]

Listen, great being! Dharmakāya is pure and total consciousness. Other than pure and total consciousness there is no dharmakāya that can be the result of alteration: thus enlightenment is not something other than consciousness.

Saṃbhogakāya is pure and total consciousness. Other than pure and total consciousness and the forms that issue from it, there is no other saṃbhogakāya.

Nirmāṇakāya is pure and total consciousness. Other than pure and total consciousness that emanates, there is nobody else that acts for the good of beings.

All the Buddhas of the three times, too, are nothing other than pure and total consciousness. The Buddhas of the past achieved self-realization perceiving the authentic nature of their mind. As they have understood the authentic and unaltered nature of their mind, the Buddhas of the present now act for the good of others. The Buddhas to come in the future have never been taught to correct the self-arising state of their mind, so already now, they do not alter their mind by meditating on something. Instead they follow the path of "not correcting."

Those who do not understand that all the phenomena of the universe are pure and total consciousness seek self-realization in vain, correcting and striving. However, as they do not understand, even though they strive and correct themselves for many kalpas, they do not accede to effortless bliss.

Listen! As the three kāyas are not produced by altering the nature of mind, when the teachers of the three dimensions teach that one has to correct, they do not transmit the fundamental reality. However hard they try to make the necessity to alter something appear as truth, this pertains to the provisional teaching and not to the definitive one.

[42. *The chapter on the state that cannot be altered*, 141.2–142.4]

Listen, great being! I am the teacher of all the teachings: from my three natures there manifest the three teachers, thus I teach three kinds of teachings. The disciples who follow these teachings are of three categories, too. Who are the teachers? The teacher that communicates the essence of existence, the teacher that communicates the nature of existence, the teacher that communicates through the meaning of words.

The teacher that communicates the essence manifests the empowering flow from the unborn condition and thereby discloses the fundamental state of all the phenomena of existence.

The teacher that communicates the nature manifests all the phenomena of existence in the dimension of its own form and teaches that no other nature exists.

The teacher that communicates through the meaning of words summarizes the meaning of all the teachings and transmits it to the ignorant beings of the three worlds by means of words and explanations. This is the nature of the teacher.

Now I will explain the three categories of disciples. As soon as they start on the path, disciples of atiyoga beyond effort acquire certainty and abide on the level of enlightenment.

The Vidyādhara [and Bodhisattva] disciples from the first to the tenth levels of realization who have not yet achieved enlightenment although they are very near it are still on the level of [the path of] meditation.[210]

The disciples who practice mental aspiration abide at the level of performance of virtuous action in order to extinguish the poisons of the passions. These are the categories of the disciples of the three teachers. [...]

Listen, great being! The dharmakāya teaching concerns the authentic nature, which is impossible to divide. "Authentic nature" denotes that all the phenomena of existence are the nature of mind. Whoever meditates altering this condition does not understand the dharmakāya teaching.

The true essence of enlightenment that does not manifest visibly is precisely the authentic nature: those who meditate on it and alter it do not perceive the true nature of their own mind.

The phenomena of manifestation and the essence of enlightenment that never manifests are both the authentic nature of mind: not understanding it, everyone perceives it in his own way. But even if the Buddhas of the three times were to seek this nature, they would not find it!

[43. *The chapter that explains [the nature of] the teacher*, 142.5–143.7; 144.1–144.5]

Listen, great being! The state of non-action is precisely my nature. I do not act: as for me, from the beginning, all is accomplished, my being itself is non-action. As this is my nature, in its regard there is no question whatever of entering into action.

The "nature of nature" is the natural state that cannot be modified. Sattvavajra, do not try to alter this pure and total consciousness that cannot be altered! If you alter it, you would alter me, the source. All the phenomena of existence are only my nature.

Listen, great being! My nature is unchanging: if you meditate on it, you are trying to correct and transform it. I am original self-perfection: if you try to achieve me through effort, you will alter me. You cannot reach me by treading a path. You do not find me by seeking. You do not purify me through training yourself.

Have no view about me: I am beyond [being an] object! Do not tread a path to reach me: I am beyond a path! Do not train yourself to purify me: I am beyond hindrances! I have no abode whatsoever and cannot become an object to which to address the mind. I know no conceptual elaborations and transcend the objects of thought.

All the phenomena conceived by the mind are only my nature. Whoever seeks to reject or to block them will not encounter me, the source, for another three kalpas: in reality, that which they believe they must reject is my very nature itself.

[44. *The chapter that demonstrates how total perfection does not give results to those who are unsuitable,* 145.7–146.7]

Listen, great being! My view is not something on which to meditate, because it concerns me, the source, and one cannot meditate on me: I, that am the source, cannot become an object of meditation. By nature I abide in all, without ever being altered. [...]

The view of total perfection is not to be meditated on because the qualities of my mind are the extraordinary qualities of pure and total consciousness. Thus self-sacrifice is not necessary in seeking to realize them: being beyond causes and conditions, there is no need to strive to obtain them. Being the fruit that already exists in nature, there is no need to seek them elsewhere. Being the natural condition itself, there is no need whatever to meditate. Never having been born, they cannot be destroyed. Not depending on anything, there is no need to seek a state of meditation.

Whoever meditates on me will not encounter me precisely on account of that meditation. As I am the manifestation of the fundamental nature, [in my state] suffering does not arise, and consequently, there is no need to try to eliminate it. As I am self-arising, unborn, and indestructible, there is no need to block the senses tied to the interdependence of ignorance.

Being utterly pure by nature, the fundamental condition does not need to be purified. Being pure from the beginning, it does not need to be cleansed. Being ever self-perfected, there is no need of effort to attain it. Even seeking everywhere, nothing impure can be found: all is the essential condition that manifests in the form that is always good.[211]

From the beginning, the phenomena that appear as objects of the six senses, too, are this very nature and nothing else. Whoever tries to meditate and strives to realize this condition is like a blind man [vainly] pursuing the sky.

[45. *The chapter that demonstrates that there is no view on which to meditate,* 149.1–149.2; 150.7–151.6]

Listen, great being! In total perfection there is no commitment to keep. The nature of the source that is pure and total consciousness is unborn and beyond concepts. Thus when the miracle of the birth of the variety of phenomena manifests, by recognizing that all objects are this same nature and that they transcend judgement and concepts, whatever appears one remains [in the self-arising state] without trying to grasp it, without accepting it or rejecting it. In this way [one complies with the four commitments]: absence, omnipresence, singleness, and self-perfection, beyond any rule or vow to keep. [...]

For me, the source, there is no commitment to keep. As I am beyond causes and conditions, there is no need to try to attain me through effort. As I am self-perfected, there is no need to adopt a conduct. As I am primordial wisdom, there is no need to try to know me. As I am self-arising, there is no need of causes and conditions. As I am beyond good and bad, there is no need to accept me or reject me.

Being without material substance, I am called "absent." Since my wisdom is without interruption, even though it cannot be experienced as something concrete, I am called "omnipresent." As all is one single thing in the nature of mind, I am called "single." As all the phenomena of existence are perfect in the knowledge of pure and total consciousness, I am called "self-perfected."

[46. *The chapter that demonstrates that there is no commitment to keep*, 153.6–154.2; 156.6–157.3]

Listen, great being! I, the source, am total perfection, and as this perfection exists spontaneously by nature, from the beginning there is no need to try to acquire a capacity for spiritual action. [...]

The manifestation of dharmakāya in the form of saṃbhogakāya teaches mahāyoga disciples that the essence is the totality of one's state. [However its realization is said to require] visualization of the various deities in the maṇḍala of one's pure mind, each with its own color and attributes characteristic of its specific family. [These are:] the deity of pacifying activity for pacifying; the deity of flourishing activity for enriching; the deity of power for subjugating; the deity of wrathful activity for eliminating. In this way one realizes the levels of Vidyādhara of "long life" and of Mahāmudrā.[212] But however hard one strives, the state beyond effort and action is not realized through the four activities.

As total perfection transcends cause and effect, it is not realized by trying to obtain it. [...]

Listen, great being! Do not meditate visualizing with your mind! Do not turn wisdom into an object of conceptual thought! It is of no use to mumble formulae or to recite mantras. It is of no use to form ritual gestures with your hands. It is of no use to concentrate on visualizing the radiation and re-absorption [of light]. Remaining in the natural condition, abide in unmovable self-perfection.

Being in the natural state, nobody can correct it. Remaining in this authentic condition beyond effort means not acting, and precisely this is the supreme action. Those who understand this have no need to perform the various [ritual] actions: without acting they remain in the fundamental state.

Whoever is in the natural state "just as it is" realizes the true meaning that cannot be altered.

[This is the meaning of *teshinnyid*]: *te* means "authentic"; *shin* means "unaltered"; *nyid* denotes the authentic condition. There is no enlightenment outside the natural state.

[47. *The chapter that demonstrates that there is no capacity for spiritual action to seek*, 158.3–158.4; 159.3–159.7; 161.1–161.5]

Listen, great being! From my single natural condition the three teachers manifest without interruption [as a quality of mine]. They teach six fundamental methods for understanding my single natural condition to the three categories of disciples that arise from the miracle of birth.

The view is the foundation for understanding the natural condition and the means to recognize it. However, as the essential condition is the unborn that transcends all objects of thought, even though one tries to scrutinize it through a view, one is not able to do it.

The commitment is the foundation for the elimination of one's defects and the means to avoid any interruptions. However, as the essential condition is not an object to protect, even trying to maintain it, one is not able to.

The capacity for spiritual action is the foundation for realization and the means to achieve it through striving. However, as the essential condition cannot be the result of a quest, it is not achieved through actions.

The path is the foundation for reaching the goal by pursuing a gradual process and the means to attain a level of stability. However, as the essential condition is not the goal of a path it is not reached by pursuing a gradual process.

The levels of realization are the foundation for attaining stability and the means to obtain that stage where there is no longer any need to train oneself. However, as all is already in the essential condition, there is no need to train oneself to attain a level of stability.

Wisdom is the foundation for true understanding and the means to recognize the essential nature. However, as the essential condition cannot become an object of understanding, self-arising wisdom is not something to conceptualize.

Listen, great being! As pure and total consciousness is the foundation of existence, even if the [teachers of the] various vehicles teach the six foundations of view and behavior to their disciples who are conditioned by cause and effect, and even if on the basis of their capacity of comprehension, the disciples try to realize the essential nature through these [six], this nature can never become the object of a quest. As the very fact of seeking it amounts to altering it, [such disciples] do not encounter their own mind, which is the unaltered foundation.

Listen, great being! This is the meaning of "there is no view on which to meditate." As the root of existence does not lie outside oneself, it is not possible for a subject to take itself as an object; consequently, there cannot be an object that is not oneself. Thus there is no view on which to meditate.

This is the meaning of "there is no commitment to keep." Even if one tries to curb one's mind, it cannot be blocked. As it is self-arising wisdom, there is no need to protect it.

Listen, this is the meaning of "there is no spiritual action to seek." As from the beginning, total perfection transcends cause and effect, believing that a spiritual capacity can manifest as the effect of a cause by means of striving [does not correspond] to total perfection that does not confirm any effect. Thus, as the capacities for spiritual action are self-perfected and are not the result of effort, it is said that there is no action that needs to be sought.

This is the meaning of "there is no path to tread." The Buddhas of the three times and the beings of the three worlds all tread the path of pure and total consciousness, and in the nature of consciousness there is no duality of Buddhas and sentient beings. Thus there is no path that consciousness has to tread to reach itself.

This is the meaning of "there is no level of realization to attain by training." People conditioned by cause and effect wish to train themselves in order to attain the level of pure and total consciousness, the ultimate dimension of existence. However, precisely by training they alter it and so do not realize it.

This is the meaning of "there is no wisdom to objectify." As from the beginning, any object is self-arising wisdom, wisdom cannot have itself as its object.

[*48. The chapter that discloses how the ground of all phenomena is Kunjed Gyalpo*, 162.4–165.1]

Listen, great being! I, the supreme source, abide in everybody as the essence of enlightenment. The nature of pure and total consciousness is the palace of the ultimate dimension of reality: in this immense universe of mind there abide all the Buddhas of the three times and all the beings of the three worlds, none excluded. This [nature] is the abode and the universal level where all abide beyond the limits of joining or separating from it. So it is not to be deemed a goal to reach through training, otherwise one runs the risk of altering one's mind: by altering mind one does not achieve perfection. This, then, is the abode and the universal level! [...]

There are six levels of realization resulting from practice, whose names are: total light, lotus-endowed free of attachment, vajra holder, dense array, great accumulation of the cakra [of letters], level of Vajradhara, indivisible level of Samantabhadra beyond cause and effect. However, as the nature of mind is beyond causes and conditions, there is no fruit that can be the result of a practice. In reality, [these six levels] are merely so many ways of manifestation of the nature of mind.

In fact, as everything that manifests as clarity through the five sense doors points to uninterrupted self-arising wisdom, one speaks of "total light."

As [in this state] there is no judging the object or forming attachment to it, one speaks of "lotus-endowed free of attachment."

As pure and total consciousness is beyond birth and cessation, one speaks of "vajra holder."

As in one's true nature, the boundless natural condition, self-arising wisdom manifests as the dimension of non-discursive equanimity, one speaks of "dense array."

As the nature of pure and total consciousness is a maṇḍala that embraces all the phenomena of enlightenment, one speaks of "great accumulation of the cakra of letters."

As the Body, Voice, and Mind are without beginning or end, one speaks of "level of Vajradhara."

As pure and total consciousness is beyond the dualism of cause and effect and all the phenomena that manifest from it have always been beyond all considerations of good and bad, of acceptance and rejection, one speaks of "indivisible level."

Thus all the Buddhas of the three times and the beings of the three worlds issue from the ultimate dimension of pure and total consciousness and abide therein. For this reason the ultimate dimension of pure and total consciousness is called the "level of universal experience."[214]

[*49. The chapter that demonstrates that in total perfection there is no progressing through the levels of realization*, 165.3–165.6; 166.6–168.1]

Listen, great being! What is called "the wisdom of wisdom" is knowledge that has existed from the beginning. Self-arising wisdom is primordial knowledge. The wisdom that judges an object, as it derives from the object itself, cannot be "self-arising."

Clarity does not manifest merely by remaining in a state without an object. Thus, self-arising wisdom is wisdom that concerns primordial knowledge. [...]

As wisdom arises of itself, one should not meditate concentrating on it. Not meditating, one does not accumulate the karmic tendencies of meditation.[215] The fundamental condition, free of karmic tendencies, is the true state of knowledge of the Buddhas of the three times. The essence of the knowledge of the Buddhas of the three times does not depend on an object because from the beginning it rests in a state of equanimity.

Listen, great being! The state of self-arising wisdom of all the Buddhas of the three times, being free of concepts from the beginning, should not be constructed by the mind. It is beyond all the objects of judgement. By remaining in the non-conceptual condition, atiyoga practitioners realize the state of knowledge of the Buddhas.

Listen, great being! The state of enlightenment lies in self-arising wisdom. In fact, by not judging objects this wisdom is not contaminated by the karmic tendencies of discursive thought.

Karma is produced by the tendencies of meditative absorbtion, while in the non-conceptual state there are no karmic tendencies.

The five self-arising wisdoms of the non-conceptual state manifest as the five natural doors of the mind, the five senses, and are without interruption. When the nature of pure and total consciousness manifests, the self-arising wisdoms shine uninterruptedly and distinctly. As they appear spontaneously, they should not be denied: in this way one does not accumulate the karmic tendencies resulting from a meditative absorbtion devoid of thoughts. [...]

Listen, great being! Understand properly the meaning of these words in the experience of the state of pure presence!

Self-arising wisdom abides in the five sense objects, but the five wisdoms do not crave the five objects: the five sense objects manifest as the five wisdoms. As these themselves are the wisdom that has existed from the beginning, there is no dualism between objects and wisdoms! Thus the object, too, is self-arising wisdom. [...]

Disciples [of the three teachers] give diverse names to my single nature on the basis of the way they conceive me. Some call it "pure and total consciousness"; others, "ultimate dimension of phenomena"; others, "condition of space." Others call it "self-arising wisdom"; others, "dharmakāya"; others, "saṃbhogakāya"; others, "nirmāṇakāya." Others call it "Body, Voice, and Mind"; others, "omniscience"; others, "totality of phenomena"; others, "the three wisdoms" or "the four wisdoms"; others, "the five wisdoms"; others, "the emptiness-dimension and primordial wisdom." These are the names they attribute to the single self-arising pure and total consciousness on the basis of the views they hold about me.

[*50. The chapter that discloses self-arising wisdom*, 168.3–168.4; 168.7–170.1; 170.2–170.4; 170.7–171.4]

VI. THE CONCLUDING TEACHINGS

Listen, great being! The teachers of the three dimensions, my emanations, explain that it is necessary to tread a path and to that end they teach five or three paths. As they assert that by treading these paths one achieves one's aim, their notion of attainment is based on the principle of cause and effect, and this does not correspond to total perfection in which there is no path to tread.

Through the five paths—of accumulation, of application, of seeing, of meditation and of the final attainment [also called "of no more learning"]—they fulfil the two accumulations and [believe they] finally succeed in eliminating the dualism of subject and object. However, this realization, which [they believe] enables them to see the truth due to meditation, does not correspond to the path in which there is no path to tread, thus it should not be defined as "effortless bliss."

The three paths of the secret teaching of the "fruit" are the contemplations on the essential nature, on the total manifestation [and on the syllable]. As they are the way to realize the three dimensions,[216] one meditates to become accustomed to them. Through the four "approaches and accomplishments" that entail the application of the principle of cause and effect to self-arising reality, one proceeds gradually and thus does not attain the level that transcends the effort of practice.

As one's mind, beyond conceptual elaborations, is the ultimate dimension of existence, [it is] in this freedom from concepts [that] all the Buddhas abide. So, do not follow a gradual path!

Mind, which is unhindered, is clear like the sky: in it there abide all the Buddhas of the three times. So, do not follow a gradual path!

Mind, which is unaltered, is the authentic, fundamental condition: in it all the Buddhas of the three times are spontaneously perfected. So, do not follow a gradual path!

If you start to follow a path based on ignorance, you will never attain your goal and will never achieve true understanding. Following a gradual path, one does not attain the level of enlightenment. Enlightenment is mind free of concepts and it is not achieved by following a gradual path.

Meditating on the view, you encounter the object of contemplation; however, this contemplation does not lead to the equanimity of the state free of concepts.

Keeping a commitment, one remains tied to the resolution not to break it; however, due to this concept, one does not find the equanimity of the non-conceptual state.

Seeking to acquire the capacity for spiritual action, one practices the methods of realization; however, meditation directed to the acquisition of something is far from the equanimity of the state free of concepts.

Training to progress along the levels of realization, one practices the methods for stabilizing the state of calm;[217] however, meditation tending to perfection is far from the equanimity of the state free of concepts.

Seeking to understand the ultimate nature of existence, one practices the methods of meditation for clarity;[218] however, meditation directed to clarifying something is far from the equanimity of the state free of concepts.

Seeking to clarify wisdom, one practices the methods of conceptual meditation; however, meditation that seeks to clarify understanding is far from the equanimity of the non-conceptual state.

Listen, great being! Meditation based on desire, however clear it may be, does not bring about realization of happiness free of desires. The total bliss of non-action is realized through the non-conceptual state and the absence of desire. Not meditating [conceptually] and not accumulating karmic tendencies, self-arising wisdom is not subject to the power of karma.

Self-arising wisdom, the essence of dharmakāya, is not realized through effort, but conversely, by just remaining in the natural condition. It transcends all the aims of the practices, for that which is called "aim" is only a name: in reality "enlightenment" itself is only a name.

Using the definition of "enlightenment" is a characteristic of the provisional teachings and not of the definitive ones.

[51. *The chapter that demonstrates that there is no path to tread*, 172.2–174.3]

Listen, great being! If you want to realize all the Dharmas, do not base yourself on the desire to obtain! The mind that kindles desire makes one lose everything instead of obtaining. As the true nature transcends cause and effect, those desirous of the fruit should not engage in its cause: it is realized by just remaining in the natural condition free of concepts. Give up all meditations based on desire!

Being without desires, one obtains everything. Practicing meditation, one clings to desire, but this is not at all right because in reality there is nothing to grasp. All the paths based on action seek to realize self-perfection that transcends effort, but they do not succeed: self-perfection is present just as it is without needing to act and is not attained through action.

As it moves everything away, desire is a grave hindrance to realization. The karmic tendencies that derive from a path of meditating based on desire bind the mind to the idea of grasping something and consequently, they move happiness away. Conversely, not grasping anything, one obtains all happiness, because happiness is the true natural condition.

This unalterable condition is the single state of consciousness of all the Buddhas: it is pure bliss utterly without desire or the idea of grasping anything. [In it] the state that transcends concepts is not deemed an object to aim for, nor does one cling to the non-discursive state.[219] The true meaning of this "not doing" is realized by stopping desiring. Grasping nothing and being free of attachment, one practices supreme contemplation. Precisely this, complete and perfect from the beginning, is supreme realization that transcends the ideas of something to let go of and something else to hold.

Listen, great being! Meditating on diversity does not clarify the one. Meditation aimed at clarifying something is not true meditation. Even though the fundamental condition is one alone, creating a division between Buddhas and sentient beings and between happiness and suffering, [some] teach the acceptance of happiness and the rejection of negativity: however, this doesn't concur with the definitive teaching.

Listen, great being! Do not turn what is one into two! Happiness and suffering are one in the state of enlightenment. Buddhas and sentient beings are one in [the nature of] mind. All that exists in the animate and inanimate world is one in the fundamental nature. Truth and falsehood, too, are one in the fundamental nature. Do not accept happiness, do not reject suffering! Remain in the natural condition and you will attain everything.

Getting attached to happiness is suffering. If one does not judge the manifestation of clarity, it itself is self-arising wisdom. If wisdom is not defiled by karmic tendencies, can it ever be stained by action? Wisdom tied to cause and effect is based on conceptual meditation, and this "conceptual wisdom" gives birth to karmic tendencies.[220] As in this way [self-arising] wisdom is subjected to tendencies, do not meditate on conceptual wisdom! Meditating on conceptual wisdom, one moves away from the equanimity of the non-discursive state, and contemplation is afflicted by the disease of effort.

Listen, great being! I, the source, am pure and total consciousness, and as all is pure and total consciousness, apart from it nothing exists. From [pure] consciousness there manifest the sundry teachings based on the physical characteristics and beliefs of beings, tied to specific perception of forms and colors. All of this is an emanation of the compassionate energy of wisdom and not something other than the natural condition.

Enlightenment itself is not something other than the natural condition, thus it is the fundamental nature of all the Buddhas of the three times. Aside from the fundamental nature, there is no enlightenment. Aside from enlightenment, there exist no sentient beings. The non-conceptual state of beings is the essence of the state of enlightenment. Before the manifestation of pure and total consciousness, there are neither Buddhas nor sentient beings. Thus it is the nature of mind that should be praised more than all the Buddhas! It is unchanging and has never been subject to change: even if one wants to alter it, its nature does not move one iota. Thus the teachers who divide the single nature in nine vehicles and eighty-four thousand methods do not understand the meaning of the one. Not understanding the one, they do not understand the totality. Thus, understanding the single state of mind is supreme understanding! [221]

[52. *The chapter on the immovable, desireless state*, 174.7–177.7]

All phenomena neither cease nor do they ever vanish; their nature is clarity that never moves from the essence. Those who, conditioned by desire and basing themselves on the principle of cause and effect, seek to realize reality that has never "moved," do not transmit my teaching.

Being without desires, I realize everything: without desiring it, the nature is already realized. The very word "realize" is not part of my language but of the language of those who base themselves on cause and effect.

I am the great enemy of all speculative artifice that tends to exaggerate or to diminish reality. Without judging the conjectures of being or not being, of realizing or not realizing, I remain in the condition of equanimity. I, the forebear of the Enlightened Ones, teach nothing else apart from this condition of equanimity! [...]

This supreme equanimity, whose nature is total purity, is an unchanging condition beyond all attachments. It transcends the dualistic object and any position of the mind. If, moved by desire, one seeks to obtain it as if it were something concrete, one falls into attachment and does not find the non-conceptual state of equanimity.

The fundamental condition has always been in nature: wanting to seek it and to obtain it is the same as seeking one's mind elsewhere. However, even if we were to cut into small pieces the space of existence, the sky, the three worlds, and all living beings, still we would never find the abode of mind.

Mind has the nature of the sky: it has no borders and its space is not subject to diminution.

Mind, which has the nature of the sky, cannot be found, and the same applies to the nature of all existence.

The authentic, natural condition cannot be altered: even if one practises the meditation methods tied to the manifestation of energy,[222] the essence of the authentic condition is not changed. [...]

There is no difference of quality or of size between the state of the Body, Voice, and Mind of the Buddhas and the body, voice, and mind of beings. The fundamental nature beyond concepts abides in equanimity, and in this state there is no distinction between dharma and non-dharma. Sentient beings are not deemed a cause nor are Buddhas deemed their effect.

Teachers who teach cause and effect are mistaken. The whole of existence, which emanates from me, is the same: all is one without any distinction between good and bad!

[53. *The chapter that demonstrates that the nature of all phenomena is the immovable state,* 179.2–179.6; 179.7–180.5; 180.6–181.2]

First of all, to enable understanding of the ultimate nature, the ten dolungs on manifestation are taught. [Then,] in order to eliminate doubts and concepts and to grant certainty, the ten dolungs that precisely disclose [the nature] are taught. [To enable understanding that] the natural wisdom of self-arising wisdom does not depend on cause and effect, the ten dolungs beyond cause and effect are taught. [To enable understanding] that the self-arising wisdom of the supreme source need not be sought through action and effort, the ten dolungs on perfection beyond action are taught. [To enable understanding] that the self-arising wisdom of the supreme source itself establishes knowledge of its nature, the ten dolungs that establish knowledge are taught.

There are five necessities tied [to the five subdivisions]. The dolungs on manifestation serve to discern truly the ultimate nature because when the ultimate nature is precisely understood, there is no longer need of view, conduct, or commitment or to tread a path. The dolungs that precisely disclose [the nature] serve to achieve certainty free of errors, and, by possessing precise certainty of the nature of mind, to overcome the need to seek to realize enlightenment. The dolungs that do not depend on causes and conditions serve to overcome the need to apply effort, and, as there is no longer any need for effortful action, to abide in bliss beyond effort. The dolungs on perfection beyond action serve to perfect [knowledge of] the uncreated nature, and, having perfected the [knowledge of] nature beyond action, [to realize] primordial self-perfection. The dolungs that establish knowledge serve to establish the knowledge, based on the principle of all five [subdivisions of the] dolungs, that the Buddhas of the three times, the beings of the three worlds, and the whole animate and inanimate universe is causeless, self-arising, and beyond action.

[54. *The chapter that demonstrates that all teachings are contained in the nature of Kunjed Gyalpo,* 182.4–183.7]

Listen, great being! All that exists in the animate and inanimate universe, all the expressions and meanings, are only pure and total consciousness.

The dimension of emptiness and the space of the sky are nothing other than pure and total consciousness beyond concepts and free of hindrances.

The manifestation of the elements—space, air, water, earth, and fire— is the nature of pure and total consciousness. The three worlds— of desire, form, and formless—are the manifestation of the three natures of pure and total consciousness. The teachers of the three dimensions that teach this, too, are the three natures of pure and total consciousness.

The uninterrupted wisdom of consciousness manifests as the world of desire. The nature of consciousness manifests as the world of form. The essence of consciousness, which is unborn, manifests as the formless world.

The unborn essence beyond concepts is dharmakāya. Consciousness that enjoys its own nature is saṃbhogakāya. The emanation of consciousness that benefits beings through mind is nirmāṇakāya.

The moment they discover the equanimity of the non-conceptual state, even beings of the hell realms and of the other realms of saṃsāra who have fallen prey to the suffering of heat and cold, of hunger and thirst, of foolishness and speechlessness, can liberate themselves in the authentic, natural condition.

As it does not conceptualize the object, self-arising wisdom is beyond all considerations of defects or qualities deriving from karmic tendencies. Without accepting the qualities or rejecting the defects, [in this state] one does not seek to obtain happiness or to eliminate suffering.

The authentic condition has never moved away from itself: even though one may want to transform it, it does not change. Even though one may aspire after it, there is nothing that can be obtained. [...]

Listen! Human beings and divine beings find it hard to understand. Distracted by sense objects, they remain ignorant and are made content by anything that is taught to them. When they learn the principle of the absolute truth and relative truth based on the provisional teachings of cause and effect, their minds are appeased by the dualism of truth and falsehood and they nurture this dualism for several kalpas.

So, first of all, one must teach in a precise manner the nature of one's consciousness. Once it has been communicated, one encounters the infallible path that transcends seeking and from the very first moment, one is on the level which does not entail effort. In this manner, one connects with the path beyond seeking and with the state where there is no longer any meditation, obtaining stability in happiness that transcends all effort.

On realizing the nature of one's consciousness, the qualities manifest spontaneously and already perfected without needing to seek them. There is no longer need to cultivate good intention or to follow a gradual path, no need to train oneself to achieve the levels of realization or to meditate on the view, no need to strive to observe rules and discipline strictly.

Great being, teach all this! Do not practice in the worldly way, meditating on [the form of] a deity as the activity of the body, reciting mantras and formulae as the activity of the voice, and visualizing and concentrating as the activity of the mind.

[55. *The chapter that demonstrates that no phenomenon exists that does not derive from bodhicitta,* 186.4–187.5; 188.4–189.3]

Teacher of teachers, supreme source, I have understood the true nature thus: all phenomena are one in the true nature. The palace of the ultimate dimension of reality is the supreme source, its fame resounds. This divine abode in the dimension of space, too, is the supreme source. The teacher of unborn dharmakāya, too, is the supreme source. The saṃbhogakāya of perfect enjoyment, too, is the supreme source. The nirmāṇakāya of the potentiality of the energy of wisdom, too, is the supreme source. The world of desire, tied to passion, is the supreme source. The world of form, tied to pride, is the supreme source. The formless world, tied to the mental body, is the supreme source. The Buddhas of the past epochs that abide in your state are the supreme source. The Buddhas of the present who act for the benefit of beings are the supreme source. The Buddhas of the future who will spring forth from your state are the supreme source. The practitioners of the four yogas who aspire to your state are the supreme source. The whole animate and inanimate universe composed of the five elements is the supreme source. Apart from the supreme source, there are no Buddhas or sentient beings, and no animate and inanimate universe or any other phenomenon exists.

Thus spoke Sattvavajra.

[56. *The chapter in which Sattvavajra declares his understanding of the nature of Kunjed Gyalpo*, 189.6–191.1]

The teachings of the teachers of the three dimensions speak of cause and effect, specifying that by practicing engaging on the cause one produces the fruit. Using the terms "Buddhas" and "sentient beings," they explain that the mind must obtain the fruit of enlightenment. But this is not my teaching.

My nature transcends the duality of cause and effect: as there is no duality whatever between Buddhas and sentient beings, enlightenment is not something that the mind needs to obtain. I, the supreme source, am the nature of consciousness, self-arising wisdom.

[57. *The chapter on the entrustment of the teaching*, 192.2–192.4]

6 The Further Tantra: the Teachings on Understanding

I. INTRODUCTION

Listen! This is my way of understanding. I am the unborn nature, and thus I understand that all phenomena arising from it are likewise unborn and self-arising.

Listen well, great being! Recognizing that I am unborn, I understand that the three teachers, too, are unborn and so are the three kinds of teachings, the disciples, the places, and the epochs. I understand that the Buddhas of the past are unborn, and so are the Buddhas of the present and those to come in the future.

Listen! Just as I, that am the teacher and the source, understand, you too, Sattvavajra, must understand! If you do not understand thus you will not perceive my nature and, consequently, you will not understand the ten fundamental natures. If you ignore the real meaning of the ten natures, how can you understand the ten teachings on non-meditation? [...]

Understand that the Buddhas of the three times are unborn. Understand that the six classes of beings are unborn. Understand that earth, water, fire, air, and space are unborn. Understand that the three worlds and the three existences are unborn. Understand that the five sense objects are unborn. Thus, all phenomena are pure and total consciousness, and pure and total consciousness is the supreme source. Understand that the supreme source was never born!

I am the root of all phenomena; if you understand that I am the fundamental unborn dimension, you will perceive all the rest in the same way.

[*58. The introductory chapter on understanding,* 200.3–201.2; 201.4–201.7]

II. UNDERSTANDING THE TRUE MEANING OF THE TEN NATURES

1. On the View

Understand well, Sattvavajra! In terms of the source, the root of all phenomena, there is no such thing as an observer and an object to observe. Whoever understands the essence without deeming it the object of the view understands my nature.

Listen! All the phenomena of existence, without exception, abide in the supreme source in a condition of birthlessness. Let those who want to understand the fundamental meaning understand my nature! [...]

Were I not to teach this definitive teaching, the posterity of the supreme source, who is the forebear of all the enlightened ones, would be interrupted, and everybody would continue to transmigrate.

Listen! Thus, Sattvavajra, overcome the idea of having or not having a view. As having a view means covering the true meaning with concepts, do not base your understanding on the view of cause and effect!

In the atiyoga vehicle in which nothing is confirmed, trying to observe and to examine [the true nature] amounts to interrupting perception of it. Thus, understand that the true nature of the source, the unaltered essence, cannot be perceived by basing oneself on a view.

Listen! I, the supreme source, pure and total consciousness, am the mirror in which all phenomena are reflected. Although lacking self-nature, everything manifests clearly; without need for a view, the nature shines clear. Understanding that the essential unborn condition is not an object to observe dualistically is the great understanding!

[*59. The chapter on the unborn state,* 202.2–202.4; 203.4–204.2]

2. On Commitment

The teachers of the three dimensions, my emanations, teaching on the basis of the diverse capacities of the disciples, convey the understanding that the source is something to maintain by commitment.

Some understand that they have to keep their vows and discipline pure, others observe the Vidyādhara vows, while others base themselves on the numerous fundamental and secondary rules. But however deep their scrutiny, they do not achieve true understanding.

The commitment of the supreme source is beyond the dualism of keeping or not keeping. Whoever understands the meaning of "beyond keeping or not keeping" understands my commitment.

Listen! I, the supreme source, teacher of teachers, am the equality of all phenomena in pure and total consciousness that is the root. Thus, I am the fundamental essence of all commitments. Understand that I am beyond the dualism of keeping or not keeping!

Listen! Like the unborn sky, the commitment of the view of the supreme source transcends all limits: whoever understands this well understands the commitment of the supreme source. [...]

Listen! As the single root of all phenomena is consciousness, the single root of the commitment is not something to keep: this means having understood one's unborn mind.

Through [the four points of] absence, omnipresence, singleness, and self-perfection all commitments are transcended. The commitments of the supreme source refer to understanding the unborn state.

According to whether or not one understands that the fundamental essence is not something to protect, and on the basis of the subdivision in [the teachings of] the "provisional meaning" and of the "definitive meaning" the necessity or lack of necessity of a commitment to keep is taught.

Listen! As in this way one understands that there is no commitment to keep, this understanding equals the state of the Buddhas of the three times. Practitioners without this understanding are really in contradiction with the essence of their mind. Those who observe the commitment of the teachers of the three dimensions instead of keeping my commitment will find it difficult to encounter the true meaning for hundreds and thousands of kalpas

Thus, as you have received my teaching, understand that there is no commitment to keep!

[60. *The chapter on the commitment that need not be kept*, 204.3–205.2; 205.4–206.5]

3. On the Capacity for Spiritual Action

Sattvavajra, understand well! The teachers of the three dimensions, emanated from my nature, take the most appropriate form for their disciples and give them to understand that in order to realize the goal, it is necessary to acquire the capacity for spiritual action. In terms of the body, it is necessary to engage in mudrās; of the voice, to recite of mantras; of the mind, to visualize the radiation and re-absorption [of light]. They do not understand that one can attain self-realization leaving free the three doors of body, voice, and mind.

Listen! My capacity for spiritual action is not something to seek by means of action. [...]

Listen! My capacity for spiritual action is not something that has to be sought. As benefit for oneself is already spontaneously perfect, there is no need for action. As benefit for others is the equality of the ultimate dimension, it does not need to be sought. Understand this well!

Listen! As all is already accomplished in pure and total consciousness, within it there is no need whatever to act. Whoever could ascribe the definition of "acting" or "not acting" to the very essence of enlightenment, which is uncreated and beyond action?

Listen! In order to obtain my capacity for spiritual action, there is no need to form mudrās with the body, to recite mantras with the voice, or to visualize radiation and re-absorption with the mind. The enlightenment of all the Buddhas of the past, present, and future depends solely on understanding the true nature of spiritual capacity: non-action. As [the enlightenment of] the Buddhas of the three times is based on understanding, you too, Sattvavajra, [should] understand well my words!

Listen! The teachers of the three dimensions teach those attracted by the multiplicity of the characteristics of concepts the teachings on actions for pacifying, increasing, conquering, and wrathfully eliminating on the basis of the variety of their disciples' concepts. [...]

Listen! I, the source, the supreme teacher, teach that all actions are the path of concepts. Understanding the true meaning of spiritual action that transcends action, all beings can become the supreme source.

[61. *The chapter on understanding the nature of the three doors beyond action and seeking*, 206.4–207.1; 207.1–207.7; 208.3–208.4]

4. *On the Maṇḍala*

Understand, Sattvavajra! The teachers of the three dimensions, my emanations, teach disciples attracted by the multiplicity of characteristics the need to visualize the maṇḍala and the gaṇacakra.[223] Those who follow the path of the three dimensions seek to gain understanding by means of the multiplicity of characteristics, and for hundreds and thousands of kalpas they do not understand that there is no maṇḍala to visualize. [...]

This is my maṇḍala: the maṇḍala that arises from oneself is already perfect because everything is complete in its essence and is beyond the possibility of growth or diminution. Without needing to visualize it, instantaneously it is the perfect maṇḍala.

Listen! [This is the meaning of the word maṇḍala, in Tibetan *khyil-khor*]: *khyil* or "center" denotes the true essence; *khor* or "circumference" means that this essence possesses the bliss of saṃsāra and nirvāṇa in its entirety. This is the essence and the root of all maṇḍalas; all maṇḍalas are contained in it.

Listen! The maṇḍala of the supreme source is the maṇḍala in which all is perfected in essence. Whoever understands this perfection becomes expert in the meaning of "there is no maṇḍala to visualize."

Listen! With the unborn maṇḍala of pure and total consciousness, I, the supreme source, teacher of teachers, without coming and going, fill the whole universe. Only through knowledge does one accede to the unborn.

Listen! Whether or not the maṇḍala of the five wisdoms manifests depends on knowledge or ignorance. Thus, there exist the distinct notions of having or not having to visualize. However, when one has supreme understanding, this distinction no longer exists. So without tarrying over words, Sattvavajra, understand the meaning well! Whoever understands immediately abides in the state of the supreme source. [...]

Listen! Just as I taught you that the five passions are pure and total consciousness that was never born, you too, Sattvavajra, teach thus to your disciples on the basis of your own understanding!

[62. *The chapter on understanding that the maṇḍala is not to be created by visualization*, 208.6–209.2; 209.3–210.2; 210.5–210.6],

5. On Initiation

Sattvavajra, understand well! I am the teacher supreme source, and the teachers of the three dimensions which are my emanations teach that there are methods of conferring initiation. Attached to the path of concepts, they do not see my nature.

Listen! I am the teacher supreme source, and as my nature creates all and pervades all, I have no other aim. Understand thus that I am beyond conferring or not conferring [an initiation].

The various types and levels of initiations are taught to individuals attracted by the variety of characteristics. To those abiding in the meaning of the unaltered state, I teach the natural condition that is not conferred [by initiation].

Listen! As the nature of the supreme source pervades all, teach those practitioners who recognize and understand what it means to abide in the natural condition beyond conferral that there is no need to receive initiation!

Listen! I, the supreme source, teacher of teachers, understand and teach that it is not necessary to receive an initiation. Once one has obtained the power of one's pure unborn mind,[224] there is no longer any need for the effort of the initiation of the ten natures. One no longer places one's hopes in initiation into mantras and mudrās and is no longer attached to initiation into the sacred symbols and objects.

Recognizing the purity of one's mind, one no longer meditates on the deity with characteristic attributes and no longer distinguishes between planets, constellations, and particular astrological conjunctions.

Listen! My way of understanding is not shared by the teachers of the three dimensions, consequently, the true meaning of the ten natures is hindered. Thus, my nature is not understood.

Listen! I, the supreme source, teacher of teachers, teach the teachers of the three dimensions, my first disciples, the unaltered, authentic, and natural condition. There is no need to rely on a worldly "deity" to visualize or to depend on gaṇacakras or on initiation. As all is perfected in the power of pure unborn presence, leaving it as it is without seeking anything, all goals are spontaneously realized.

Listen! I am the teacher supreme source, and the teachers of the three dimensions are created by me. What they teach is also created by me: however I have no need to create myself!

Listen! Whoever understands the nature of the source in this way recognizes that it is the nature of all: thus understand my nature and do not depend any longer on initiations based on attachment to conceptual characteristics!

[63. *The chapter on the power of understanding the self-arising state*, 210.7–212.5]

6. *On the Path*

Listen! The nature of the supreme source, teacher of teachers, abides in the single condition of the unborn. However, as it is difficult to realize the meaning of the "unborn," in order to lead their followers on satisfactory paths, the teachers of the three dimensions, my first disciples, teach that it is necessary to tread gradual paths. Thus, to lead those of lesser capacity towards the true meaning, they transmit provisional teachings.

Listen! [They teach that] by following the gradual paths of accumulation, of application, of seeing, of meditation, and of the final attainment it is possible to realize the fruit after hundreds of kalpas, within seven lives, within three lives, etc. However in this manner they do not enable people to understand my path.

Listen! I will explain to you the path of the supreme source. As the true nature is unborn, I transcend the limiting definition of taking up or not taking up [a path]: thus there is no need to tread a gradual path. The five paths are conditioned by concepts. However, as I transcend the objects of concepts, I cannot be reached by following a conceptual path.

Listen! My path has no stages and is always equal in the immense sphere of the unborn: understanding this single nature, one discovers the futility of treading a gradual path.

Listen! In order to attain me, teacher of teachers, the supreme source, there are no stages related to a gradual path. Self-arising wisdom is instantly perfect: leaving the natural condition as it is, one finds oneself at the goal without ever having started the journey! Thus, Sattvavajra, do not pursue me in a gradual manner!

Listen! I am boundless like the sky. Just as trying to reach the bounds of space means troubling oneself to no avail, there is no disease worse than that of those who seek to realize my nature by following a gradual path! So you too, Sattvavajra, teach my nature to your disciples. Thus they too will understand that all is my nature, and they will no longer remain attached to the paths with worldly characteristics and will no longer get involved in discussions based on words. Abiding calmly in the unaltered state, they will reach the other shore, and they will meet the path of the universal essence!

The universal path of the supreme source has never been altered and cannot be trodden in a gradual manner: those who follow it in a gradual manner do not understand the real meaning of enlightenment and will never realize my nature. Understand thus the real meaning of "no path to tread."

[64. *The chapter on understanding that there is no path to tread,* 212.7–214.4; 214.5–214.6]

7. On the Levels of Realization

Sattvavajra, understand well! The teaching of the supreme source, teacher of teachers, whereby there is no need to train oneself in order to progress through the various levels, is not appropriate to all and is difficult to grasp.

Listen! In order to enable those of lesser capacity, attracted by the multiplicity of concepts, to progress, the teachers of the three dimensions, my emanations, teach the ten and the six levels. What they teach, their disciples understand. However, all of this pertains only to the sphere of concepts.

Listen! These are the six levels: total light, vajra holder, Vajradhara, dense array, lotus-endowed, level of Vajrasattva.[225] They are taught to practitioners following a gradual path according to the type of contemplation and deity.

Listen! This is the level of the teacher supreme source. As all the phenomena of existence are one single thing in the ultimate dimension of the unborn, there is no distinction between the various levels of realization. Understand that there is only one level!

If one is not on my level, the diverse levels of understanding that can be attained are merely projections of personal concepts and do not allow one to meet me, the source.

Listen! The nature of the level of the supreme source is the spontaneous perfection of pure presence, never altered or improved through progress. Even training to progress, one would not meet the true meaning, whereas understanding the true nature brings instantaneous self-perfection.

Listen! As, notwithstanding its having no origin, the level of the single vehicle of pure and total consciousness, the source, is all-pervading, seeking to achieve understanding by following a gradual path is like trying to reach the bounds of space. If instead one leaves the natural condition as it is, without following a gradual path, one self-liberates.

Listen! I, the supreme source, teacher of teachers, manifest as the essence of the levels of realization, thus in me there are no higher or lower levels. Understand the meaning of my level!

Even though I manifest clearly in front of everybody, the disciples of the three dimensions [try to] understand me [enclosing me] in concepts. However, the state of the supreme source is so deep that, however much they scrutinize it, they do not see it.

Listen! The teachers of the three dimensions, my first disciples, transmit teachings suitable to diverse dispositions: for each vehicle of the Body, Voice, and Mind they teach a level of realization, a path, and a fruit. But until my level is understood, the diverse levels do not enable one to discover the fundamental path. Thus the nature of mind is the universal vehicle, the level of pure and total consciousness. Understand this fundamental level that I am teaching you!

When you recognize that the true nature of realization does not depend on progress, you will finally abide on the level of pure and total consciousness, the source!

[65. *The chapter on understanding that there is no progressing through the levels of realization*, 215.1–216.7]

8. On Conduct

Listen! I am the teacher supreme source. Among the teachers of the three dimensions emanated from me, some understand that it is necessary to behave by accumulating virtues and eliminating negative deeds; others, that one should accept the pure and reject the impure; still others, that one can employ both pure and impure. However, in this way, they do not understand the meaning of transcending [the constraint of] behaving or not behaving in a certain manner.

Those who comply with these conducts seek to purify themselves by means of antidotes; consequently, their understanding remains bound to a contrived concept. They do not understand behavior beyond accepting and rejecting.

Listen! This is the behavior of the supreme source. As [all concepts of] virtue and vice, of accepting and rejecting, of pure and impure, of big and small are only one single thing in unborn pure and total consciousness, understand that there is nothing to accept or reject! Understand the nature beyond pure and impure! Understand the state where there is no difference between doing and not doing! Understand what cannot be split into center and border! Understand that the root is unborn pure and total consciousness!

Listen! This is the behavior of the supreme source. Whatever action one does, no conflict [with the true nature] arises: on recognizing that doing and not doing are both the unborn, any action one performs remains the unborn.

Listen! My behavior, like that of the sky, cannot be limited or measured. Being non-dual, it transcends the limits of being and non-being. Understand this to be the behavior of pure and total consciousness, the source!

Understand that the five sense objects are the behavior of pure and total consciousness! Understand that the five passions are the behavior of pure and total consciousness! Understand that the five ornamental causes [the five elements] are the behavior of pure and total consciousness! Understand that the three worlds and the three existences are the behavior of pure and total consciousness!

I, the forebear of all the Enlightened Ones, have never taught a behavior that ignores the meaning of the unborn!

[66. *The chapter on understanding that there is no conduct to accept or to reject*, 217.2–218.3]

9. *On Wisdom*

The teachers of the three dimensions, emanated from me, understand that it is necessary to eliminate hindrances in order to realize wisdom. This is what they teach their disciples, and this is what the disciples understand: attached to their own personal goals, they do not become disciples of mine.

Listen! I teach my disciples that all visible and audible phenomena are one single thing in the unborn fundamental condition. Therefore, I do not give rise to the distinction between hindering and not hindering, and consequently, I do not teach that wisdom can ever be hindered.

I do not deem the concepts of "hindering or not hindering" dualistic, I do not judge in quantitative terms the true meaning where there is no goal, and do not seek to give rise to the essence by basing myself on cause and effect.

Listen! My teaching does not correspond to what is taught by the teachers of the three dimensions. I do not measure the unborn, single condition in order to define the quantity of its characteristics, I do not judge in terms of consciousness and object, and I do not rely on antidotes. As knowledge and ignorance are one single thing in the ultimate dimension of the unborn, I do not divide what is one by means of dualistic thought. I do not produce judgements, I do not constrain perception within or follow a method of alternation [to abide in the true nature], yet I know everything instantaneously. Understand this, Sattvavajra!

Listen! My wisdom cannot be fathomed, and it transcends all numbers. Explaining diverse wisdoms related to specific qualities does not lead to true understanding.

Listen! My wisdom does not involve judgement and it transcends conceptual elaboration. It is supremely serene, without even an infinitesimal particle, just like the sky: hence it is called "unborn." Without ever separating from single self-arising wisdom, the diverse forms manifest distinctly in clarity without being altered. Whoever understands and realizes this [state] is the child of the supreme source.[226] Sattvavajra, realize this knowledge of unborn wisdom!

Listen! I am wisdom, the supreme source: I dispel the view of ignorance, I sever all the nets of hindrances, I make the light of wisdom blaze forth.

I am the source, self-arising wisdom. No wisdom exists that does not derive from me, all wisdoms are my manifestation: thus I am called "supreme wisdom." Those who wish to see their passions shine forth as wisdom must understand this teaching of mine!

[67. *The chapter on understanding that knowledge has no hindrances*, 219.4–221.2]

10. On Self-perfection

I am the teacher, the supreme source. I am self-perfected and not the object of a quest. I will show you my nature: understand it well!

Listen! I am the teacher, the supreme source. As my nature is difficult to understand, the teachers of the three dimensions, emanated from me, teach that I must be sought through specific means. How?

[The śrāvakas] teach that on entering the path of the four noble truths, it is necessary to strive to renounce the passions and to increase wisdom.

Attached to the path [of the twelve links] of interdependence, [the pratyekabuddhas] teach that it is necessary to strive to block the passions and to obtain wisdom.

After having introduced their disciples to the path of the two truths, [the Bodhisattvas] teach that it is necessary to obtain the fruit through striving and training oneself.

On the basis of the effort of dualistic actions, [the followers of kriyā] deem realization to be abiding in the manifestation of the deity.

On the basis of the effort of action and meditation, [the followers of ubhaya] deem the fruit can be obtained by means of accepting and rejecting.

On the basis of the effort of the three contemplations, [the followers of yoga] believe they can obtain the fruit by means of accepting and rejecting.

On the basis of the effort of meditation entailing the radiation and re-absorption [of light], [the followers of mahāyoga] believe they can obtain the fruit that transcends accepting and rejecting.

On the basis of the effort of meditation on cause and effect, [the followers of anuyoga] believe they can obtain the fruit of the three kāyas of Vajrasattva.

Listen! All these results entail quest and effort; however, they do not enable understanding of my nature. [...]

Listen! I, the teacher, the source, pure and total consciousness, am all-pervading like the sky, therefore I am in contact with everything and benefit everybody: thus there is no need to seek me and to obtain me through effort.

What I have taught you serves to enable you to understand that there is nothing to seek or to strive for. Transmit to my disciples this understanding that you have now obtained!

Listen! As I am self-perfected and beyond seeking, I have transmitted this understanding to you. Through it you will come to understand all phenomena in the same way that I understand them. Then, heartened by awareness that there is nothing whatever to obtain by effort, you will become the supreme source. Thus, wise Sattvavajra, transmit the knowledge "beyond effort" to those who have sacrificed themselves for many kalpas so that they too might abide effortlessly on the level of the unaltered state.

[*68. The chapter on understanding that self-perfection cannot be the result of a quest,* 221.4–222.4; 222.6–223.3]

III. CONCLUSION

Then Sattvavajra spoke to the supreme source, pure and total consiousness:

You are the supreme source. All phenomena of existence have been created by you, supreme doer. Everything is a manifestation of yours. Yet, in you who are the supreme doer, there is no need to act: everything is already accomplished from the beginning. [...]

Marvellous Sattvavajra, Body, Voice and Mind of all the Victorious Ones! Now that you have taken possession of the secret treasure, you are the supreme lion of speech. You are the Mind that understands the great secret. You are the Voice that expresses the ocean of secrets. You are the Body endowed with all the self-perfect qualities. You are the scion of the Victorious Ones. Like me, the supreme source, be the forbear of all the Victorious Ones! Dispel darkness everywhere! Be the teacher of all yogins! Transmit this further secret teaching, supreme among all secrets, to yogins!

[69. *The chapter that praises understanding*, 223.4–223–6; 224.7–225.3]

7 The Final Tantra: The Teachings on Meditation

I. INTRODUCTION

Sattvavajra, now experience the true state![227] Do not get distracted even for an instant from understanding of the single sphere of your mind that has no origin!

In the state of enlightenment, which is the true nature of existence beyond meditation, there is no duality between meditating and the object of meditation. So, if you leave the natural condition as it is without meditating, this is meditation!

The universal aim is that which has no origin, but if you recognize that thoughts and concepts, too, are this nature, then whatever arises in your mind, whatever you think about, you will never get distracted from the natural condition which has no origin. Thus, if you understand that whatever you think of is meditation, in whatever state you find yourself, without needing to meditate, there will be no distraction.

Listen! The teachers of the three dimensions, who have arisen from me, teach those who are attracted by conceptual meditation that which is most suitable to them and consequently, they uphold that it is necessary to meditate.

Listen! The single teacher, the supreme source, is wisdom of pure self-arising presence: the teachers [of the three dimensions] too are naturally comprised within it.

This single teacher teaches that there is no meditation to do and that his very teaching is beyond explanation and intellectual characteristics: the teachings [of the three dimensions] too are comprised within it.

The supreme abode of Akaniṣṭha, of pure unaltered presence, also contains the celestial abodes [of the three dimensions].

All the phenomena of existence are contained in pure and total presence, the essence. The three classes of disciples, too, and the various epochs are contained in it. There is nothing that is not spontaneously contained in self-arising wisdom.

This teaching on how to find the natural state without needing to meditate does not confirm assertions of the type "There is need to meditate" or "There is no need to meditate." Nor does it take into consideration the [dualistic] mind that grasps at hope and fear, at imagining or denying things through concepts.

[*70. The chapter that demonstrates whether or not it is necessary to meditate,* 227.1–228.3]

II. THE STATE OF NON-MEDITATION OF THE TEN NATURES

1. On the View

The teachers of the three dimensions, my emanations, teach methods of conceptual meditation to those involved in conceptual characteristics.

[The śrāvakas] teach meditation on the calm state, [the pratyekabuddhas,] that on the deep state.[228]

[The Bodhisattvas] teach meditation on the absence of identity that represents the union of calm state and deep vision.

[Followers of kriyā], having as their basis the concept of purity, visualize [themselves and the deity as] servant and lord.

[Followers of ubhaya], having as their basis the separation of view and conduct, abide in meditation in order to achieve union.

[Followers of yoga], on the basis of the state that transcends characteristics, abide in meditation endowed with characteristics.

[Followers of mahāyoga], having as their basis the purity of their own mind, abide in radiation and re-absorption of the three [contemplations].

[Followers of anuyoga], mainly having as their basis the purity of cause and effect, abide in contemplation of light. All these are conceptual meditations and do not represent my teaching.

This is my teaching. All is contemplation of the purity of the unborn, whether or not one meditates. All the phenomena of existence are the "object" of meditation without being conditioned by a particular method. Leaving them freely as they are is meditation!

Listen! As these secret instructions on "non-meditation" refer to the true meaning that transcends words and definitions, in reality the

Kunjed Gyalpos of the past have never taught anything, the Kunjed Gyalpos of the future will never teach anything, and the same applies to the Kunjed Gyalpos of the present.

Listen! The supreme source, teacher of teachers, transmits the fundamental meaning precisely. Speaking of meditating or not meditating in regard to the fundamental meaning that transcends all affirmations and negations is like fighting against the air!

The state in which there is no distraction from knowledge cannot be defined either as "concrete" or as "not concrete." As it transcends all limits and the very concept of "beyond limits," it cannot be confined within the limited definition of "meditating" or "not meditating."

Listen! Just as for me, the teacher of teachers, the supreme source, it is impossible to use the definitions of "meditating" or "not meditating," so you too, Sattvajra, and you practitioners abiding in the true meaning, try to be in this state!

Listen! The supreme source, teacher of the three times, has never defined the state of pure and total consciousness, saying, "It is thus!" It is not doing so now, and never will do so!

When one understands that there is no view on which to meditate, alternating between meditation and non-meditation becomes a deviation.

When one realizes the supreme unborn state, there is no longer even the concept of erring and not erring.

[71.*The chapter on the inseparability of view and state of knowledge*, 228.5–230.4*]*

2. On Commitment

As long as they remain on the path of conceptual characteristics, the teachers of the three dimensions, my emanations, distinguish between "keeping" and "not keeping" [the commitment], and in consequence they teach that it is necessary to observe the main and secondary rules.

Listen! From the beginning I, the supreme source, am the natural condition, and as this nature transcends the dualism of subject and object, whoever understands all phenomena in this manner does not even form the idea of keeping or not keeping.

Listen! I am the source, unaltered pure and total consciousness, I do not depend on antidotes and do not give birth to the consideration of an object. The commitment of the self-arising and self-perfected state of pure presence cannot be breached or damaged. Thus it is not something one has to guard intentionally.

Only authentic pure presence, unaltered by conceptual ideas, gives access to the fundamental meaning. As in the unborn state of consciousness dharmakāya has only one taste, I transcend the limit of "entering" or "not entering" it.

Listen! Sattvavajra, experience the true state! Unless the secret state of pure presence, the fundamental essence, arises, then even an expert in words and definitions will not meet my teaching.

From the beginning, this supreme state, in which there is no [commitment] to keep, pervades everything without needing to be guarded: unless one gains experience, any other way of keeping [the commitment] becomes an incurable disease!

Listen! This is the commitment of my state: through undistracted presence, without needing to make any alteration, all material phenomena manifest naturally as wisdom. When one masters pure presence, the limit of keeping or not keeping is transcended.

When all phenomena of existence are mastered through clarity as the self-arising essence, one is beyond the concepts of knowledge and ignorance regarding the total manifestation of the supreme source! [...]

I am the supreme source, pure and total consciousness, and as I transcend all assertions and negations, I do not think of anything and do not meditate on anything!

I do not correct body, voice, or mind: I let them relax. I do not discern planets, constellations, propitious dates and times. I do not visualize anything, nor do I use mudrās or mantras. The source, which is pure and total consciousness, does not know the boundary between keeping and not keeping [the commitment]!

[72. *The chapter that demonstrates that one cannot deviate from view and meditation*, 230.7–232.2; 232.4–232.6]

3. *On the Capacity for Spiritual Action*

I am the supreme source and, as my state transcends objectification by thought, it cannot at all become something on which to meditate.

Listen! Consciousness is the essence of the authentic condition, and I have never corrected this condition. Being self-arising, I have neither causes nor conditions, so leave body, voice, and mind in the relaxed state, without striving! Followers of methods tied to effort do not meet me, the source.

Listen! As my capacity for spiritual action knows no doing, I do not get involved in the effort of activities. Having no aim, I do not give birth to the consideration of "meditating."

As this state is beyond union and separation, maintain its presence without forgetfulness! When thoughts manifest as the unborn, without doing anything one accomplishes all the actions.

Listen! I am the teacher, the supreme source, and even though I have created all the spiritual actions of the Buddhas, the truth is, self-arising wisdom being perfect without the need to act, the natural condition has never acted.[229] Remain in the unaltered natural condition!

When mind and mental events[230] arise in this unaltered natural condition, that is the state of the enlightened ones; if one has the capacity to remain in the unborn, all ideas tied to action and effort can be overcome.

Sattvavajra, experience the natural condition! Naturally and undistractedly maintaining the view that liberates thoughts in their very condition, one overcomes action and effort. In this way all that arises liberates itself in itself.

Sattvavajra, experience the natural condition! Do not correct the body, do not control the senses, do not curb the voice: there is no action whatever to do. Wherever mind turns, leave it in the unperturbed state!

Experiencing this spiritual capacity that transcends action, even without acting at all one achieves all goals.

Listen! In the total bliss of the natural state that transcends effort, do not engage body, voice, or mind, do not correct them nor direct them towards a goal.

Do not get stuck in any idea, leave aside all concepts: remain in the bliss of self-arising wisdom. Precisely this is the state of self-arising clear light, the capacity for spiritual action of the state of the supreme source.

Sattvavajra, experience the natural condition! In order to accede to the unaltered natural state, there is no need of logic nor antidotes to correct anything. Remain in knowledge without altering anything!

Listen! This natural activity that transcends actions is not accomplished through effort of body, voice, and mind. When one is in the state of the supreme source, its capacity for spiritual action manifests already self-perfected!

[73. *The chapter that demonstrates how to abide in the condition "as it is" without acting and seeking*, 233.1–234.7]

4. On the Maṇḍala

Sattvavajra, experience the natural condition! I, teacher of teachers, the supreme source, teach that the essence cannot be created: this means that the natural condition transcends the distiction between central [deity] and secondary [deities of the maṇḍala].

Listen! When one clearly masters the supreme state of pure presence, the supreme wisdom of understanding enables the obtainment of the essence that transcends all effort. Precisely this is the maṇḍala of the supreme source.

Listen! Here is how the supreme source, teacher of teachers, manifests the essence in the maṇḍala of the Body: all visible phenomena abide in the unborn ultimate dimension. As the essence is beyond accepting and rejecting, [the maṇḍala of the Body] manifests from me, the source.

Listen! Here is how the supreme source, teacher of teachers, manifests the essence in the maṇḍala of the Voice: all audible phenomena abide in the Voice that issues from the unborn ultimate dimension and actually are the essence of the Voice that transcends explanation. Thus [the maṇḍala of the Voice,] too, manifests from me, the source.

Listen! Here is how the supreme source, teacher of teachers, manifests the essence in the maṇḍala of pure presence: all thoughts and concepts are recognized as the unborn supreme source itself.

The Body, Voice, and Mind of the supreme source are the three maṇḍalas of the unaltered natural condition. Understanding that they are instantaneously perfected without needing to be created, one accedes to the fundamental meaning of self-perfection.

Sattvavajra, experience! If you remain in this supreme maṇḍala of the self-arising essence, maintaining the natural condition and relaxing body, voice, and mind, you will be in my state!

The Kunjed Gyalpos of the past accomplished their aims remaining in the natural condition; the same applies to the present Kunjed Gyalpos and to those to come in the future.

[74. *The chapter that demonstrates how to abide in the fundamental meaning*, 235.2–236.5]

5. On Initiation

Sattvavajra, experience the natural condition! When one clearly masters the supreme state of pure presence, one no longer depends on initiation into a sensation of bliss tied to conceptual characteristics.[231] When understanding arises, one remains naturally in the non-conceptual state.

Listen! In the pure presence that arises after having received the empowerment of the supreme source,[232] material phenomena manifest continuously as the unaltered natural state. This is the supreme path to nirvāṇa that does not depend on causes and circumstances. [...]

Listen! This state of the [supreme] source in which pure presence holds sway cannot be expressed in words and transcends objectification by the mind; it appeases all thoughts and cannot be conceptualized; it is all-pervading like the sky and cannot be confined within a limited space.

Sattvavajra, experience the natural condition! When one transcends [the duality of] meditating and non-meditating, there is no longer either the wish to enter the state of meditation nor worry about leaving it, so one must not have the idea of "entering" the state of equality or of meditating on it. Without needing to receive an initiation or to obtain a siddhi, without altering anything, one abides in the state of the supreme source.

Listen! I am the teacher supreme source, the self-arising essence that is not something on which to meditate: the clarity of wisdom cannot be achieved by effort.

[*75. The chapter on the power of pure instantaneous presence*, 237.2–237.3; 237.5–238.1]

6. On the Path

Sattvavajra, listen! Now, without distraction, experience understanding of the single sphere of your unborn mind!

Similar to the sky, the path of the fundamental essence of the non-conceptual state is all-pervading. Thus there exists nothing other than the unborn that is not already meditation.

As it transcends objectification by analysis, this essence cannot be the target of concepts. As it is not the goal of a process, this essence that transcends conceptual characteristics cannot be reached by following a gradual path. Remaining in the bliss of the non-conceptual state, without following a gradual path or training to attain the various levels, one realizes self-perfection.

Listen! This path of the supreme source remains ever the same in the ultimate dimension of existence: thus it is not something that needs to be trodden.

When one is always together with the fundamental essence, there cannot any longer be distraction. As everything is already unified in the single sphere, there is no place to reach.

Sattvavajra, experience this reality! Unless you experience the state of "non-meditation" then even meditating for hundreds of kalpas on the basis of conceptual characteristics, you will not understand my state.

The state of the supreme source transcends all the characteristics of the object of thoughts: to find oneself in what is not subject to action, there is no need to perform any action. [...]

Sattvavajra, experience well the true state! I, the teacher, supreme source, have guided all the Buddhas of the three times, so now you too follow my path well! The Buddhas of the past have followed the unborn path, as will the Buddhas of the future, and it is precisely in the unborn that the Buddhas of the present abide. Thus the supreme source is the universal path!

Listen! From the first moment, practitioners who enter this path and meditate [according to it] find themselves on the level of the Enlightened Ones without their thoughts getting attached to the state of knowledge and without upholding a limited position. The fundamental path is beyond [the concept of] "entering" and "not entering" on a path.

Listen! The moment they receive transmission of knowledge of the supreme source, practitioners who have the capacity to accede instantaneously to the natural state are able to maintain the presence of movement of thoughts and to become familiar with it. Aside from this there is nothing to meditate on nor a state to enter: teach thus!

Listen! I am the teacher, the source, pure and total consciousness: all created phenomena issue from pure and total consciousness and are precisely the path leading to the unborn nature of mind. But the path to the happiness of the unborn is not something that can be "entered." By becoming familiar with it, the fortunate Bodhisattvas who know this path understand the fundamental essence beyond treading a path and beyond a quest such that they no longer have any doubts about the state of the supreme source.

[76. *The chapter on how to abide on the path of the fundamental essence,* 239.3–240.1; 240.2–241.2]

7. *On the Levels of Realization*

Listen! Even if the teachers of the three dimensions speak of diverse levels of realization, the level of the supreme source has no stages. On the other hand, what they teach their disciples is precisely the difference between one stage of realization and another.[233]

Listen! The supreme source, teacher of teachers, teaches that there are neither hindrances nor differences of levels for those who understand the essence and the method of the unborn nature of equality.

My nature is not something limited by the three times that can be entered and exited, neither can it become the object of thought. It cannot be subjected to any partial viewpoint nor sought as an object with specific characteristics. This is the true state of the supreme source!

Listen! My state cannot be found through indications by words or scriptures, nor can it be established through logical justifications or definitions. Never having been born, it cannot cease. It can neither be increased nor diminished. It is not endowed with conceptual characteristics, but not even this refutation can define it.

Listen! As I, the supreme source, teacher of teachers, empower all the phenomena of existence in the nature of the unborn, when one achieves understanding, everything becomes integrated in this state. [...]

The fundamental essence of non-meditation is maintaining undistracted presence: this is the secret instruction! This supreme source, pure and total consciousness, does not derive from explanations and verses [of the scriptures], nor does it depend on having or not having meditated. The true essence transcends all mantras and mudrās.

Listen! Those who follow the level I teach will free themselves of accepting and rejecting. Being in the all-pervading state free of directions, they will overcome the limit of "big and small." Abiding in the true dimension of phenomena, they will transcend the dualism of understanding and not understanding. So, Sattvavajra, remain perfectly at this instantaneous level!

[77. *The chapter that demonstrates that the true meaning is beyond any progress*, 241.6–242.5; 242.6–243.2]

8. On Conduct

Listen! I, the supreme source, teacher of teachers, display only the unborn nature of pure and total consciousness and do not teach that in order to attain the unaltered authentic state one needs to enter the dualism of accepting and rejecting.

The unborn nature transcends affirmations and refutations, while accepting and rejecting ineluctably imply affirming and refuting. Whoever enters the fundamental meaning realizes the state beyond affirming and refuting. On transcending all thoughts, one understands the true nature beyond accepting and rejecting.

Sattvavajra, experience the fundamental nature! I am the authentic fundamental nature, and judgements tied to accepting and rejecting cannot alter me: one acquires familiarity with my state through naturally existing supreme bliss. On understanding the supreme source, all returns to abide in the essence.

Thus, this essence is not something to accept or reject, neither is it an entity subject to birth and cessation, nor can it be defined as good or bad, pure or impure. Therefore it is said to transcend objectification by analysis or reasoning.

Sattvavajra, experience now! Meditating and the object of meditation are both the unaltered nature of pure and total consciousness, beyond the consideration of meditating or not meditating.

Listen! I, the supreme source, pure and total consciousness, do not teach my disciples accepting and rejecting. I do not teach dividing that which is one. I do not teach reasoning and analyzing in order to transcend analysis and reasoning. I do not teach correcting something in order to attain the unaltered condition. I teach that remaining naturally in the very condition of everything one does and perceives, without thinking of anything, is the way to self-liberate!

Sattvavajra, experience now! As the natural condition of enlightenment, beyond accepting and rejecting, is like the sky, the body and mind should not be altered. As [in this state] there is no attachment caused by mental judgement, there is nothing on which to meditate.

Like the sky, this state is utterly serene, beyond all impurities. [Abiding in it] one does not enter into the idea of an object, nor does one make knowledge one's object.

Sattvavajra, experience well now! Do not let yourself get caught up in judging sense objects, yet at the same time do not retain the mind within: without using antidotes, without purifying body and mind,[234] understand that the unaltered condition of body and mind is the fundamental essence itself!

Listen! Remaining effortlessly relaxed in the behavior of the supreme source, all aims are realized. As all is unified in this essence, there is nothing any more to accept or reject. As there is no hope or fear, the state beyond suffering is no longer the goal of meditation.[235]

Whoever understands my behavior completely transcends any definition of "entering" or "not entering" the unborn state of equality of the three times. This is the meaning of "nothing to accept or reject."

[78. *The chapter that demonstrates that in equality there is neither acceptance nor rejection*, 243.4–245.4]

9. On Wisdom

The supreme source, teacher of teachers, teaches that the unhindered essence is the true state of knowledge. All the phenomena of existence are one single thing in the ultimate unborn dimension. Thus, in the state of Mind, the unborn essence, there is no distinction between being or not being hindered.

Sattvavajra, now experience well! As all is one single thing in the ultimate unborn dimension, those who wish to relinquish hindrances and to accept the unhindered state do not concur with the true meaning. According to the teaching of the supreme source, pure and total consciousness, by experiencing the unborn, all the phenomena that are continuously "being born" manifest as the essence. Whoever abides in the state that, like the sky, transcends analysis and judgement[236] understands that hindering and not hindering both abide in pure and total consciousness.

Listen! The aim of this teaching that the supreme source transmits to disciples is to clarify the meaning of wisdom that cannot be hindered: in fact, it abides in the self-arising essence that does not depend on causes or conditions. It is the state of knowlege that, once understood, brings one beyond affirming and refuting.

So, Sattvavajra, experience now! Self-arising wisdom is beyond all objects of the mind: do not make "understanding" become an object on which to fix. As it transcends any object, it does not in any way curb ordinary mental consciousness. As all material phenomena manifest as the essence, it does not meditate at all. As forms manifest as the essence, it has no room at all for the dualism of hope and fear.

Listen! The teacher of teachers, the supreme source, teaches his disciples the unaltered state, enabling them to understand definitively the unaltered essence that is the root of all phenomena. Understanding the single fundamental nature, all is unified in the state of the supreme source, that is the universal nature. So, whoever knows perfectly the supreme source also becomes expert in all infinite phenomena. Whoever acquires familiarity with my state acquires familiarity with [the nature of] every thing.

Sattvavajra, experience well! The conclusion of everything is understanding and acquiring familiarity with the essence of what one perceives through sight and hearing. Whatever form the essence assumes, one understands its unborn nature. Undistracted presence beyond hope and fear is the true state of knowledge.

Sattvavajra, now experience well! Whatever form phenomena assume is only a means that symbolizes the supreme source: do not enter into conflict with this method of teaching!

Once my children have understood that all is the unborn state, they no longer think in terms of saṃsāra and nirvāṇa: the fundamental nature is totally beyond judgement and analysis!

[79. *The chapter on the state that knows no hindrances,* 245.6–247.5]

10. On Self-perfection

Sattvavajra, now experience well! I, the teacher supreme source, teach that all the phenomena of existence without exception are the nature of unborn mind.

Listen! As the nature of mind is self-perfected, I do not teach the dualism of realizing and not realizing. I do not judge in the dualistic terms of happiness and suffering. I am free from hope for nirvāṇa and fear of saṃsāra.

As the nature of self-perfected mind manifests everywhere, I do not try to communicate that all is empty and that all has never arisen.[237] As the fundamental essence transcends judgement and analysis I do not get attached to the idea of realizing and establishing.

Listen, Sattvavajra. Now experience well! Just as I do not judge the self-perfected essence that transcends analysis in terms of realizing and not realizing, you do the same!

Listen! Those who get attached to the concept that in the self-perfected essence beyond action and seeking there is nothing to integrate are like children fighting the air: they do not see my nature. The minds of those who believe that integration consists in giving up something are still enslaved by hope and fear: but how can a practitioner who remains attached to the limit of "without limits" ever attain the essence of self-perfection?

Listen, Sattvavajra! Experience well! On perceiving the utterly pure unborn state, one no longer deems appearances as concrete or gets attached to it.[238] When appearances self-liberate in the unborn, without needing to meditate on emptiness, one self-liberates by understanding the authentic condition.

I, the supreme source, teacher of teachers, teach that all the phenomena of existence are unborn and totally pure. Thus whatever thing is "born" I understand as the essence.

Listen! The teachers of the three dimensions that emanate from me all speak of the "unborn nature of mind," but even if they discuss at length the meaning of "without self-nature,"[239] they do not understand the true "unborn."

Thus, the aim of this teaching of mine is to communicate the essence and to enable one to remain in this state without being distracted. However, it does not at all imply the application of effort, purification of the mind by means of antidotes, concentration on an object, or withdrawal of the mind within. As whatever manifests is the fundamental nature, enter my state, the supreme source!

Listen! The supreme source, teacher of teachers, teaches disciples the unaltered nature of mind. The yogin who understands that all is the unborn has no need to apply effort regarding the ten natures.

In the nature of pure and total consciousness there is no dualism of subject and object and nothing to reject: when understanding conquers everything else and one is really in this dimension the state of self-perfection of the supreme source manifests spontaneously.

[*80. The chapter that demonstrates the key to the fundamental meaning,* 247.7–249.6]

III. CONCLUSION

If, Sattvavajra, you understand well this teaching on pure and total consciousness that is the root of all the vehicles, the root that is enclosed in the supreme source, you will become the Victorious One of the Victorious Ones, the supreme source. So, Sattvavajra, teach this state to my disciples! Teach that saṃsāra and nirvāṇa are one in the ultimate dimension! Teach that cause and effect are already perfect in the same instant!

[*81. The chapter that demonstrates the key to the fundamental meaning,* 253.4–253.7]

Teacher of teachers, supreme source! You are the root that manifests from the self-arising wisdom of your single Mind, so I pay homage to you, the essence of phenomena!

Teacher of teachers, supreme source! Dispelling the path of ignorance, you make the light of wisdom shine everywhere. I pay homage to you, supreme source!

Being self-arising, all the phenomena that manifest to perception transcend any cause and condition. Illuminating the authentic unaltered condition of the fundamental essence, [you enable one to understand that,] however much one may examine the state of the supreme source, self-arising wisdom is free of the limits of center, range, and depth. It is the origin of everything and transcends all thoughts. It is beyond birth and cessation, beyond concepts, and pacifies everything. [On discovering that] in this state there is no concept of holy and mean, those who [used to] nurture concepts [finally] attain bliss beyond effort and are thus given heart. Abiding in the supreme source, the root of phenomena, means being beyond all effort.

Thus spoke Sattvavajra.

[*82. The chapter of praise*, 255.2–256.1]

This teaching that directly discloses knowledge of the essence of enlightenment and that transcends any base must be given to those who have faith, who keep their commitments, and are diligent; who have compassion, have forbearance, are saddened [by saṃsāra], and do not change their mind; and who are capable of offering without attachment but with faith and delight their own body, their children, their spouse, servants, and property. All of this being a sign of faith and commitment, as they understand the fundamental meaning [such disciples] are worthy to receive [this teaching].

The fundamental meaning and the teaching of the unborn should be transmitted to whomever shows signs of having renounced fame and of being free from pride, of not sparing body and life in order to realize the fundamental sense, and not violating orders.

"Now that I have found the essential teaching, how can I any longer be conditioned by the characteristics of worldly things? Now that I have found the teaching, I will act in accord with the teacher's instructions!" This teaching should be transmitted to anyone who takes this commitment.

"Teacher, as long as you and I are alive, until body and life separate, I will act in accord with your instructions!" The *Kunjed Gyalpo*, essence of the teaching, should be imparted to anyone who takes such a vow.

In brief, one's body and life too must be offered up, let alone material things, land and livestock! Even though they do not need them, the teachers will accept all things and offer them to the Three Jewels.

[*83. The chapter that indicates to whom the teaching should be transmitted*, 256.6–257.5]

Listen! The teacher of teachers, the supreme source, will disclose to you his diverse names.

As all perceptible phenomena, those created, those being created, and those to be created, manifest self-perfected in me without my needing to act, I am called "supreme source."

Listen! As I, the fundamental essence, am without impurities, and I, being self-perfected and not to be sought, am not the object of a quest nor of striving, I am called "pure and total consciousness."

Listen! As in the uncreated, primordially existing ultimate nature, the essence that transcends causes and conditions and that cannot be sought shines equanimously and unhindered in all directions, I am called "self-arising wisdom."

Listen! As all perceptible phenomena without exclusion manifest in me, I, the unaltered authentic condition, am beyond dualistic division and all limits. Thus I am called "the mirror of phenomena that explains the scriptures."

Listen! As the true essence of the unaltered, authentic condition utterly embraces saṃsāra and nirvāṇa, [thanks to me] everything self-liberates from the net of acceptance and rejection, of grasping and attachment. Thus I am called "the vehicle of the fundamental meaning."

Listen! As the Buddhas of past, present, and future do not see or conceive anything but the unborn, I am the unaltered sphere that transcends the dualism of subject and object. Thus I am called "the mirror of the view."

Listen! As I, the essence and the unaltered authentic condition, transcend all conceptual elaborations tending to confirm or deny me, the Buddhas of the three times originate from me. Thus I am called "mother of the Victorious Ones."

Listen! As I, the unborn and unaltered supreme source, completely possess all the necessary qualities without needing to seek them, I transcend all seeking and striving. Thus I am called the "king of tantras."

[*84. The chapter that illustrates the diverse names*, 259.1–260.3]

Epilogue: On the Nature of Samantabhadra

A Conversation with Chögyal Namkhai Norbu

Question: Is it possible to conceive of a being that has never entered into dualism, into saṃsāra?

Answer: Reading certain tantras it would seem that originally, by the magic of knowledge and of ignorance, on one side there arose Samantabhadra, the first Buddha, and on the other side beings who transmigrate. However, this should be mainly understood as a metaphor to enable us to discover our real condition. If we deem Samantabhadra an individual being, we are far from the true meaning. In reality, he denotes our potentiality that, even though at the present moment we are in saṃsāra, has never been conditioned by dualism. From the beginning, the state of the individual has been pure and always remains pure: this is what Samantabhadra represents. But when we fall into conditioning, it is as if we are no longer Samantabhadra because we are ignorant of our true nature. So what is called the primordial Buddha, or Ādibuddha, is only a metaphor for our true condition.

Question: What does it mean, then, that Samantabhadra is the "first" enlightened one and that he has never transmigrated?

Answer: We cannot talk about the true condition of the primordial state in terms of "before" and "after," as if there was somebody before and then something else arose. These are all limited concepts, and it is necessary to go beyond time. Samantabhadra means our state, and should not be interpreted as God in the sense of a supreme entity who is the only creator, for example.

Question: In some texts it says "Recognizing his state, Samantabhadra self-liberated, while we, who did not recognize it, started to transmigrate." If Samantabhadra is our own state, why does it say this?

Answer: Samantabhadra is our knowledge, the state of knowledge that has always remained as it is. Even though it says that Samantabhadra "self-liberated," actually there is nothing to liberate. From the very beginning Samantabhadra is free from the concept of liberation, but when we are ignorant of our condition then we cannot speak of liberation: Samantabhadra does not manifest.

Question: Couldn't this lead us to think that two entities co-exist within us: one transmigrates, while the other does not?

Answer: It's not a matter of two entities. The point is we are ignorant of our condition and this is the cause of samsaric vision, but there are not two entities. Our condition is only one, but it is as if it were a wrapped jewel that we cannot see. Samantabhadra is dharmakāya, is bodhicitta that is spoken about so much in Dzogchen. But unless one knows it, it remains merely a word. Then the concept also arises: "There is something inside us [that does not transmigrate]." This is already a sign of ignorance, isn't it?

Question: Could we then say that we are a manifestation of Samantabhadra?

Answer: No, we ourselves are Samantabhadra, but because we don't understand it, we are ignorant of it. This ignorance produces dualistic vision and leads us to formulate the question: "Where is Samantabhadra? Inside us or outside us?" But we do not find anything, because, as I have just said, this is a sign of ignorance.

Question: But if all beings are Samantabhadra, can we say that there are infinite Samantabhadras?

Answer: We could also think that there are infinite Samantabhadras, but when we are in the state of Samantabhadra, what does "infinite" mean? This is already a limited viewpoint. The true condition is beyond numbers. If we think in terms of an "individual being" this means that we are limiting, and consequently everything becomes complicated. If we want to understand, then we must not limit.

Question: In every tantra there is a dialogue, such as the dialogue between dharmakāya and saṃbhogakāya in the *Kunjed Gyalpo* tantra. What is the real meaning of this?

Answer: It is a way of communicating knowledge. The transmission of knowledge comes from the state of rigpa that has never been stained and has never been hindered. This is the Ādibuddha, or "primordial Buddha," Kunjed Gyalpo.

Question: Is the state of Ādibuddha, or Kunjed Gyalpo, something universal, present in all beings?

Answer: The state of Kunjed Gyalpo is knowledge, and in knowledge there is not even the concept of "one and two," otherwise we have already entered into dualism. Also the concept of "individual" presupposes dualistic vision. But Samantabhadra is beyond all this, isn't he?

Appendices

APPENDIX ONE
Transmission of the Four *Kāyas* According to the *Bai ro 'dra ' bag*

Note: The following is a summary of a section of Chapter One of the Bai ro 'dra 'bag, *Bibliography no. 16, Lhasa, ff. 3a.1-5b.4.*

First of all, in the Akaniṣṭha dimension, for those able to understand, there arose the Mantrayāna, particularly the marvellous atiyoga teaching, through four diverse transmissions: of the svabhāvikakāya, of the dharmakāya, of the saṃbhogakāya, and of the secret kāya (*gsang ba'i sku*).

The teaching of the svabhāvikakāya originated from the immeasurable vastness of the fundamental nature (*dharmadhātu*) in the all-pervading dimension of total self-perfection. The place where the teaching is transmitted is the heavenly palace of pure presence (*rig pa*) beyond concepts, adorned with the ornaments of wisdom that is all-penetrating without material hindrances, without center or border. The teacher is the svabhāvikakāya [or dimension of the fundamental nature], the essence of the self-arising state of enlightenment in the aspect of the five kāyas. The assembly consists of all the Vidyādharas of self-perfection, regents of the Buddhas of the three times, inseparable from the dimension of the fundamental nature. The epoch is infinite time. The teaching is not communicated by word or symbol but through the natural clarity of the dharmakāya. The moment the assembly realizes the state of the teacher, they become inseparable from it in a condition of total equality. The teachings are collected by Samantabhadra, absorbing in the space of pure presence the contents of atiyoga.

Regarding the teaching of the dharmakāya, the place is the ultimate Akaniṣṭha, a heavenly palace that is the manifestation of clarity, without outside or inside. The teacher is the dharmakāya Samantabhadra who abides in the state of total bliss beyond union and separation. The assembly consists of saṃsāra and nirvāṇa in their entirety, and in particular of the vidyādharas of self-perfection in their saṃbhogakāya manifestations, inseparable from the state of dharmakāya. The time is the absolute equality of the fourth time, the indivisibility of past, present, and future. The teaching is not transmitted by word or symbol: Samantabhadra transmits knowledge of the fundamental nature by means of the empowering flow. In this way the disciples realize the state of the teacher, the nature that transcends birth and cessation and become equal to Samantabhadra. The teachings are gathered by Vajrasattva, absorbing in the space of pure presence the teachings on the phases of creation, of completion, and of total perfection, and in particular the contents of atiyoga.

Regarding the teaching of the saṃbhogakāya, the place is the palace of the fundamental nature of Akaniṣṭha in the pure dimension of Sukhāvatī, a heavenly abode made of precious substances that gives the impression of being inside looking out and of being outside looking in. The teacher of this maṇḍala dimension, who can be one of the five Tathāgatas and in particular Vajrasattva, is endowed with all the characteristic signs of the saṃbhogakāya, with a profusion of jewels and other ornaments. The time is the time of contemplation of pure presence. The teachings are communicated through the symbols of the manifestation of a saṃbhogakāya Buddha that pervades the ten directions without front or back. The disciples who realize this state become vidyādharas of the five kāyas. The teaching consists of the three series of creation, completion, and total perfection, but particularly the three series of outer tantras. The teachings are collected by Guhyapati Vajradhara.

Regarding the teaching of the secret kāya, the place is the repository (*za ma tog*) of the secret mother, where immaculate bliss gives birth to all the Buddhas. The teacher is the secret kāya, a form of total bliss of the saṃbhogakāya that confers the secret empowerment (*gsang dbang*). The assembly consists of the vidyādharas of the five kāyas and in particular of the saṃbhogakāya. The time is the time of the secret empowerment. The teaching consists of the deep secret empowerment and of the empowerment of wisdom tied to the immaculate bliss of emptiness. The disciples who realize the wisdom of total bliss achieve enlightenment and become equal to the teacher. The teachings are gathered by Guhyapati Vajrapāṇi.

APPENDIX TWO

The Lineage of Teachers from Oḍḍiyāna and India After Mañjuśrīmitra

Note: The names are given according to the spellings found in the original texts, except in the case of obvious errors.

Bibliography no. 21, p. 138:

1. 'Da' he na ta lo
2. Sras thu bo Ha ti
3. Sras mo Pa ra ni
4. gNod sbyin mo byang chub (rGyal po yon tan lag gi bu mo)

5. rMad 'tshong ma Pa ra na
6. Kha che'i mkhan po Rab snang
7. Urgyan kyi mkhan po Ma ha ra ja
8. Sras mo Go ma de byi
9. A rya A lo ke
10. Khyi'i rgyal po Gu gu ra ja
11. Drang srong Ba sha ti
12. rMad 'tshong ma bDag nyid ma
13. Nāgārjuna
14. Gu gu ra ja phyi ma
15. 'Jam dpal bshes gnyen phyi ma
16. Lha'i mkhan po Ma ha ra
17. Bu dha kug ta
18. Śrī Siṃha
19. dGe slong ma Kun dga' ma
20. Vimalamitra

Bibliography no. 30, p. 298:

1. Dha he na te lo
2. Sras thu bo Ra ja ha sti
3. Sras mo Sarani
4. Klu'i rgyal po
5. Ku ku ra ja
6. Nāgārjuna
7. Khyi'i rgyal po phyi ma
8. gNod sbyin mo Byang chub
9. sMad 'tshong ma Bud dha ma ti
10. 'Jam dpal bshes gnyen phyi ma
11. A rya pa lo
12. O rgyan gyi mkhan po Dha he
13. Drang srong Bhi sha ti
14. Sras mo Go ma de bi
15. Kha che'i rgyal po Rab snang
16. rGyal po Devarāja
17. Dharmaraja
18. Buddhagupta
19. Śrī Siṃha

Bibliography no. 13, p. 86:

1. rGyal po Dha na ta lo
2. Sras thu bo Ra ja has ti
3. Sras mo Wa ra ni
4. Klu'i rgyal po 'jog po
5. Sras mo gNod sbyin mo byang chub
6. gZung ma a ra li
7. sLob dpon Akshobhya
8. Khyi'i mkhan po slob dpon Kukurāja
9. sMad 'tshong ma buddha samaya
10. sMad 'tshong ma buddha samati
11. O rgyan gyi mkhan po Mahārāja
12. Sras mo Go ma de wi
13. sLob dpon Aloke
14. Khyi'i mkhan po phyi ma
15. Lha'i mkhan po Mahārāja
16. Drang srong Bha shi ta
17. gZung ma bDag nyid ma
18. sLob dpon Nāgārjuna
19. sLob dpon Devarāja
20. 'Jam dpal bshes gnyen phyi ma ('Jam dpal bzang po)
21. Rigs 'dzin dge bsnyen legs pa
22. sLob dpon Sangs rgyas gsang ba
23. sLob dpon Śrī Siṃha

Bibliography no. 7, p. 582:

1. rGyal po Dha na ta la
2. Du bo Rajati
3. Sras mo Me tog gsal
4. Klu rgyal dga' bo
5. gNod sbyin mo Byang chub ma
6. gZugs tshong ma Sa ra ni
7. Kha che'i gnas brtan Rab snang
8. O rgyan gyi dge slong Mahārāja

9. Sras mo Go ma de wa
10. Acarya Aloke
11. Kukurāja snga ma
12. Drang srong Bhashi
13. sMad tshong ma bDag nyid ma
14. Nāgārjuna
15. Kukurāja phyi ma
16. 'Jam dpal bshes gnyen phyi ma
17. Drang srong Devarāja
18. Bhutikuna
19. Śrī Siṃha
20. Vimalamitra
20b. dGe slong ma Kun dga' mo

Bibliograpy 32, p. 402:

1. rGyal po Danatalo
2. rGyal bu Rājahati
3. Warani
4. Klu 'jog po
5. gNod sbyin mo
6. Barini
7. Kha che'i mkhan po Rab snang
8. Budha Kukurāja
9. O rgyan mkhan po Mahārāja
10. Gomadewi
11. Aloki
12. Kukurāja phyi ma
13. Drang srong Bhashita
14. bDag nyid ma
15. Klu sgrub
16. 'Jam dpal bshes gnyen phyi ma
17. rNam snang Budhagupta
20. Śrī Siṃha
21. Kun dga' mo

APPENDIX THREE
Dzogchen Scriptures Tied to the Transmission of Vairocana

Note: In this appendix are listed the teachings received, translated, and transmitted by Vairocana according to some traditional texts. The list is not meant to be exhaustive.

A: Teachings received from Śrī Siṃha
rGyud nyi shu rtsa lnga

Bibliography no. 8, p. 318:

1. *Nam mkha' che rgyas pa'i rgyud*
2. *Nam mkha' che rgyas pa phyi rta'i (spyi ti'i. rgyud)*
3. *Nam mkha' che grol ba'i rgyud*
4. *Tika rgyal po'i rgyud*
5. *Byang sems thig le'i rgyud*
6. *Ye shes thig le'i rgyud*
7. *Man ngag 'phreng ba'i rgyud*
8. *gSang ba rgyal po'i rgyud*
9. *Shes rab ye shes thig le'i rgyud*
10. *dByings rnam par dag pa'i rgyud*
11. *Man ngag snying po'i rgyud*
12. *sNying po sid dhi'i rgyud*
13. *Nam mkha' che rtsa ba can gyi rgyud*
14. *Nyag gcig dgongs pa'i rgyud*
15. *bSam gtan gcig pa'i rgyud*
16. *bSam gtan brgyud pa'i rgyud*
17. *sGo mang gi rgyud*
18. *Nam mkha' che dbang gi rgyal po'i rgyud*
19. *Nam mkha' che yi ge med pa'i rgyud*
20. *Rin chen 'bar ba'i rgyud*
21. *Rin chen sgron me'i rgyud*
22. *Rin chen phreng ba'i rgyud*
23. *Nges pa snying po'i rgyud*
24. *rDo rje gsang ba'i rgyud*
25. *Ye nas sangs rgyas kyi rgyud*

Bibliography no. 24, p. 75:

1. *Nam mkha' che rgyas pa'i rgyud*
2. *Nam mkha' che rgyas pa spyi ti'i rgyud*

3. *Nam mkha' che grol ba'i rgyud*
4. *Yang tig rgyal po'i rgyud*
5. *Byang chub sems kyi thig le'i rgyud*
6. *Ye shes thig le'i rgyud*
7. *Man ngag 'phreng ba'i rgyud*
8. *gSang ba rgya mtsho'i rgyud*
9. *Shes rab ye shes kyi rgyud*
10. *dByings rnam par dag pa'i rgyud*
11. *sNying po spyi ti'i rgyud*
12. *Nam mkha' che bsams kyi rgyud*
13. *Nyag gcig dgongs pa'i rgyud*
14. *bSam gtan gcig pu'i rgyud*
15. *bSam gtan brgyud pa'i mdo rgyud*
16. *bKra shis sgron ma'i rgyud*
17. *Nam mkha' che dbang gi gal mdo'i rgyud*
18. *Ye shes sgron ma'i rgyud*
19. *Nam mkha' che yi ge med pa rtse mo'i rgyud*
20. *Rin po che 'bar ba'i rgyud*
21. *Rin po che sgron me'i rgyud*
22. *Rin po che phreng ba'i rgyud*
23. *Khams gsum sgron ma'i rgyud*
24. *Nges pa snying po'i rgyud*
25. *rDo rje rab tu gsang ba'i rgyud*
26. *Ye nas sangs rgyas pa'i rgyud*

Bibliography no. 3, p. 283:

1. *Nam mkha' che rgyas pa'i rgyud*
2. *Nam mkha' che rgyas pa phyi ma'i rgyud*
3. *Nam mkha' che grol ba'i rgyud*
4. *Yang tig rgyal po'i rgyud*
5. *Byang chub sems kyi thig le'i rgyud*
6. *gSang ba rgyal po'i rgyud*
7. *Shes rab ye shes thig le'i rgyud*
8. *dByings rnam par dag pa'i rgyud*
9. *Man ngag snying po'i rgyud*
10. *sNying po spyi ta'i rgyud*
11. *Nam mkha' che can gyi rgyud*

12. *Nyag gcig dgongs pa'i rgyud*
13. *bSam gtan gcig bu'i rgyud*
14. *bSam gtan brgyud pa'i mdo*
15. *sGo mangs kyi mdo*
16. *Nam mkha' che dbang gi gal po'i rgyud*
17. *Nam mkha' che yi ge med pa'i rgyud*
18. *Rin chen 'bar ba'i rgyud*
19. *Rin chen sgron me'i rgyud*
20. *Rin chen 'phreng ba'i rgyud*
21. *Khams gsum sgrol ma'i rgyud*
22. *Nges pa snying po'i rgyud*
23. *rDo rje gsang ba'i rgyud*
24. *Ye bsangs rgyas pa'i rgyud*

Lung chen bco brgyad

Bibliography no. 6, p. 349.5:

1. Rig pa'i khu byug
2. rTsal chen sprugs pa
3. Khyung chen lding ba
4. rDo la gser zhun
5. Mi nub pa'i rgyal mtshan
6. rTse mo byung rgyal
7. Nam mkha'i rgyal po
8. bDe ba 'phrul bkod
9. rdzogs pa spyi chings
10. Byang chub sems tig
11. bDe ba rab 'byams
12. Srog gi 'khor lo
13. Thig le drug pa
14. rdzogs pa spyi gcod
15. Yid bzhin nor bu
16. Kun 'dus rig pa
17. rJe btsun dam pa
18. bsGom ma don grub

Bibliography no. 16, f. 62b:

1. Rig pa'i khu byug
2. brTsal chen sprugs pa
3. Thig le drug pa
4. Khyung chen lding ba
5. Mi nub pa'i rgyal mtshan
6. Yid bzhin nor bu
7. rJe btsan dam pa
8. Yid spyod rgyal po
9. Rin chen kun 'dus
10. bDe 'jams
11. Srog gi 'khor lo
12. Sems kyi ti ka
13. Nam kha'i rgyal po
14. bDe ba 'phra bkod
15. sPyi 'chings
16. rDo la gser zhun
17. rTse mo byung rgyal
18. rMad du byung ba

Bibliography no. 30, pp. 298ff.:

1. Khyung chen
2. Rig pa'i khu byug
3. Nam mkha' che
4. Thig le drug pa
5. rTsal chen
6. Sems sgom
7. rMad byung
8. Yid bzhin nor bu
9. rTse mo byung rgyal
10. sPyi gcod
11. sPyi chings
12. bDe ba 'phra bkod
13. Srog gi 'khor lo

14. Rin chen kun 'dus
15. sKye med rang rig
16. bDe ba rab 'byams
17. Nam mkha rgyal po
18. rJe btsun dam pa

Bibliography no. 8, p. 320:

1. Rig pa'i khu byug
2. rTsal chen
3. Khyung chen
4. Byang sems sgom pa rdo la gser zhun
5. Mi nub rgyal mtshan nam mkha' che
6. gNad du gyur pa
7. rJe btsan dam pa
8. Yang tig
9. Srog gi 'khor lo
10. Yid bzhin nor bu
11. Kun 'dus
12. Nam mkha' che rgyal po
13. rTse mo byung rgyal
14. bDe 'byams
15. bDe ba phra bkod
16. rTogs chen
17. Phyir chings

Bibliography no. 24, p. 78:

1. Rig pa'i khu byug
2. Rig pa rTsal chen
3. lTa ba Khyung chen
4. rDo la gser zhun
5. Mi nub rgyal mtshan nam mkha' che
6. Ye shes rMad du byung ba
7. bsGom don grub pa
8. rJe btsun dam pa
9. sKye med ti la ka
10. Srog gi 'khor lo
11. Yid bzhin nor bu

12. Rin chen kun 'dus
13. Nam mkha' che ba rgyal po
14. rTse mo byung rgyal
15. bDe ba rab 'byams
16. bDe ba phra bkod
17. sNa tshogs gter chen
18. bKa' lung gi spyi chings

Bibliography no. 3, p. 294:

1. Nam mkha' che
2. Khyung chen
3. rTsal chen
4. Rig pa'i khu byug
5. sGom pa don drug ma
6. rMad du byung ba
7. Nam mkha'i rgyal po
8. rDo la gser zhun
9. bDe la phra bkod
10. Byang chub sems thig
11. Kun btus
12. bDe 'jam snying po
13. rdzogs pa spyi spyod
14. Yid bzhin nor bu
15. rJe btsan dam pa
16. sPyi rgyud spungs pa
17. rTse mo byung rgyal

Bibliography no. 6, p. 349.6:

1. Rig pa'i khu byug
2. rTsal chen sprugs pa
3. Khyung chen lding ba
4. rDo la gser zhun
5. Mi nub pa'i rgyal mtshan
6. rTse mo byung rgyal
7. Nam mkha'i rgyal po
8. bDe ba 'phrul bkod
9. rdzogs pa spyi chings

10. Byang chub sems tig
11. bDe ba rab 'byams
12. Srog gi 'khor lo
13. Thig le drug pa
14. rdzogs pa spyi gcod
15. Yid bzhin nor bu
16. Kun 'dus rig pa
17. rJe btsun dam pa
18. bsGom pa don grub

Other teachings

Bibliography no. 16, ff. 62-65:

Man ngag rgya mtsho'i klong
Klong sde'i skor
rGyud sde'i skor
Ke'u tshang gi skor
Gab pa'i skor
Shan 'byed pa bram ze'i skor
La zlo ba rgyal po'i skor
Rang grol mngon sum gyi skor
rTsa ba'i rgyud lnga
Yan lag gi rgyud nyi shu rtsa lnga
Klong dgu la sogs pa sprul sku dga' rab rgyal ba'i bka' man ngag bco brgyad
Rig 'dzin gyi gnyen yig bzhi
Ku ku ra dza nyi ma'i snying po 'od dang ldan pa
Śri Siṃha'i rgyan 'phreng 'od gsum dang bSam gtan nyams kyi sgron ma

B: The first teachings translated by Vairocana on his return to Tibet from Oḍḍiyāna

Bibliography no. 16, f. 77b:

Man ngag chos

Nam mkha' che legs pa'i bstod gyur pa
Yul ni kun la 'jug pa'i sham bu brtags (Khyung chen)
Ku bhyug
rTsal chen phu dung
Byang sems don drug

rGyud lung chos

gShin rje'i gtam rgyud
Rin chen mdo rgyud
dBang bskur rgyal po'i rgyud
Nam mkha' che la sogs pa rgyud lnga
rMad du byung ba
Kun byed rgyal po
mDo bcu

rGya mtsho klong

Nang sngags tan tra sde bco brgyad
Ma ha yo ga'i rgyud sde bcu drug

[Bai ro tsa na nyid kyis mdzad pa'i chos]

sNyan rgyud thugs kyi snying khu'i rgyud mdo

Bibliography no. 15, p. 432:

Nam mkha' che
Legs pa'i stod gur
Yul rnams kun la 'jug pa'i sham bu btags (=Khyung chen)
Khu byug
rTsal chen phu dungs
Byang sems don grub
rGyud lung chos
gShin rje'i gtam rgyud
Rin chen 'od rgyud
dBang bskur rgyal po'i rgyud
Nam mkha' che la sogs pa'i rgyud lnga
rMad du byung ba
Kun byed rgyal po
mDo bcu
rGya mtsho klong
Nang sngags tan tra sde bco brgyad
Ma ha yo ga'i rgyud sde bcu drug

Bai ro tsa na nyid kyis mdzad pa'i chos

sNyan brgyud thugs kyi snying khu

C: Teachings transmitted to rGyal mo g.Yu sgra snying po

Note: This section is based exclusively on Klong chen chos 'byung, *Bibliography no. 3, pp. 292-298. I have also consulted the edition in two volumes published in Delhi in 1975, where these lists are given on pages 46-60 of the second volume.*

According to this tradition, rDzogs chen *scriptures are divided into four categories: the external teachings* (phyi skor), *the internal teachings* (nang skor), *the secret teachings* (gsang skor) *and the treasure cave* (ke'u tshang skor) *teachings. The external teachings include nine series:* rgyud sde, sems sde, klong sde, bam po'i skor, mdo lung, rdzogs chen ma bu'i skor, man ngag rdzong 'phrang gi skor, man ngag snyan brgyud kyi skor, man ngag bsam btan gyi skor. *The internal teachings include six series:* bram ze'i skor, rig pa'i skor, gab pa'i skor, rmad du byung ba'i skor, snying po'i skor, rdzogs chen lde mig gi skor. *The secret teachings include nine series not listed here. The treasure cave teachings include six series:* 'phrul gzhi zab mo skor, rin po che rgyas pa'i skor, nyi ma'i 'khor lo zab mo skor, rgyal po'i bla gter zab mo skor, za 'og ber khyim zab mo skor, rgyud pa tha ma zab mo skor. *Other teachings are also listed. I have met some difficuties in coordinating these lists and I have not yet come across other texts that might help clarify the different categories. My main purpose has been to list as many* rDzogs chen *texts as possible for future reference.*

I. rDzogs pa chen po phyi skor (A ti phyi skor sems phyogs)

1. rGyud sde'i skor

[rGyud sde chen po bcu drug]

rTsa ba'i rgyud lnga

1. *bKra shis mi 'gyur gsal bar gnas pa'i rgyud*
2. *Yon tan rdzogs pa rnam par rol pa'i rgyud*
3. *Yul kun la 'jug pa rnam dag rol pa'i rgyud*
4. *Thig le rgya mtsho 'jug pa la gnas pa'i rgyud*
5. *Rin po che bkod pa rnam par 'byed pa'i rgyud*

Yan lag gi rgyud bdun

1. *Kun tu bzang po che ba rang la gnas pa'i rgyud*
2. *Ye shes rang la dbab cing rang la gnas pa'i rgyud*
3. *Mi 'gyur gnas pa'i rgyud*
4. *bKod pa rgyan gyi rgyud*
5. *Don gsal ba mthar phyin pa'i rgyud*
6. *gSal ba rang grol gyi rgyud*
7. *dKyil 'khor rdzogs pa'i rgyud*

bShad pa'i rgyud bzhi

1. *rMad du byung ba' i rgyud*
2. *Kun byed rgyal po'i rgyud*

3. *Byang chub sems dpa' ye shes rol pa stong nyid kyis brgyan pa'i rgyud*
4. *De kho na nyid ston pa gsang ba rol pa'i rgyud*

[Kun byed rgyal po ma bu dgu skor]

1. Kun byed rgyal po rtsa ba'i rgyud thos pa'i shes rab la gdams pa le'u lnga bcu rtsa bdun pa
2. rGyud phyi ma bsam byung gi shes rab la gdams pa le'u bcu gnyis pa
3. rGyud phyi ma'i phyi ma sgom byung gi shes rab la gdams pa le'u bcu lnga pa
4. Kun byed bshad pa'i rgyud mdo bcu
5. sPyi'i bshad rgyud 'khor ba rtsad gcod
6. lTa ba nam mkha' dang mnyam pa'i rgyud le'u bcu gsum pa
7. bsGom pa rgya mtsho dang mnyam pa'i rgyud le'u bdun pa
8. sPyod pa nyi zla dang mnyam pa'i rgyud le'u bcu gcig pa
9. 'Bras bu rin po che dang mnyam pa'i rgyud le'u bcu bzhi pa

including commentaries and pith instructions

2. Sems sde'i skor

Note: The text says in India there existed seventy-seven teachings of sems sde, *but only eighteen of them were translated.*

Sems sde'i rgyud bco brgyad (lung chen bco brgyad)

1. Nam mkha' che
2. Khyung chen
3. rTsal chen
4. Rig pa'i khu byug
5. sGom pa don drug ma
6. rMad du byung ba
7. Nam mkha'i rgyal po
8. rDo la gser zhun
9. bDe la phra bkod
10. Byang chub sems thig
11. Kun btus
12. bDe 'jam snying po
13. rdzogs pa spyi spyod
14. Yid bzhin nor bu
15. rJe btsan dam pa
16. sPyi rgyud spungs pa
17. rTse mo byung rgyal
18. missing

3. Klong sde'i skor (Klong skor gsum)

Note: In India there existed eighteen series of klong sde, *but only three of them were translated.*

1. Thugs rje klong nag ma bu gnyis
2. Klong dkar po la rgya mtsho'i klong ma bu gnyis
3. Klong chen rab 'byams ma bu bzhi

Klong sems kha sbyor [combined Klong sde and Sems sde]

1. Sems sde rtsa ba bco brgyad
2. bsKal pa dum bu'i rgyud bco brgyad

4. Bam po'i skor (Bam po brgya skor)

Note: In India there existed twenty thousand sections of this category, but only a hundred of them were translated.

1. sNang ba'i bam po
2. sTong pa'i bam po
3. Ye shes kyi bam po
4. lTa sgom spyod pa 'bras bu'i bam po etc.

5. mDo lung gi skor

1. mDo lung
2. mDo rtsa gnyis
3. mDo 'grel

6. rDzogs chen ma bu'i skor

1. Ma stong pa'i ye shes
2. Bu rig pa'i ye shes

7. Man ngag rdzongs 'phrang ('phreng) gi skor

1. bKa' rdzogs
2. gNyan rdzogs

8. Man ngag snyan brgyud kyi skor

1, 2. Man ngag che chung

9. Man ngag bsam gtan gyi skor

1. bSam gtan brgyad bcu pa

II. rDzogs pa chen po nang skor

1. Bram ze'i skor (bcu gnyis)

1. rGyud drug
    - 1.1. rGyud kyi snying po le'u nyi shu rtsa brgyad
    - 1.2. Ye shes ting rdzogs kyi rgyud le'u nyi shu rtsa bdun pa
    - 1.3. 'Khor ba thog mtha' gcod pa'i rgyud le'u bdun pa
    - 1.4. Nam mkha' klong yangs kyi rgyud le'u sum cu tham pa
    - 1.5. rMad du byung ba'i rgyud le'u nyi shu rtsa brgyad
    - 1.6. bKa' lung spyod pa don yod pa'i rgyud
2. Lo rgyud
3. 'Phrul gyi lde mig
4. 'Khor lo gsum
    - 4.1. Man ngag srog gi 'khor lo
    - 4.2. lTa ba spyod pa'i 'khor lo
    - 4.3. gTan tshigs sgra'i 'khor lo
5. Rin po che rgyan gyi man ngag (gNad la dbab pa'i skor)

2. Rig pa'i skor

3. Gab pa'i skor

4. rMad du byung ba'i skor

5. rDzogs chen lde mig gi skor

III. Ati gsang ba'i skor

Note: In India there existed three main categories: gsang rgyud chen po, yang tig, *and* spyi tig. *Among these, only the "nine profound series"* (zab mo skor dgu) *were translated into Tibetan.*

(Zab mo skor dgu)

IV. rDzogs chen ke'u tshang skor

1. 'Phrul gzhi zab mo skor

2. Rin po che rgyas pa'i skor

3. Nyi ma'i 'khor lo zab mo skor

4. rGyal po'i bla gter zab mo skor

5. Za 'og ber khyim zab mo skor

6. rGyud pa tha ma zab mo skor

Other teachings:
[bShad thabs gnyis]

I. mKhas pa pan di ta'i lugs

1. Thig le'i sde bzhi
2. 'Jam dpal sde bzhi
3. Big par ta sde bzhi, etc.

II. Ku su lu rnal 'byor pa'i lugs

1. sNags kyi rtsa ba gsum
    - 1.1. rGyud thams cad kyi rtsa ba 'Jam dpal dgongs pa 'dus pa
    - 1.2. Lung thams cad kyi rtsa ba mkha' 'gro ma drwa ba'i 'khor lo
    - 1.3. Man ngag thams cad kyi rtsa ba 'khor lo lngas bskor ba

III. Grub mtha' bkod pa'i man ngag

1. Lhun grub ji bzhin bkod pa'i rgyud
2. Dri med rnam dag gi rgyud
3. gSang ba rig pa bkod pa'i rgyud
4. Dri med 'od gsal gyi rgyud
5. rGyud gser mgo mgo can
6. Lung tho yig can
7. Man ngag phra yig can

IV. Rang grol mngon sum du ston pa'i man ngag

1. Ye shes rdzogs pa ('i rgyud)
2. Ye shes gsang ba ('i rgyud)
3. Rig pa rang gsal mchog gi rgyud
4. mKha' sa mun ta nam mkha' dang mnyam pa'i rgyud
5. sNying po don gyi rgyud

V. Yan lag gi rgyud nyi shu rtsa lnga

Plus teachings by different masters:

1 .sPrul sku dGa' rab kyi bka'i man ngag phran bu bco brgyad

2. Rig 'dzin gyi chos bzhi
    - 2.1. Rin po che rang gi gter gtad pa (by 'Jam dpal bshes gnyen)
    - 2.2. Byang chub kyi sems rin po che bdud rsti chu rgyun che mchog rgyan gyi 'khor lo (by Lha bdud rtsi chos kyi rgyal po)

2.3. Sa'i rim pa gsum du bsdus pa'i man ngag (by Klu rgyal dge ba dpal 'bar)

2.4. Byang chub kyi sems rin po che gsang ba thugs kyi sgron ma (by gNod sbyin ma byang chub ma)

3. Dri med gsang sgron (by gNod sbyin ma byang chub ma)
4. Byang chub kyi sems nyi ma'i snying po 'od dang ldan pa (by Kukurāja)
5. Rin po che'i rgyan (by Śrī Siṃha)
6. Rin po che'i phreng ba (by Śrī Siṃha)
7. bSam gtan don gsum pa (by Śrī Siṃha?)

APPENDIX FOUR
Tantras of the *rDo rje sems dpa' nam mkha' che*

Abbreviations:

TS=mTshams brag edition of the *rNying ma'i rgyud 'bum*

DK=Dil mgo mkhyen brtse edition

BGB=*Bai ro rgyud 'bum*

1. *rDo rje sems dpa' nam mkha' che rgyas pa yi ge med pa'i rgyud* (TS, Ka, 586-592; DK, Ka, 495, 499; BGB, A, 375-381)
2. *rDo rje sems dpa' nam mkha' che gsang ba'i snying po rnal ma don gyi rgyud* (TS, Kha, 415-443; DK, Ga, 65-87)
3. *rDo rje sems dpa' nam mkha' che kun tu bzang po gsang ba snying po'i rgyud* (TS, Kha, 443-529; DK, Ga, 537-606)
4. *rDo rje sems dpa' nam mkha' che bram ze rgyas pa'i rgyud* (TS, Kha, 529-556; DK, Ga, 629, 651)
5. *rDo rje sems dpa' nam mkha' che rgyas pa zhes bya ba rnal 'byor pa'i rgyud* (TS, Kha, 556-595; DK, Kha, 332-362)
6. *rDo rje sems dpa' nam mkha' che rgyas pa zhes bya ba rnal 'byor ma'i rgyud* (TS, Kha, 595-646; DK, Ka, 362-398; BGB, Ka, 329-395)
7. *rDo rje sems dpa' nam mkha' che rtsa ba'i rgyud skye ba med pa* (TS, Ga, 81-119; BGB, Ka, I, 291-381)
8. *rDo rje sems dpa' nam mkha' che rgyal po rgyas pa'i rgyud* (TS, Ga, 119-165)
9. *rDo rje sems dpa' nam mkha' che'i rgyud ces bya ba* (TS, Ga, 165-191)

APPENDIX FIVE
Index of chapters of the *Kun byed rgyal po* and of *mDo bcu*

Kun byed rgyal po, mTshams brag edition:

rTsa ba'i rgyud

1. Gleng gzhi'i le'u
2. Chos nyid mngon du phyung nas bstan pa'i le'u
3. Ji ltar byung ba'i khung bstan pa'i le'u (chos thams cad kyi sngon rol du byed pa po nga byung ba)
4. Nyid kyi mtshan bshad pa'i le'u (nyid kyi rang bzhin mtshan gyi chos nyid bshad pa)
5. Don 'grel gyi le'u
6. rTsa ba gcig pa'i le'u (chos thams cad nyid kyi rang bzhin la rdzogs pa)
7. rNam grangs bsdus pa'i le'u (nyid kyis byas pa las byung ba'i chos rnam par dbye ba'i chos)
8. Chos kyi rang bzhin las chos nyid kyi yul kun la bkod pa'i le'u (byas pa'i chos thams cad de bzhin nyid du gcig pa las/ de bzhin nyid las rang bzhin rnam pa gsum snang bar gyur pa ste so sor snang ba)
9. Gol sgrib skyon sel gyi le'u
10. Phun sum tshogs pa shin tu bkod pa'i le'u (nyid kyi rang bzhin phun sum tshogs pa)
11. Chos thams cad kyi rtsa ba byang chub kyi sems kun byed rgyal po nyid kho nar 'dus pa'i le'u
12. Nges par lung khungs bstan pa'i le'u (chos thams cad kyi khung kyi mdo)
13. Sems kyi bshad lugs kyi le'u (lung thams cad kyi rgyal po yin pa'i phyir/ chos thams cad kyi spyi lung bshad pa'i bshad lugs)
14. sKal med la gsang ba'i le'u (nyid kyi gsang ba dam pa'i gdams ngag)
15. Rang bzhin rnam pa gsum mngon du phyung ba'i le'u (nyid kyi lung chen po mngon du phyung ba'i lung)
16. Sems dpa' rdo rje la gdams ngag phog pa'i le'u
17. sKu gdung gtad pa'i le'u
18. bTsal bas mi 'grub pa'i le'u (chos thams cad kyi chos nyid nga yin pa'i lung)
19. Ma btsal lhun gyis grub pa'i le'u
20. Chos thams byang chub kyi sems kun byed las byung ba'i khungs kyi le'u
21. gTan tshigs bshad lugs kyi le'u (chos thams cad kyi khungs kyi rgyal po yin pa'i phyir/ nyid las byung ba'i tshig)
22. Mi gnas yul gyi le'u (sems rnal du gzhag pa'i phyir/ bya med rdzogs pa'i lung khungs chen po-khyung chen lding ba)

23. lTa ba yul med kyi nam mkha'i dgongs pa bstan pa'i le'u
24. Bya med rdzogs pa phyag rgya 'gyur med kyi le'u (bya med rdzogs pa'i lung phyag rgya bzhugs tshul gyi le'u)
25. Rang sems ston par phyung ba'i le'u (khams gsum gyi sems can la rang gi sems ston pa yin par bstan pa)
26. Bya med rdzogs pa bsgom du med pa'i le'u (sems las byung ba'i chos chen po lnga ston par phyung ba'i rtags su ma skyes pa'i byang chub kyi sems ston par zhal gyis bzhes pa-rdo la gser zhun)
27. Bya med rnam dag dbyings kyi lung bstan pa'i le'u (nyid kyi gdams ngag dang mthun pa'i lung chen po rim gyis bstan pa-rtsal chen sprugs pa)
28. Bya med rdzogs pa 'gyur med btsal gyis mi rnyed pa'i le'u (nyid kyi rang bzhin 'gyur ba med pa)
29. dGongs pa rnal du gzhag pa'i le'u (sems rnal du gzhag pa)
30. rDo rje sems dpa'i rang bzhin mi nub pa'i rgyal mtshan gyi le'u
31. rDo rje tshig drug pa'i le'u (kun byed nyid kyi rang bzhin bya med rdzogs pa lhun gyis grub pa)
32. Nges pa tshig bzhi'i le'u (ma byas don grub kyi lung)
33. Nges pa'i lung dang drang ba'i lung bstan pa'i le'u (nyid kyi rang bzhin rtogs par dka' ba)
34. dGongs pa 'dus pa'i mdo lung gi le'u (sangs rgyas thams cad kyi dgongs pa nyid la 'dus pa'i mdo)
35. rDzogs pa chen po'i gzhung bstan pa'i le'u (nyid kyi bstan pa gzhan gyi spyod yul ma yin pa/ rdzogs pa chen po'i gzhung 'di rgyu 'bras rtsol sgrub las 'das pa 'di bstan)
36. sKu gsung thugs su 'dus pa'i le'u (chos thams cad kyi rang bzhin nyid kyi sku gsung thugs su 'dus pa)
37. bsGom du med pa'i mdo lung gi le'u (rdzogs pa chen po'i chos nyid bsgom du med pa)
38. lTa spyod kyi gol sgrib bstan pa'i le'u ('khor gyi ston pa'i bstan pa gol sa dang sgrib par gyur pa)
39. rGyal ba'i snying po'i le'u (nyid kyi rang bzhin thams cad la gol sa dang sgrib pa med pa rgyal ba'i snying po yin pa)
40. Byang chub kyi sems kyi rang bzhin bstan pa'i le'u (rgyu 'bras kyi theg pa bgrod lam nor bas/ rdzogs pa chen po las gol dang sgrib par gyur pa)
41. Ngo bo gcig pa'i le'u (chos thams cad kyi rang bzhin nga yin pa)
42. bCos su med pa'i le'u (chos thams cad byang chub kyi sems kho nar sangs rgyas pa)
43. sTon par zhal gyis bzhes pa' i le'u (chos thams cad kyi ston pa nyid yin par zhal gyi bzhes pa)
44. rDzogs pa chen po skal med don med kyi le'u (nyid la bya ba med pa'i don)

45. lTa ba sgom du med pa'i le'u (rdzogs pa chen po la lta ba sgom med kyi mdo lung)
46. Dam tshig bsrung du med pa'i le'u (rdzogs pa chen po dam tshig bsrung du med pa)
47. 'Phrin las bstal du med pa'i le'u (rdzogs pa chen po las phrin las bstal du med pa)
48. Chos thams cad kyi gzhi ma kun byed nyid yin par zhal gyis bzhes par bstan pa'i le'u
49. rDzogs pa chen po sa la sbyang du med pa'i le'u (thams cad nga la gnas pa)
50. Rang byung ye shes bstan pa'i le'u (byang chub kyi sems rang byung ye shes la sgrib pa med pa)
51. Jam la bgrod du med pa'i le'u (rdzogs pa chen po'i lam la bgrod du med pa)
52. Ma g.yos 'dod pa med pa'i le'u (bya med rdzogs pa ma g.yos pa 'dod pa med pa)
53. Chos thams cad rang bzhin g.yos pa med pa'i le'u
54. mDo lung thams cad kun byed nyid kyi rang bzhin du bsdus pa bstan pa'i le'u
55. Chos thams cad byang chub kyi sems las med pa'i le'u
56. Sems dpa' rdo rjes kun byed rgyal po'i rang bzhin rtogs pa'i sgo nas bsgrags pa'i le'u
57. bsTan pa gtad pa'i le'u

Phyi ma'i rgyud (rTogs pa bshad zhes bya ba'i rgyud phyi ma)

58. rTogs pa gleng gzhi'i le'u
59. sKye ba med pa'i le'u (lta ba bsgom du med par rtogs pa)
60. bSrung med dam tshig gi le'u (dam tshig bsrung du med par rtogs pa)
61. sGo gsum bya btsal med par rtogs pa'i le'u ('phrin las bstal du med par rtogs pa)
62. dKyil 'khor bskyed du med par rtogs pa'i le'u
63. Rang 'byung rtogs pa'i dbang gi le'u (dbang la bskur du med par rtogs pa)
64. Lam la bgrod du med par rtogs pa'i le'u
65. Sa la sbyang du med par rtogs pa'i le'u
66. sPyod pa blang dor med par rtogs pa'i le'u
67. Ye shes sgrib pa med par rtogs pa'i le'u
68. lHun grub btsal du med par rtogs pa'i le'u
69. rTogs pa bsgrags shing bstod pa'i le'u

Phyi ma'i phyi ma'i rgyud (bsGom pa'i mdo lung)

70. bsGom du yod med bstan pa'i le'u
71. lTa dgongs dbyer med pa'i le'u (don gcig pa lta ba bsgom med kyi dgongs pa)
72. lTa sgom 'dar med pa'i le'u (bsrung du med pa'i de bzhin nyid du gnas pa)
73. Ji bzhin pa la bya btsal dang bral bar gnas pa'i le'u (bya med bstal ba dang bral bar rtogs pa)
74. sNying po don la gnas pa'i le'u (snying po 'du 'bral med par gnas pa'i le'u)
75. Rig pa dbang sgyur la gnas pa'i le'u (rig pa dbang sgyur la gnas pa'i don)
76. sNying po lam la gnas pa'i le'u (snying po don gyi lam)
77. Don la sbyang med kyi le'u
78. mNyam pa la blang dor med par bstan pa'i le'u
79. Mi sgrib pa'i le'u (rang 'byung snying po'i don la sgrib pa bsal du med pa'i dgongs pa)
80. lHun grub re dogs bcad pa'i le'u (lhun grub re dogs las 'das pa'i dgongs pa)
81. dGongs don lde mig gi le'u
82. rJes su bstod pa'i le'u
83. bsTan pa gang la gzhag pa'i le'u
84. mTshan gyi rnam grangs bstan pa'i le'u

Colophon: byang chub kyi sems kun byed rgyal po/ lta ba nam mkha' ltar mtha' dbus med pa'i rgyud/ nam mkha'i snying po mchog gi don/ gsang ba mchog gi mdo lung brgyad cu rtsa bchi pa rdzogs so/ rgya gar gyi mkhan po dpal gyi seng ge dang/ dge slong bai ro tsa nas bsgyur cing zhus te gtan la phab pa'o.

Kun byed rgyal po, alternative index of the rTsa ba'i rgyud

I. ***mNgon du phyung ba'i mdo lung*** **(*chos nyid mthong bar bya ba'i phyir/ mngon par sangs rgyas che bar bstan pa*)**

Ten fundamental chapters: 1, 10, 2, 11, 3, 20, 15, 25, 21, 6; and chapter 16.

II. ***Nges par bstan pa'i mdo lung*** **(*chos nyid de nyid kun byed nges rtogs phyir/ chos dbyings sangs rgyas che bar bstan pa*)**

Ten fundamental chapters: 4, 33, 13, 12, 5, 32, 36, 34, 29, 17; and chapter 55.

III. ***rGyu 'bras 'das pa'i mdo lung*** **(*rgyu 'bras log pa'i zhen pa bzlog pa'i phyir/ bdag nyid sangs rgyas che bar bstan pa*)**

Ten fundamental chapters: 41, 14, 38, 9, 35, 19, 18, 8, 40, 52; and chapter 7.

IV. ***Bya med rdzogs pa'i mdo lung*** **(*de yin sangs rgyas che bar bstan pa*)**

Ten fundamental chapters: 22, 30, 24, 28, 27, 31, 23, 26, 44, 56; and chapter 43.

V. ***gTan la 'bebs pa'i mdo lung*** **(*sangs rgyas med pa'i che bar bstan pa*)**

Ten fundamental chapters: 48, 39, 45, 37, 46, 47, 49, 51, 50, 53; and chapter 42.

mDo bcu, mTshams brag edition (*mDo 'grel chen po bcu*)

I. ***Chos thams cad rdzogs pa chen po byang chub kyi sems su 'dus pa'i mdo*** **(*Byang chub sems kyi mdo*) [tied to the *mNgon du phyung ba'i mdo lung* of the *Kun byed rgyal po*]**

1. gLeng gzhi'i le'u
2. rGyu 'bras gcig pa'i le'u
3. dPe don gcig pa'i le'u
4. rTsa ba byang chub sems kyi le'u
5. Don gyi 'grel pa'i le'u

II. ***rTsa ba gcig la don gnyis 'byung ba'i rnam par bgrang ba'i mdo*** **(*rNam par bgrang ba'i mdo*) [tied to the *rGyu 'bras 'das pa'i mdo lung* of the *Kun byed rgyal po*]**

1. 'Jig rten pa'i theg pa bstan pa'i le'u
2. 'Jig rten las 'das pa'i le'u
3. Don gyi 'grel pa'i le'u

III. *Phun sum tshogs pa'i mdo* [tied to the *mNgon du phyung ba'i mdo lung* of the *Kun byed rgyal po*]

1. sTon pa phun sum tshogs pa'i le'u
2. 'Khor phun sum tshogs pa'i le'u
3. bsTan pa phun sum tshogs pa'i le'u
4. gNas phun sum tshogs pa'i le'u
5. Dus phun sum tshogs pa'i le'u
6. Phun sum tshogs pa'i mdo'i don gyi 'grel pa

IV. *Bye brag 'byed pa'i mdo* [tied to the *rGyu 'bras 'das pa'i mdo lung* of the *Kun byed rgyal po*]

1. Yo ga bzhi'i bye brag phye ba'i le'u
2. Yo ga rnam pa bzhi'i don gyi 'grel pa bye brag 'byed pa'i mdo bzhi

V. *Khyad par 'phags pa'i mdo* (*Che ba lnga'i mdo*) [tied to the *mNgon du phyung ba'i mdo lung* of the *Kun byed rgyal po*]

1. Khyad par 'phags pa'i che ba lnga bstan pa'i le'u
2. Don gyi 'grel pa

VI. *Gol sgrib ston pa'i mdo* [tied to the *rGyu 'bras 'das pa'i mdo lung* of the *Kun byed rgyal po*]

1. Gol sgrib bstan pa'i mdo'i le'u
2. Don gyi 'grel pa

VII. *gTan la 'bebs pa'i mdo* [tied to the *gTan la 'bebs pa'i mdo lung* of the *Kun byed rgyal po*]

1. Lung gsum man ngag bzhis gtan la dbab pa'i mdo'i le'u
2. Don gyi 'grel pa

VIII. *Nges par ston pa'i mdo* [tied to the *Nges par bstan pa'i mdo lung* of the *Kun byed rgyal po*]

1. Nges par ston pa'i mdo bstan pa'i le'u
2. Don gyi 'grel pa

IX. *Theg pa yas phubs theg pa dgu'i mdo* [tied to the *mNgon du phyung ba'i mdo lung* of the *Kun byed rgyal po*]

1. Theg pa yas phub kyi mdo
2. Don gyi 'grel pa

X. *Yongs su rdzogs pa'i mdo* [tied to the *gTan la 'bebs pa'i mdo lung* of the *Kun byed rgyal po*]

1. Yongs su rdzogs pa'i mdo
2. Don gyi 'grel pa

and:

1. Don gyi 'grel pa lnga po
2. bsTan pa gtad pa'i le'u

Notes

1. For the Tibetan terms a phonetic transcription system has been used in which, by and large, consonants are pronounced as in English and vowels as in Italian. In the notes and parentheses (except for the more commonly used terms) the Wylie transliteration has been used. The Wylie transliteration for most of the terms has also been given in the index at the end of the book.

2. When capitalized, the term Tantra denotes the totality of the characteristic system of these teachings.

3. From *gZhi lam 'bras bu'i smon lam* (p. 445.5), from the cycle of teachings of the *Klong chen snying thig*, a *gter ma* of 'Jigs med gling pa (1730-1798); Bibliography no. 25.

4. From *bSam gtan mig sgron*, by gNubs chen sangs rgyas ye shes (ninth century), Bibliography no. 33, p. 13. 3. The *Supreme Peak* (*rTse mo byung rgyal*) is one of the fundamental texts of the rDzogs chen sems sde.

5. Outside the context of rDzogs chen the term *lung* may denote a quotation from an important scripture. Its Sanskrit equivalent, corresponding to the meaning of "tradition," appears to be *āgama*.

6. The final three of the ten *bhūmis* of the Mahāyāna path are known as the "three pure levels" (*dag pa sa gsum*). Bodhisattvas on these three levels are able to perceive the pure *saṃbhogakāya* dimension. The *vidyādharas*, or *rig 'dzin*, are beings who have attained realization through practice of Tantra and in particular of rDzogs chen.

7. According to some sources the *Kun byed rgyal po* was also taught by another of the twelve primordial teachers, brTse bas rol pa'i blo gros. See Chapter 1, section II.

8. In the mTshams brag edition of the *rNying ma rgyud 'bum*, published at Thimpu in 1982, respectively vol. Ka, pp. 1-262; vol. Ka, pp. 262-288; vol. Kha, pp. 1-278; vol. Ga, pp. 165-191; vol. Ga, pp. 191-355.

9. Literally, *Samantabhadra*, in Tibetan *Kun tu bzang po*, means "always good" or "good in all circumstances." Depicted as a naked, unadorned, sky-blue Buddha, he represents the primordial *dharmakāya* state present in all beings.

10. Vajrayana, or "*vajra* vehicle," denotes the tantric teachings, as do its synonyms Mantrayāna and Guhyamantra. In the tantric teachings the *vajra*, a word that also designates a characteristic ritual object, represents the primordial, indestructible state of the Body, Voice, and Mind.

11. The most ancient tradition of rDzogs chen teachings in Bön is contained in the *Zhang zhung snyan brgyud* cycle, the *Oral Transmission of Zhang Zhung*, revealed by Tapihritsa and written down by sNang bzher lod po about the eighth century. See Chögyal Namkhai Norbu, *Drung, Deu & Bön* (Dharamsala 1995), Chapter 15, section 11.

12. The four conceptual limits (*mu bzhi*) denote the dualism of "birth and cessation," of "eternity and nothingness," of "being and non-being," and of "vision and emptiness."

13. *Lhun grub rdzogs pa chen po'i ston pa dang bstan pa'i byung tshul brjod pa'i gtam nor bu'i phreng ba*, MS, Bibliography no. 34, pp. 11. 7–17.1.

14. The five perfect conditions (*phun sum tshogs pa lnga*) are the teacher, the teaching, the assembly, the place, and the time. They are also called the "five certainties" (*nges pa lnga*) of the *saṃbhogakāya*.

15. Bibliography no. 34, pp. 21.5–23.6.

16. The colophon of the *Klong chen chos 'byung*, whose original title is *Chos 'byung rin po che'i gter mdzod bstan pa gsal bar byed pa'i nyi 'od*, written in 1362, bears the name of rGyal sras Thugs mchog rtsal, identified by some, including 'Jigs med gling pa, as Klong chen pa. Notwithstanding this many scholars remain in doubt over the identity of the author of this work.

17. *dGongs pa 'dus pa*, the fundamental text of anuyoga.

18. Akaniṣṭha, in Tibetan *'og min*, "the highest," designates the pure dimension where the Tantric teachings originated. The texts speak of different types of Akaniṣṭha related to as many levels of manifestation of wisdom.

19. Bibliography no. 3, pp. 5–6. The three analytical vehicles or "analytical causal vehicles" (*rgyu'i mtshan nyid kyi theg pa*), respectively those of the śrāvakas, of the pratyekabuddhas (both Hīnayāna), and of the Bodhisattvas (Mahāyāna), include the teachings of the sūtras, defined as "analytical" inasmuch as they mainly cultivate a gradual or "conceptual" understanding of *śūnyatā* before arriving at direct perception of it. The Chinese Ch'an and Japanese Zen traditions are exceptions.

20. See Appendix One.

21. Bibliography no. 4, p. 22.3ff.

22. Vajradhara (rDo rje 'chang) represents the principle of the state of enlightenment, understood in particular as the origin and unification of the "five Buddha

families." In the modern Tantric tradition he is the equivalent of Samantabhadra of the ancient tradition.

23. The most ancient reference to the tradition of the twelve teachers (*ston pa bcu gnyis*) is found in the tantra *Rig pa rang shar* (Bibliography no. 28, pp. 612.2ff.), but the first source to list the names of the twelve teachers together with the teachings they transmitted, etc., seems to be the *Lo rgyus rin po che'i mdo byang*, a chapter of the *Bi ma snying thig* contained in the *g.Yu yig can* section (Bibliography no. 29, pp. 162ff.). Other important sources are the *Theg mchog mdzod* by Klong chen pa (Bibliography no. 10, pp. 12.5ff.), the *mKhas pa'i dga' ston* by dPa' bo gstug lag phreng ba (Bibliography no. 7, pp. 562.14ff.) and the *Ma rig mun sel*, belonging to the *gter ma* cycle rediscovered by sTag sham nus ldan rdo rje (Bibliography no. 20, pp. 8.4ff.). The sources mainly used here that give more descriptive details, are the *Lo rgyus rin po che'i mdo byang* and the *Ma rig mun sel*. See also Dudjom Rinpoche (Bibliography no. 35), *The Nyingma School*, pp. 135ff.

24. The seventeen tantras (*rgyud bcu bdun*) of the Man ngag sde series. The principal one is the *sGra thal 'gyur*.

25. In the context of Tantra and of rDzog chen the *ḍākinīs* (*mkha' 'gro ma*) are immaterial beings of female appearance that protect the teachers and the teachings.

26. According to the *Ma rig mun sel* this Buddha taught the mother tantras of *prajñā* (*shes rab kyi chos ma rgyud*).

27. Buddhist philosophy contemplates four kinds of birth: miraculous (such as in the case of devas), from an egg, from heat and humidity, and from the uterus. The tradition of the twelve teachers also follows this principle.

28. According to the *Ma rig mun sel*, on the other hand, he taught the four series of tantras of method or *upāya* (*thabs kyi chos rgyud sde bzhi*).

29. Tib. *sa yi tshil zhag* or *sa zhag*.

30. See the Preface by Chögyal Namkhai Norbu. According to the *Ma rig mun sel*, he taught the six *pāramitās* (*pha rol tu phyin pa drug*).

31. The seven heroic Buddhas (*sangs rgyas dpa' bo bdun*) who according to the sutric tradition have already appeared in our kalpa.

32. The *Ma rig mun sel* speaks of a "pagoda of the yakṣas, wrathful manifestation of Vajrapāṇi" as this Buddha's place of birth.

33. The six classes of beings are the devas, the asuras, and the humans, called the "three higher states"; and the animals, the pretas, and the hell beings, called the "three lower states."

34. The *Ma rig mun sel* specifies that he taught the father tantras as the outer teaching, the mother tantras as the inner teaching, the *Rig pa rang shar* as the secret teaching, and the *'Khor 'das rang grol* as the supreme teaching.

35. According to the *Ma rig mun sel*, the yakṣa Legs spyod was a prevous incarnation of dGa' rab rdo rje.

36. Among the ten tantras to subjugate gross negativities (*rags pa 'dul ba'i rgyud bcu*) the *Ma rig mun sel* mentions the tantras of Hayagriva, of Vajrakilaya, of Yamāntaka, of Ekajati, etc.

37. The Vinaya is the section of the Buddhist scriptures concerned with the discipline and rules of monastic conduct.

38. That is, a *pipal* (*Ficus religiosa*), the same tree under which Buddha Śākyamuni obtained enlightenment at Bodhi Gaya.

39. "The Immutable" (*mi g.yo ba*), the eighth of the ten *bhūmi* that mark the Bodhisattva's ascent to total realization.

40. Although it does not mention the "seven special tantras" (*phra bdun rgyud*) the *Ma rig mun sel* quotes, among others, the following titles: *Kun byed rgyal po, Khu dbyug rol pa, Sems lung chen mo, Kun tu bzang po che ba rang la gnas pa, Nam mkha' che, Chub pas rol pa, Ye shes mchog, 'Khor lo gcod pa, Thig le bra rgyud, 'Bar ba chen po, Nor bu phra bkod.*

41. The *Theg mchog mdzod* (Bibliography no. 10) relates that this master taught the sūtras, the kriyā tantras and the anuyoga scriptures (*lung a nu yo ga*). The *Ma rig mun sel* also mentions the *Ati bkod pa* and adds that as his testament he left the *Sras gcig sa bon gyi rgyud* and the *'Das rjes tha ma.*

42. The *Ma rig mun sel* also mentions the *rGyud phyi ma'i phyi ma stong gsum za byed* and the *Pad ma'i dum bu.*

43. The twelve great deeds that mark the spiritual career of the Buddha, from the decision to descend from the pure Tuṣita dimension and take birth on earth to entry into *parinirvāṇa.*

44. See, for example, *mKhas pa'i dga' ston*, Bibliography no. 7, p. 565.20, and Reynolds, *The Golden Letters* (Bibliography no. 46), pp. 205ff.

45. In fact, Asaṅga, who formulated the yogācāra, or cittamātra, philosophy, lived in the fourth century. Moreover, the Buddhist University of Nālandā was not founded until the fifth century.

46. Apart from this common factor, the Klong sde and Man ngag sde lineages differ greatly both in the biographical accounts of the early teachers and in the lineage after Śrī Siṃha.

47. Most Western scholars give the Sanskrit for dGa' rab rdo rje as Prahevajra or Praharṣavajra. However the *Bi ma snying thig* (Bibliography no. 29, p. 194.4) mentions the name Vajra Prahe.

48. See, for example, Reynolds, *The Golden Letters*, pp. 179-189.

49. There are two editions of the *Bai ro 'dra 'bag*, which in its present form derives from no later than the thirteenth century: a wood-block edition published in Lhasa (the same as the one published in Dehradun) and the edition published in Leh in volume eight of the *Bai ro rgyud 'bum*. The two versions differ somewhat in some points. Here I have mainly adhered to the Lhasa edition although at times it proved necessary to insert details from the Leh edition. For a history of the origin

of this text and of its *gter ma* and *bka' ma* versions as well as a summary of its complete contents, see Karmay, *The Great Perfection* (Bibliography no. 37), pp. 31ff.

50. "*Vajra* recitation" (*rdo rje'i bzlas pa*) consists in combining the sound of the three syllables *OṂ ĀḤ HŪṂ* with a particular breathing technique. These syllables symbolize the Body, Voice, and Mind of all the Buddhas.

51. The base (*gzhi*) and the fruit (*'bras bu*) constitute the potential condition of enlightenment present in all beings and its concrete realization, made possible by means of the aspect of the "path" (*lam*). See Chapter 3, section III.

52. The five families of the Tathāgatas, presented in this section in the sequence vajra, ratna, padma, karma, and buddha, or tathāgata, represent the pure aspect of the five *skandhas* and of the five elements of every individual. This section also forms large part of the first chapter of a tantra of the Sems sde, the *Ye shes gsang ba zhes bya ba'i rgyud* (Bibliography no. 27, 727–783).

53. *Bai ro 'dra 'bag* (Bibliography no. 16, Lhasa ed.), ff. 17b.3–21a.3.

54. Most of the Man ngag sde texts give Uparāja as the name of dGa' rab rdo rje's grandfather and Sudharmā as the name of his mother.

55. The guardians of the teaching, or *dharmapāla*, are immaterial beings whose function is to assist practitioners and to protect the teachings.

56. *Bai ro 'dra 'bag*, ff. 21a.3–22b.2. Other sources specify that dGa' rab rdo rje's first disciples were ḍākinīs.

57. Art, medicine, grammar, logic, and philosophy.

58. The three *piṭakas* or baskets of Buddhist scriptures: *Sūtrapiṭaka*, *Vinayapiṭaka*, and *Abhidharmapiṭaka*.

59. The name *mu steg pa* (*tīrthika*) designates all the followers of philosophies that adhere to an erroneous view of reality, attributing to it concrete and permanent existence (*rtag pa'i lta ba*) or, conversely, denying any continuity after death (*chad pa'i lta ba*).

60. *Klong dgu bam po nyi khri* in Tibetan. The classification of "nine spaces" is specific to the rDzogs chen teachings. The *Klong chen chos 'byung* (Bibliography no. 3, p. 292) enumerates the "nine spaces" and the number of the chapters and sections of each on the basis of the following list: unborn space (*skye ba med pa'i klong*); space of the fundamental essence (*snying po don gyi klong*), space unborn from the origin (*gdod nas ma skyes pa'i klong*), space that transcends words (*tshig las 'das pa'i klong*), space beyond concepts (*spros pa dang bral ba'i klong*), ineffable space (*brjod du med pa'i klong*), space of the essential condition (*de kho na nyid kyi klong*), space that transcends all limits (*mtha' kun dang bral ba'i klong*), space of non-duality (*gnyis su med pa'i klong*). Other sources give different lists.

61. Yamāntaka (gShin rje gshed), a wrathful manifestation of Mañjuśrī, is the *yi dam* of one of the eight *sādhanas* (*sgrub pa bka' brgyad*) of mahāyoga of which Mañjuśrīmitra was the main holder.

62. The celebrated *rDo la gser zhun*, probably composed by Mañjuśrīmitra on the basis of the *Byang chub sems sgom*, one of the eighteen *lungs* of the Sems sde. A translation and commentary by N. Norbu and K. Lipman can be found in Mañjuśrīmitra, *Primordial Experience* (Bibliography no. 39).

63. *Bai ro 'dra 'bag*, ff. 22b.2–24a.6.

64. This version can be found in *sNyan brgyud rdo rje zam pa'i lo rgyus 'bring po gdams ngag dang bcas pa* (Bibliography no. 9, pp. 316.2–325.1) and is repeated, with a few variations, in Bibliography no. 13, pp. 83.3–86.2. For a brief account of the "symbolic transmission" received by Mañjuśrīmitra see also another section of the *Bai ro 'dra 'bag* (ff. 36a, ff.) The "Vajra Bridge" *(rdo rje zam pa)* contains the Klong sde teachings transmitted by Vairocana to sPang mi pham mgon po. See Dudjom Rinpoche's *The Nyingma School*, p. 540.

65. *A HA HO YE* (or *'E*) are the four sacred syllables forming the basis of the instructions of the rDzogs chen Klong sde.

66. *Bai ro 'dra 'bag*, ff. 24a.6–24b.2. The supreme *siddhi* corresponds to total realization while the ordinary *siddhi* are limited powers, usually acquired through specific tantric practices.

67. For the diverse lists of teachers from India and Oḍḍiyāna in the Sems sde lineage see Appendix Two. The *Bai ro 'dra 'dag* (ff. 37b, ff.) reports also lineages that are different and shorter than the one given in this section.

68. The three levels of enlightenment (*sangs rgyas sa gsum*) in the tantric teachings are called "Total Light" (*kun tu 'od*), "Lotus-Endowed" (*pad ma can*), and "Great Accumulation of the *cakra* of Letters" (*yi ge 'khor lo tshogs chen*).

69. Elsewhere called Sārāni (Bibliography no. 30) and Warani (Bibliography no. 13).

70. The nāgas (*klu*) are semi-divine beings dwelling in water domains; their worship is widespread in India, Nepal, and Tibet.

71. In Tantra there are four empowerments, or initiations, that serve to "ripen" the practitioner's consciousness: the vase empowerment (*bum dbang*), the secret empowerment (*gsang dbang*), the wisdom empowerment *(shes rab ye shes kyi dbang)*, and the word empowerment (*tshig dbang*). In Tibetan *dbang* literally means "power" and is closely tied to the term *byin rlabs*, rendered as "empowering flow."

72. The five wisdoms (*ye shes lnga*) are the purified aspect of the five passions. They are: the wisdom of *dharmadhātu* (*chos dbyings ye shes*), corresponding to ignorance; mirror-like wisdom (*me long ye shes*), corresponding to anger; the wisdom of equality (*mnyam nyid ye shes*), corresponding to pride; discriminating wisdom (*sor rtogs ye shes*), corresponding to attachment; action-accomplishing wisdom (*bya grub ye shes*), corresponding to jealousy.

73. The three poisons (*dug gsum*) are the three main emotions or passions that cause rebirth—anger, attachment, and ignorance.

74. The term *gnod sbyin mo*, or *yakṣini*, the female yakṣa, may denote that this teacher was of non-human origin.

75. Elsewhere (Bibliography no. 13) called gZung ma Arali. The designation *smad 'tshong ma* (prostitute) may denote the sub-caste of origin of this teacher.

76. The lowest of the four castes in India.

77. These two lines refer to two practices characteristic of mahāyoga: sexual union (*sbyor ba*) and rites of elimination (*sgrol ba*) of evil entities symbolized by an effigy called *linga* that is ritually pierced.

78. In general, the term *mkhan po,* or *upādhyāya,* designates the abbot of a Buddhist monastery.

79. Elsewhere (Bibliography no. 30) called Dhahe.

80. These lines allude to the characteristic principle of Tantra whereby the five aggregates (*skandha*), the five elements and the other factors of the personality described in the sūtra teachings are in reality divine manifestations of the energy of the primordial state.

81. This may be same person as Vidyādhara Āryapalo mentioned in other sources (Bibliography no. 30).

82. Elsewhere (Bibliography no. 30) called Bhishati.

83. Elsewhere (Bibliography no. 30) called sMad 'tshong ma Buddhamati and (Bibliography no. 13) gZung ma bDag nyid ma. In *Bai' ro 'dra 'bag* she is also called *dge slong ma* (*bhikṣuṇī*) bDag nyid ma.

84. In the sutric teachings the "great mother" (*yum chen mo*) is synonymous with Prajñāpāramitā, the wisdom beyond the limits of the intellect, the pure recognition of emptiness. In the inner tantras this same principle takes on the meaning of the potentiality of the energy of the five elements, symbolized by Samantabhadrī, the consort of Samantabhadra.

85. Buddhagupta (spelled Bhutakugta in the *Bai ro 'dra 'bag*) is the author of the *sBas pa'i rgum chung,* a small Dzogchen text rediscovered among the Tun Huang manuscripts. It has been the subject of study and commentary by Chögyal Namkhai Norbu in *The Small Collection of Hidden Precepts* (Bibliography no. 19). See also Karmay, *The Great Perfection.*

86. Vimalamitra is famous especially for having transmitted in Tibet the rDzogs chen teachings of the Man ngag sde series, subsequently redacted in the *Bi ma snying thig* cycle. His hagiography can be found in diverse Western publications, including Thondup, *The Tantric Tradition of the Nyingmapa* (Bibliography no. 43), pp. 54-56.

87. *Bai ro 'dra 'bag,* ff. 24b.2–31b.3.

88. See Tulku Thondup, *The Tantric Tradition of the Nyingmapa,* pp. 51-52.

89. An allusion to the practices for the accumulation of merit and the purification of karmic hindrances, generally regarded as indispensable for the attainment of realization.

90. Yang dag, a manifestation of Vajrapāṇi, is a *yi dam* belonging to the cycle of eight *sādhanas* of mahāyoga.

91. *Tsampa* (*rtsam pa*, in the text *spags*), roasted barley flour, is the staple diet of Tibetans.

92. *rDo rje sems dpa'i sgyu 'phrul drwa ba* (*Vajrasattvamāyājāla*), also known as *gSang ba snying po* or *Guhyagarbha*, is the most important text of mahāyoga.

93. Method (*upāya*) and *prajñā* are the two fundamental aspects of the practice of Tantra. Method represents the manifestation of existence as the pure dimension of the *maṇḍala* and of the deity, *prajñā* is the understanding of the energy of emptiness whence the manifestation issues. In sutric Buddhism the term *prajñā* basically denotes the intuitive faculty that recognizes the true nature of phenomena, *śūnyatā*.

94. I.e., the five sense consciousnesses plus the mental consciousness.

95. The eighteen sense spheres, or elements (*khams bco brgyad*) comprise the six sense organs (five senses plus the mind), their consciousnesses and their objects.

96. Bibliography no. 9, pp. 325.2–342.1; Bibliography no. 13, pp. 96.3–103.3.

97. The events connected with the promulgation of Buddhism in Tibet during the reign of King Khri srong lde'u btsan (742-797 C.E.) are narrated in several Western publications. See, for example, Yeshe Tsogyal, *The Life and Liberation of Padmasambhava* (Bibliography no. 47), the translation of the *Pad ma bka' thang*.

98. The teachings transmitted by Padmasambhava are contained in the *mKha' 'gro snying thig* cycle, those transmitted by Vimalamitra in the *Bi ma snying thig*. Both form part of the *sNying thig yab bzhi* redacted by Klong chen pa. According to tradition Vimalamitra also transmitted the "thirteen later texts" (*sems smad bcu gsum*) of the eighteen *lungs* of the Sems sde, excluding, that is, the first five texts translated (*snga 'gyur lnga*) by Vairocana.

99. In ancient times the art of "fast walking" (*rkang mgyogs*), based on controlling the *prāṇa*, enabled yogins to travel vast distances in very short time.

100. See Yeshe Tsogyal, *The Life and Liberation of Padmasambhava*, vol. II; Yeshe Tsogyal, *The Lotus-Born* (Bibliography no. 48), the translation of the *Zangs gling ma*; Karmay, *The Great Perfection*, which contains a synopsis of the version found in the *Bai ro 'dra 'bag*.

101. From this point until Vairocana's song of the "eight dangerous passes" (*'phrang brgyad*) the translation of the text is complete. *Bai ro 'dra 'bag*, ff. 62a.3–65a.3.

102. According to other sources, before teaching the "eighteen *lungs* of Sems sde" listed here, Śrī Siṃha transmitted twenty-five tantras. See Yeshe Tsogyal, *The Lotus-Born*, pp. 91-92. Moreover, the order of the eighteen *lungs* and the short indications of their contents found in the *Bai ro 'dra 'bag* do not tally with those in the list given by Nyang ral Nyi ma 'od zer. For a complete list of the twenty-five tantras and the eighteen *lungs*, see Appendix Three.

103. For this song I have followed the Lhasa edition of the *Bai ro 'dra 'bag* (emending *'phreng la sdug* to *'phrang la sdug*), notwithstanding the *Pad ma bka' thang* (Bibliography no. 15, pp. 422-423) and other sources which give *'phrang la brdugs*,

giving rise to a different interpretation. See, for example, Yeshe Tsogyal, *The Life and Liberation of Padmasambhava*, pp. 446-448.

104. According to certain sources, *Shan 'byed pa bram ze'i skor* and *La bzlo rgyal po'i skor* together with the *Rang grol mngon sum du ston pa man ngag gi rgyud* or "tantras that directly show self-liberation" comprise the three categories of tantras of the Sems sde. See Bibliography no. 31, p. 538.6.

105. For a list of the teachings transmitted by Śrī Siṃha to Vairocana see Appendix Three.

106. The "six spheres" (*thig le drug*) represent six fundamental aspects for understanding and practicing the rDzogs chen Sems sde. They are: the sphere of the ultimate dimension (*dbyings kyi thig le*), the sphere of purity of the ultimate dimension (*dbyings rnam par dag pa'i thig le*), the sphere of the ultimate dimension of phenomena (*chos nyid kyi thig le*), the sphere of total wisdom (*ye shes chen po'i thig le*), the sphere of Samantabhadra (*kun tu bzang po'i thig le*), the sphere of self-perfection (*lhun gyis grub pa'i thig le*). See Bibliography no. 33, p. 375.1. For the five greatnesses (*che ba lnga*) see Chapter 2, section III.

107. By and large the unbroken translation of the *Bai ro 'dra 'bag* ends here.

108. For a list of these texts, see Appendix Three.

109. There is a detailed list of these teachings in *Klong chen chos 'byung* (Bibliography no. 3, pp. 292-298), with frequent allusions also to rDzogs chen texts that once existed in India but were never translated into Tibetan. For a complete list of the teachings transmitted to g.Yu sgra snying po see Appendix Three.

110. "The three statements that strike the essence" (*tshig gsum gnad brdegs: ngo rang thog tu 'phrad (sprad), thag gcig thog du bcad, gdengs grol tu 'cha'*) epitomize the whole rDzogs chen teaching in correspondence with the three series, Sems sde, Klong sde and Man ngag sde. In particular they also comprise the contents of the famous practice text, the *mKhas pa shri'i rgyal po'i khyad chos* by rDza dPal sprul rin po che (1808-1887), translated and commented upon in Reynolds, *The Golden Letters*.

111. Realization of the rainbow body (*'ja' lus*) is a phenomenon that has been amply documented in the history of rDzogs chen of both the Buddhist and Bön traditions. See, for example, Tulku Thondup, *Buddha Mind* (Bibliography no. 45), pp. 137-139. This realization was also achieved by many teachers of the Klong sde lineage.

112. For example, it is interesting to observe how early rDzogs chen works such as the *bSam gtan mig sgron* almost exclusively quote Sems sde texts, in particular the eighteen *lungs*.

113. For a general study of the *gter ma* literature see Tulku Thondup, *Hidden Teachings of Tibet* (Bibliography no. 44).

114. See, for example, the *sBas pa'i rgum chung*, Tun Huang MS, f. 1a, reproduced in Karmay, *The Great Perfection*, p. 258, where it states that this text "originates from all the *lungs* of *bodhicitta*" (*khungs ni byang chub sems kyi lung thams cad nas byung ngo*).

115. The third turning of the wheel of Dharma by Śākyamuni Buddha (following the first turning, based on the four noble truths, and the second turning, when he expounded the Prajñāpāramitā) embraces the sūtras that expound the principle of *tathāgatagarbha* as the essence of enlightenment present in all beings. See, for example, *Laṅkāvatārasūtra, Saṃdhinirmocanasūtra* and *Ratnagotravibhāga*, in many ways tied to yogācāra or cittamātra philosophy.

116. *bSam gtan mig sgron* is a text of fundamental importance for understanding the difference between the various Buddhist traditions that existed in Tibet at the time of the first promulgation of Buddhism in the ninth century. It is the first text on Dzogchen to have been written by a Tibetan teacher and the only one to treat, exhaustively and without bias, the ancient sTon mun tradition, an offshoot of the Chinese Ch'an tradition that was very widespread in Tibet at the time.

117. Bibliography no. 33, p. 290.6.

118. *Theg pa chen po'i tshul la 'jug pa'i btsan bcos* is the second great text, after *bSam gtan mig sgron*, that can be deemed a theoretical and practical treatise on the Sems sde.

119. Bibliography no. 11, p. 205.2.

120. Kaḥ Thog Monastery was known as a center of study of the three fundamental texts of the bKa' ma tradition: *gSang ba snying po* or *Guhyagarbha* for mahāyoga, *'Dus pa mdo* for anuyoga and *Kun byed rgyal po* for atiyoga. For a brief history of this monastery, see *Gangs can bod yul du byon pa'i gsang sngags gsar rnying gi gdan rabs mdor bsdus ngo mtshar pad mo'i dga' tshal* by 'Jam dbyangs mkhyen rtse'i dbang po (1820-1892), in *'Jam dbyangs mkhyen rtse'i dbang po'i gsung rtsom gces sgrig*, Si khron mi rigs dpe skrun khang, 1989, pp. 21ff.

121. This list is based on the *Chos dbyings rin po che'i mdzod kyi 'grel pa lung gi gter mdzod* by Klong chen pa (Bibliography no. 6, p. 349.5). According to tradition, the first five texts were translated by Vairocana, who also translated *Kun byed rgyal po, rMad byung* and the *mDo bcu*. The remaining texts were translated by Vimalamitra, gNyags Jñāna Kumāra, and g.Yu sgra snying po. Most of the eighteen *lungs* are contained in Volume One of the *rNying ma rgyud 'bum* (mTshams brag edition). In the same volume their names also appear as titles of separate chapters of the tantra *Rin po che dan mnyam pa skye ba med pa'i rgyud* (pp. 709-727), although the content does not tally with the original *lungs*. For a complete list of the eighteen *lungs* according to various sources see Appendix Three.

122. The first five texts from Klong chen pa's list comprise chapters 31, 27, 22, 26 and 30, respectively, of the *Kun byed rgyal po*. The only text that seems somewhat abbreviated in terms of the *lung* version is the *rDo la gser zhun*. However, it may also be the case that the version found in the *Kun byed rgyal po* is the original one and that Mañjuśrīmitra authored his text on the basis of that version.

123. The *lTa ba spyod pa'i 'khor lo* and the *lCags 'grel* (in the text, *'brel*), in *Bai ro rgyud 'bum*, vol. Nga, pp. 61-153 and 397-453, respectively.

124. For a list of these texts see Appendix Four.

125. *rTsa rgyud, bshad rgyud, yan lag gi rgyud* and *man ngag gi rgyud*, respectively.

126. This collection contains, among other things, the instructions on meditation (vol. Ka, pp. 1-120) and the exposition of the view (vol. Nga, pp. 1-168 and 329-351) of the "first five texts translated."

127. Nyang's system (*nyang lugs*) was established by the teacher Nyang mChog rab gzhon nu; Aro's system (*aro lugs*) and the Kham system (*khams lugs*) were both founded by the celebrated teacher A ro Ye shes 'byung gnas (tenth century). The instructions of these diverse Sems sde practice traditions are found in vol. Tsa of the *sNga 'gyur bka' ma*, Si khron mi rigs dpe skrun khang edition, and in the first volume of the *gDams ngag mdzod* by Kong sprul Blo gros mtha' yas (1813-1899). For the various Sems sde lineages see also *Klong chen chos 'byung*, Bibliography no. 3, pp. 392ff, where the following systems are mentioned: *khams lugs, aro'i skor, nyang lugs, rong lugs, skor lugs.*

128. In particular, the *Ye shes gsang ba sgron ma rin po che man ngag gi rgyud* (*rNying ma rgyud 'bum*, mTshams brag edition, vol. Ka, pp. 810-837) constitutes the basis of the *khams lugs* tradition. There is a commentary on this tantra in *Bai ro rgyud 'bum*, vol. Cha, pp. 111-247, under the title *rDzogs chen gsang ba'i sgron me'i rgyud 'grel chen mo.*

129. In Tibetan the four yogas (*rnal 'byor rnam pa bzhi*), or four contemplations (*ting nge 'dzin rnam pa bzhi*), of Sems sde are, respectively, *gnas pa, mi g.yo ba, mnyam nyid,* and *lhun grub*. By and large, these four stages correspond to the four yogas of Mahāmudrā practice known as: "single-pointed concentration" (*rtse gcig*), "beyond concepts" (*spros bral*), "one taste" (*ro gcig*), "beyond meditation" (*sgom med*). It would appear that the four yogas of Mahāmudrā, which date back to the teacher sGam po pa Dwags po Lha rje (1079-1153), the celebrated disciple of Mi la ras pa, are chronologically later than those of the rDzogs chen Sems sde tradition, inasmuch as the *Ye shes gsang ba sgron ma* tantra is mentioned among the texts transmitted by gNyags Jñāna Kumāra, a disciple of g.Yu sgra snying po, to A ro Ye she 'byung gnas in the tenth century (Bibliography no. 3, pp. 393-394).

130. Regarding the history of the various editions of the *Kun byed rgyal po* and of its exclusion from certain editions of the bKa' 'gyur after it was censured as not being an "authentic" Buddhist text, see Namkhai Norbu, "The History and Structure of the *Kun byed rgyal po*," in Longchenpa (Bibliography no. 38), *You Are the Eyes of the World* (Bibliography no. 38), (pp. 79-87). See also Karmay (Bibliography no. 36), "A Discussion on the Doctrinal Position of Rdzogs chen from the 10th to the 13Th Centuries"; and Dargyay (Bibliography no. 42), "A rNying ma Text, the *Kun byed rgyal po'i mdo*." Dargyay has also offered a translation of the root tantra of the *Kun byed rgyal po* in her book *The Sovereign All-Creating Mind* (Bibliography no. 41).

131. See, for example, Bibliography no. 3, p. 294.

132. Quoted by Klong chen pa in Bibliography no. 2, f. 34b.2.

133. In fact, in general there are three categories of disciples, each in its turn divided into three classes, making nine categories in all. Another division classifies practitioners in "instantaneous" (*cig char ba*), "those that skip the stages"

(*thod rgal ba*), and "gradualists" (*rim gyis pa*). See Sog bzlog pa Blo gros rgyal mtshan, *Sems sde'i khrid yig*, Bibliography no. 23, p. 380.6.

134. This sequence is given in chapter eighty-one of the *Kun byed rgyal po* and also in a section of chapter fifty-seven in the mTshams brag edition. See also Appendix Five.

135. The five greatnesses (*che ba lnga*) are *mngon par sangs rgyas pa'i che ba, bdag nyid chen por sangs rgyas pa'i che ba, chos kyi dbyings su sangs rgyas pa'i che ba, de yin pa'i sangs rgyas pa'i che ba, thams cad nas thams cad du sangs rgyas pa med pa'i che ba*: they constitute one of the cardinal points of the rDzogs chen Sems sde, and are tersely explained in one of the chapters of *Kun byed rgyal po* translated in Part Three of this work. The correspondences between the five greatnesses and the five sections of the root tantra *Kun byed rgyal po* mentioned here are based on the fourteenth chapter of *Shes bya mtha' gcod kyi rgyud*, a tantra found in the first volume of the mTshams brag edition of the *rNying ma rgyud 'bum* (vol. Ka, pp. 323-326). For the correspondences with the *mDo bcu* see Appendix Five.

136. See Bibliography no. 3, p. 254.

137. The references to the mTshams brag edition of the *mDo bcu* are the following: *Rig pa'i khu byug*, p. 453; *Khyung chen*, p. 455; *rTsal chen*, p. 453; *rDo la gser zhun*, p. 450. The remaining sections of the *Don gyi 'grel pa* concern the *rDo rje sems dpa' nam mkha' che*.

138. *La zlo gsang ba'i 'khor lo* and *Byang chub kyi sems she bya mtha' gcod kyi rgyud*, both contained in the first volume of the mTshams brag edition of the *rNying ma rgyud 'bum*.

139. *Bai ro rgyud 'bum*, vol. Ka, pp. 383-485.

140. *rdzogs pa chen po byang chub kyi sems kun byed rgyal po'i rgyud kyi dum bu*, Bibliography no. 22. It quotes chapters five, thirty-five and thirty-seven of the *Kun byed rgyal po* root tantra. It is also worth mentioning that the tantra called *rDo rje sems dpa' nam mkha' che bram ze rgyas pa'i rgyud* contains most of chapters 1, 5, 42, 43, 44, 45, 46, 47, 49, 50, 51, and 52 of the *Kun byed rgyal po* (*mTshams brag* edition, vol. Kha, pp. 529-556), although the name of the teacher is given as Kun tu bzang po instead of Kun byed rgyal po

141. *Byang chub kyi sems kun byed rgyal po'i don khrid rin chen gru bo*, by Klong chen pa, Bibliography no. 17, pp. 329-371, translated and commented on in *You Are The Eyes of the World*. According to Longchenpa himself, this guide is based on the instructions contained in a text by Vairocana, the *Sems lung rin chen sgron ma* (*The Precious Lamp of Instructions on Bodhicitta*), no longer extant.

142. *Kun byed rgyal po'i rgyud kyi bsdus don nyi zla'i drwa ba* by Klong chen pa. This text, of thirty-seven Tibetan folios, has only recently come to light again.

143. This classification is already found in ancient and authoritative texts such as *Man ngag lta ba'i phreng ba* (*The Garland of Views*), ascribed to the great teacher Padmasambhava. It has already been translated into English: see, for example, Karmay, *The Great Perfection*. According to most rDzogs chen texts, however, the

first vehicle is the *'jig rten lha mi'i theg pa* while the second unites those of the śrāvakas and of the pratyekabuddhas.

144. *Sems dpa'i rnal 'byor,* in the text.

145. *bsKyed pa (bskyed rim), rdzogs pa (rdzogs rim),* and *rdzogs pa chen po.*

146. The most common classification of the "ten natures of Tantra" (*rgyud kyi rang bzhin bcu* or *rgyud kyi dngos po bcu*) consists of: *lta ba, spyod pa, dkyil 'khor, dbang, dam tshig, 'phrin las, sgrub pa, ting nge 'dzin, mchod pa, sngags.* See, for example, the chapter of the *Byang chub kyi sems shes bya mtha' gcod kyi rgyud* tantra titled *rGyud kyi dngos po bstan pa'i le'u* (Bibliography no. 18, pp. 326-327). The list given by Klong chen pa (Bibliography no. 17, p. 345; *You Are the Eyes of the World,* pp. 34-35) has: *lta ba, sgom pa, dam tshig, phrin las, dkyil 'khor, dbang, sa sbyang ba, lam bgrod pa, sgrib pa sbyang ba, ye shes sam sangs rgyas.* See also Dudjom Rinpoche, *The Nyingma School,* vol. II, p. 164. Sometimes there are variations in the chapters of the *Kun byed rgyal po* and in other Sems sde texts also regarding the "ten absences" (*med pa bcu*) that constitute the true meaning of the ten natures.

147. In the translation of the second and third parts of *Kun byed rgyal po* the various chapters concerned with the "ten natures" are indicated with the name of the corresponding "nature" before the translation.

148. Klong chen pa gives a somewhat detailed classification of the various chapters of the *Kun byed rgyal po,* using the criterion of subdivision in sections and subsections characteristic of Tibetan Buddhist exegetical literature. The phrases that sometimes follow the translation of the title after the colon are usually based on the first lines of the corresponding chapter that serve to introduce its subject matter. For the list in Tibetan transcription see Appendix Five.

149. Bibliography no. 2, f. 6b. As regards the triad composed of *ngo bo* (essence), *rang bzhin* (nature) and *thugs rje* (energy, or the potentiality of energy), it should be noted that in the *Kun byed rgyal po, ngo bo* and *rang bzhin* are reversed so the order repeatedly found is *rang bzhin, ngo bo, thugs rje.* It may be useful to recall at this point that, as transpires from a study of rDzogs chen literature (such as, for example, the *mDzod bdun* by Klong chen pa), in this context the term *thug rje* does not mean simply "compassion." In fact, the triad *ngo bo, rang bzhin, thugs rje* concerns the "base" (*gzhi*) of the primordial state, a state in which there is no division into subject and object, into self and others, and which is free of any ethical connotation.

150. Bibliography no. 2, ff. 9a–9b.

151. I have not been able to find, in *Kun byed rgyal po* or elsewhere, any confirmation of the identification of *Khyung chen,* of *rTsal chen,* or the abbreviated version of the *rDo la gser zhun.*

152. Bibliography no. 2, f. 15a.

153. Even though Klong chen pa and other sources classify these ten chapters as the *byar med* (or *bya med*) *rdzogs pa'i mdo lung bcu,* the chapters expressly preceded, or concluded, by this epithet in the *Kun byed rgyal po* are chapters 22, 23,

24, 25, 26, and 27. According to the alternative order proposed in chapter 81 there are also other chapters pertaining to this category.

154. Bibliography no. 2, f. 17b.

155. Bibliography no. 2, f. 22a.

156. These last two subdivisions, respectively *dgongs pa kun 'dus kyi le'u gsum* and *tshig don bsdus te 'grel pa*, are found only in Klong chen pa, Bibliography no. 2, ff. 22a ff. According to other sources (Bibliography no. 22, pp. 288-289) chapters fifty-one to fifty-five contain condensed explanations of each of the five sections of the tantra.

157. The term "understanding" has been used to translate *rtogs pa*; however, it should be borne in mind that the "understanding" alluded to is not mere intellectual understanding but is instead a state of knowledge that is entirely experiential, having the same meaning as "realization."

158. For the colophons of the other versions, see the appendix by Namkhai Norbu, "The History and Structure of the *Kun byed rgyal po*," in Longchenpa, *You Are the Eyes of the World.*

159. The gSar ma, or modern tradition, includes all the Buddhist traditions that arose from the second promulgation of Buddhism in Tibet started by Rin chen bzang po (958-1055), which by and large can be subsumed in the three great schools of bKa' brgyud, Sa skya and dGe lugs.

160. Within the kriyā tantras, and this also applies to all three outer tantras, there are diverse practice methods. Clearly, the present explanation takes into consideration only the general characteristics of this system of practice. See also Tulku Thondup, *Practice of Dzogchen* (formerly *Buddha Mind*), Snow Lion, Ithaca 1995, pp. 15-22.

161. Several books on the tradition of the "Six Yogas of Naropa" are available in English. See, for example, Garma C. Chang, *The Six Yogas of Naropa* (formerly *Teachings of Tibetan Yoga*), Snow Lion, Ithaca 1997.

162. The question of the affinities and differences between Ch'an and rDzogs chen is too subtle and also too complex to be settled in a few words. It may be sufficient at present to consider that while Ch'an may be deemed the zenith of the sūtra teachings, rDzogs chen comprises the final summit of the tantric teachings, with all the theoretical and practical considerations this entails. As already stated above, the only text in Tibetan literature that deals with this issue in depth is the *bSam gtan mig sgron*.

163. At times in place of *mahāsandhi* one finds *mahāsanti* or *santimahā*. The latter is very probably in the language of Oḍḍiyāna.

164. As readers will notice, the following paragraphs do not specify the particulars of the Tibetan text in its entirety and are thus not intended literally as a "commentary" to *Kun byed rgyal po*.

165. The five aggregates, or *skandha*, are form (*rūpa*), sensation (*vedanā*), ideation (*samjñā*), volitional factors (*samskāra*), and consciousness (*vijñāna*).

166. The worlds of desire (*'dod khams*), of form (*gzugs khams*), and of formlessness (*gzugs med kyi khams*) encompass the totality of the dimensions of existence of *saṃsāra*. The last two, in particular, are the exclusive domain of the deva class.

167. The five grave deeds "without an interval" or with immediate result (*mtshams med pa lnga*) are: killing one's father, killing one's mother, killing a realized being, malevolently causing a Buddha's body to bleed, and sowing discord among the *sangha*.

168. *Rang lus ma bcos lha ma bsgom/ smra ba'i tshig dang ngag ma 'chos/ ting 'dzin ma byed sems ma 'chos.*

169. The *rDo rje sems dpa' nam mkha' che'i rgyud ces bya ba*. See Appendix Four.

170. These episodes from the life of dGa' rab rdo rje are based on the Man ngag sde tradition.

171. *bKra shis pa'i dpal, rNying ma rgyud 'bum*, mTshams brag edition, vol. Ka, pp. 499-524. A version of the *Rig pa'i khu byug* can also be found among the Tun Huang manuscripts together with a commentary, probably by Vairocana. See Karmay, *The Great Perfection*. For an overview of the "Six Vajra Verses" see Namkhai Norbu, *Dzogchen, The Self-Perfected State* (Part Two) (Bibliography no. 40).

172. The Tibetan text is: *sna tshogs rang bzhin mi gnyis kyang/ cha shas nyid du spros dang bral/ ji bzhin ba zhes mi rtog kyang/ rnam par snang mdzad kun tu bzang/ zin pas rtsol ba'i nad spangs te/ lhun gyis gnas pas bzhag pa yin.*

173. *Ma bcos mnyam pa'i rgyal po de la ni/ mi rtog chos sku'i dgongs pa de la gnas.*

174. The tantric rite of the *gaṇapūjā* (*tshogs mchod*) or *gaṇacakra* (*tshogs 'khor*), in which the sense objects are enjoyed in a state of non-duality, is based on understanding of the natural *maṇḍala* of the male and female deities present in the "*vajra* body."

175. This version of the meeting between g.Yu sgra snying po and Vimalamitra is based on chapter 83 of *Pad ma bka' thang* (Bibliography no. 15). See Yeshe Tsogyal, *The Life and Liberation of Padmasambhava*, pp. 492ff.

176. The "song of the vajra" (*rdo rje'i glu*) is a mantra belonging to the series of tantras of the *bTags grol*, many *gter ma* of which are found in the Man ngag sde.

177. *gCod* is a system of practice that unites the essence of Prajñāpāramitā, Tantra, and rDzogs chen, founded by the Tibetan lady teacher Ma gcig lab sgron (1031-1129).

178. These lines are found in *gCod yul mKha' 'gro'i gad rgyangs*, a text from the *Klong chen snying thig* cycle of *gter ma* of 'Jigs med gling pa.

179. *Rin chen gru bo*, "The Precious Ship" already mentioned above, translated under the title *You Are the Eyes of the World*.

180. I have used the terms Body, Voice and Mind with capitals to designate the pure state of the fundamental aspects of existence, corresponding to the Tibetan *sku*, *gsung*, and *thugs*.

181. In several passages of *Kun byed rgyal po* the expression "five ornamental causes" (*rgyan gyi rgyu lnga*) is used to designate the five elements.

182. The brackets repeat the phrases that are then explained word by word.

183. The five factors of realization (*byang chub lnga* in the text, but better known as *mngon byang lnga*), a method of "creation," or *bskyed rim*, are tied respectively to visualization of the moon disc (*zla ba las byang chub pa*), of the sun disc (*nyi ma las byang chub pa*), of the seed syllable (*sa bon las byang chub pa*), of the symbolic attributes (*phyag mtshan las byang chub pa*), and of the complete manifestation of the *yi dam* (*sku rdzogs pa las byang chub pa*). According to another classification the reference is to the lotus seat, the seed syllable, the symbolic attributes, the complete manifestation of the *maṇḍala* of the Body, the deity of wisdom.

184. The four miraculous actions (*cho 'phrul rnam pa bzhi*) are related to visualization, the empowering flow, the initiation, and the offerings. In Tibetan these are: *ting nge 'dzin gyi cho 'phrul, byin gyis rlabs kyi cho 'phrul, dbang bskur ba'i cho 'phrul* and *mchod pa'i cho 'phrul.*

185. Practitioners visualize themselves as the commitment deity (*dam tshig sems dpa'; samayasattva*) and visualize the wisdom deity (*ye shes sems dpa'; jñānasattva*) in front of themselves.

186. The four aspects of approach and accomplishment (*bsnyen sgrub bzhi*) are: approach (*bsnyen pa*), close approach (*nye ba'i bsnyen pa*), accomplishment (*sgrub pa*) and complete accomplishment (*sgrub pa chen po*). They constitute the four stages of the practice of transformation in mahāyoga, starting from the recitation of the mantra up to total integration with the *yi dam*. Their characteristics can vary according to the method one is using.

187. Radiation and re-absorption (*'phro 'du*) generally refer to the method of visualization of rays of light that radiate to infinity and are then re-absorbed in the center of the *yi dam*. The aim can be to accumulate merit by making offerings to the Enlightened Ones, to purify beings' negative karma, to receive the empowering flow, and so on.

188. This subdivision is also found in many Sems sde texts. See, for example *Bye brag 'byed pa'i mdo*, one of the *mDo bcu* mentioned above.

189. The four *mudrās* (*phyag rgya bzhi*) correspond to diverse methods of practice, according to their context of application. They are: *Mahāmudrā*, related to the Body; *dharmamudrā*, related to the Voice; *samayamudrā*, related to the Mind; *karmamudrā*, related to Action. In yoga tantra, for example, *mahāmudrā* refers to visualizing oneself in the form of the deity, *dharmamudrā* to concentrating on the seed syllable of the mantra, *samayamudrā* to visualizing the symbolic attributes of the *yi dam* such as the *vajra*, and *karmamudrā* to the radiation and re-absorption of the rays of light.

190. The three contemplations (*ting nge 'dzin gsum*) constitute the three initial phases of the practice of *bskyed rim* of mahāyoga and of Tantra in general. They are: contemplation of the essential nature (*de bzhin nyid kyi ting nge 'dzin*), when one meditates on the intrinsic emptiness of all phenomena; contemplation of total

manifestation (*kun tu snang ba'i ting nge 'dzin*), when one meditates on equanimous compassion for all sentient beings; contemplation on the cause (*rgyu'i ting nge 'dzin*), when one concentrates on the seed syllable of the *yi dam* deity.

191. Here the reference is particularly to the practices of sexual union tied to the third initiation of the higher tantras.

192. The ten *pāramitās* (*pha rol tu phyin pa bcu*) of the Bodhisattvas are: generosity, morality, patience, diligence, meditative absorbtion, discriminating wisdom, method, aspiration, strength, and primordial wisdom, to which correspond the ten *bhūmis* (*sa bcu*), or levels of realization.

193. The three purities (*dag pa gsum*) are: the purity of the deity and of the *maṇḍala* (*lha dang dkyil 'khor dag pa*), the purity of the ritual objects and of the substances (*rdzas dang yo byad dag pa*), the purity of the mantra and of the visualization (*sngags dang ting 'dzin dag pa*).

194. Evidently this is a reference to the three contemplations mentioned above.

195. The terms *dbyings* (here rendered "dimension of emptiness") and *ye shes* (wisdom) are the two fundamental aspects of anuyoga, tied to the principle of the three *maṇḍalas*. See *Buddha Mind*, pp. 38ff.

196. *Phra ba chos med*. For example, certain sutric philosophical systems deem that as regards the person, ultimate reality is the instant of consciousness while as regards matter, it is the indivisible atom.

197. *bDag nyid chen po*, one of the fundamental concepts of mahāyoga according to *bSam gtan mig sgron* (Bibliography no. 33, p. 200.6).

198. The expression "level of the four practices based on aspiration" (*mos spyod bzhi yi sa*) refers to the four stages of the path of application, or preparation (*sbyor lam*), when one has not yet realized knowledge of emptiness, the latter being characteristic of the path of seeing (*mthong lam*).

199. Four non-Buddhist philosophical schools of ancient India. See Dudjom Rinpoche, *The Nyingma School*, pp. 54ff.

200. In Tibetan *yang dag don gyi 'og min* and *gnas kyi 'og min* respectively.

201. In Tibetan *ma yengs ting 'dzin 'dzin pa'i rtod phur yin*. In this case "undistracted" bears a negative connotation inasmuch as it implies "effort" applied to an object.

202. Here "quality" has been used to render the Tibetan *che ba*.

203. This chapter, which corresponds to *Khyung chen lding ba*, one of the *snga 'gyur lnga*, is concise and difficult to interpret at certain points. In his summary, saying that "it is somewhat difficult to understand," Klong chen pa explains this section at greater length than is his wont. Bibliography no. 2, f. 11a.

204. The twelve links of interdependence (*rten 'brel bcu gnyis*) that underpin transmigration in *saṃsāra* are: ignorance, volitional factors, consciousness, name and form, sense sources, contact, sensation, craving, grasping, becoming, birth, old age, and death.

205. Up to this point this chapter concerns the defects of the sundry vehicles that precede atiyoga. Klong chen pa summarizes them thus (Bibliography no. 2, ff 10a.4ff): "The [pratyekabuddhas] meditate on the primordially pure nature of mind by means of the progressive and regressive method of the links of interdependence; however, as *dharmakāya* naturally abides within them, they cannot obtain a "new" purity as the fruit. The śrāvakas, who deem the absolute condition of the object to be the indivisible atom and of the subject to be the instant of consciousness, meditate on the absence of an independent entity; nevertheless, they do not understand the state of primordial enlightenment of the nature of mind. Even though they meditate on the absence of an independent entity in phenomena, the Bodhisattvas do not clearly see that this contradicts the real meaning. Practitioners of kriyā meditate on the deity as something separate from the mind; however, as the deity is the mind, they do not achieve the real condition. Practitioners of ubhaya meditate in a dualistic manner; however, outside the mind no higher wisdom exists anywhere else. Practitioners of yoga visualize themselves as the commitment deity and invoke the wisdom deity from outside, absorb it within themselves, and then meditate on the state of inseparability; nevertheless, they do not see the dualism of a meditator subject and an object of meditation. Through the stage of creation of vision, practitioners of mahāyoga perceive the single self-arising wisdom in the form of the deity and of the celestial palace; nevertheless, just as the shadow follows the body, they are not free of dualism. Through the stage of perfection tied to bliss-emptiness, practitioners of anuyoga meditate on wisdom that spontaneously arises from the ultimate dimension; nevertheless they do not transcend effort tied to the "joyous" forms [that are to be visualized]."

206. In Tibetan *shin tu rnal 'byor*, a term generally used to render atiyoga. However at times *lhag pa'i rnal 'byor* is found. The terms most commonly used in Tibetan for "anuyoga" are *rjes su rnal 'byor* and *yongs su rnal 'byor*.

207. Klong chen pa devotes nearly two and a half pages to *rDo rje sems dpa' nam mkha' che*, summarizing its main points on the basis of a subdivision in nine *mdo* or sections, which in their turn contain fifty-six subsections also called *mdo*. At the end he asserts that "this chapter forms part of the sphere of the Realized Ones and is very difficult [for ordinary people]," adding that he has given the explanations he received from his own teacher (very probably gZhon nu don grub). Bibliography no. 2, ff. 13a–15a. The present, not yet definitive translation, is based mainly on the two above-mentioned commentaries.

208. According to some commentaries to the *Guhyagarbha*, the five rituals (*cho ga lnga*) refer to gaining expertise in chanting the ritual melodies, visualizing during the mantra recitation, assuming different hand gestures (or mudrās), playing the drum, and dancing.

209. The path "with characteristics" (*mtshan bcas*) refers to the practice of visualizing the *yi dam* deity, etc. The path "without characteristics" (*mtshan med*) refers to the practice of non-conceptual contemplation.

210. That is, the level of *sgom lam,* the fourth of the five Mahāyāna paths.

211. Like the fourth line of the "Six Vajra Verses" this line, *de bzhin nyid dang rnam snang kun tu bzang,* contains the names of Vairocana and Samantabhadra.

212. There are four *vidyādhara,* or *rig 'dzin,* levels that result from mahāyoga practice: "of complete ripening" (*rnam par smin pa'i rig 'dzin*); "of long life" (*tshe la dbang ba'i rig 'dzin*); "of Mahāmudrā" (*phyag rgya chen po'i rig 'dzin*); "of self-perfection" (*lhun gyis grub pa'i rig 'dzin*).

213. Actually the *Kun byed rgyal po* lists seven, with an explanation of each related to its name: *kun tu 'od, pad ma can, rdo rje 'dzin, stug po bkod pa, 'khor lo tshogs chen, rdo rje 'chang, rgyu 'bras kun bzang dbye ba med;* however, the last two should be considered one single level. In fact Klong chen pa mentions them together as *rdo rje 'chang dbye ba med pa* (Bibliography no. 2, f. 21b). See also Chapter 6, section II.

214. *Kun spyod sa.*

215. Tib. *ting 'dzin bag chags.* This refers to the danger of shutting oneself off in states of meditative absorption, strictly tied to the practice of *zhi gnas,* or *śamatha,* which instead of leading to enlightenment can lead to rebirth in the formless worlds.

216. Contemplation of the essential nature, of total manifestation, and of the seed syllable are the causes of *dharmakāya,* of *saṃbhogakāya,* and of *nirmāṇakāya,* respectively.

217. *Sa la sbyangs pas gnas pa'i ting 'dzin byed.*

218. *gSal ba'i ting 'dzin*: here most probably a reference to tantric visualization practices.

219. This follows the bKa' ma edition: *mi rtog pa la 'dzin pa med* instead of *mi rtog pa la ting 'dzin med.*

220. *rGyu 'bras ye shes ting 'dzin rtog / rtog pa'i ye shes bag chags can.*

221. This follows the bKa' ma edition: *rab tu rtogs* instead of *rab tu dka'.*

222. *Chos kyi rol pa ting 'dzin*: in this case too the reference is to tantric visualization practices.

223. See note 174.

224. *sKye med rnam dag sems kyi dbang thob nas.* Here this refers to the *rig pa'i tsal dbang* or "empowerment of the energy of pure presence, " the only initiation, or, better, "introduction" indispensable in rDzogs chen, the path which does not depend on the methods of transformation. In any case, all the chapters of *Kun byed rgyal po* devoted to the meaning of initiation play on the double meaning of the word *dbang,* which as well as meaning initiation or empowerment also means "power," or "dominion."

225. *Kun tu 'od, rdo rje 'dzin pa, rdo rje 'chang, stug po bkod pa, pad ma can, rdo rje sems dpa'.*

226. Klong chen pa clarifies this paragraph, which embraces the essence of the practice of rDzogs chen, by commenting: "This shows that the one who, while abiding in the state of equanimous and unchangeable contemplation, clearly perceives the five sense objects that appear without judging or conceptualizing them, and gets accustomed to this state, is a practitioner of atiyoga" (*g.yo med mnyam bzhag ngang la gnas dus sgo lnga'i snang yul so sor gsal la 'dzin med rtog bral gang gis goms pa shin tu rnal 'byor pa yi gang zag tu bstan tshul*). Bibliography no. 2, f. 30a.

227. This translates the Tibetan *sgoms shig*, literally, "meditate!" or "cultivate!" I have chosen to use the term "experience!" as it provides a better rendition of its true meaning in the context of the *Kun byed rgyal po*.

228. That is, the practices of *zhi gnas* (*śamatha*) and of *lhag mthong* (*vipaśyanā*).

229. This reading follows the bKa' ma edition, which has *ji bzhin pa la 'chos par byed ma myong* in place of *ji bzhin sa las 'chos par byed ma rmongs*.

230. Mental "events" or "factors" (*sems byung*) belong to the *saṃskāra* aggregate.

231. This refers to the third initiation in Tantra (*shes rab ye shes kyi dbang*) specifically tied to the sensation of pleasure or "bliss."

232. I.e., the *rig pa'i rtsal dbang*. Cf. note 224.

233. This reading follows the bKa' ma edition, which has *sa dang sa yi rim pa'i khyad par yod* in place of *sa dang sa yi sgrib pa'i khyad par yod ces pa*.

234. This reading follows the bKa' ma edition, which has *lus sems rgyud ma sbyong* in place of *'dus sems rgyud ma sbyong*.

235. The expression *mya ngan las 'das pa*, i.e., "beyond suffering," is the Tibetan term for "nirvāṇa."

236. This reading follows the bKa' ma edition, which has *mkha' ltar rtog dpyod 'das la gang gnas pas* in place of *mkha' ltar rtogs spyod la ni gang gnas pa*.

237. *Ma byung stong pa'i don du smra mi byed.*

238. This reading follows the bKa' ma edition, which has *snang ba dngos por mi lta 'dzin mi byed* in place of *snang ba dngos por mi lta 'jig mi byed*.

239. *Rang bzhin med pa* in Tibetan, synonymous with *śūnyatā*, one of the fundamental concepts of the Prajñāpāramitā teachings and of the Mādhyamaka philosophical school.

Bibliography of Tibetan and Western Works

TIBETAN WORKS

1. *Kun byed rgyal po* (*Chos thams cad byang chub kyi sems kun byed rgyal po*), *rNying ma rgyud 'bum*: mTshams brag edition, vol. Ka, pp. 1-251, Thimphu 1982; Dil mgo mKhyen brtse edition, vol. Ka, pp. 1-220, Thimphu 1973; *sNga 'gyur bka' ma*, vol. Tsa, pp. 5-285, Si khron bod kyi rig gnas zhib 'jug khang, Sichuan; *bKa' 'gyur*, vol. Dza, pp. 1-126, The Tibetan Tripiṭaka, Peking Edition, Tokyo-Kyoto, 1957; *Bai ro rgyud 'bum*, vol. Ka, pp. 383-435, Leh 1971. (The last-mentioned edition contains only the *Phyi ma'i rgyud* and the *Phyi ma'i phyi ma'i rgyud*).

2. *Kun byed rgyal po'i rgyud kyi bsdus don nyi zla'i drwa ba*, by Klong chen pa (Klong chen rab 'byams pa) (1308-1363), photostatic reproduction of a manuscript copy from Nepal.

3. *Klong chen chos 'byung* (*Chos 'byung rin po che'i gter mdzod bstan pa gsal bar byed pa'i nyi 'od*) by rGyal sras Thugs mchog rtsal (written in 1362), Bod ljongs bod yig dpe rnying dpe skrun khang, Lhasa 1991.

4. *sGra thal 'gyur* (*Rin po che 'byung bar byed pa sgra thal 'gyur chen po'i rgyud*), in *rNying ma'i rgyud bcu bdun*, vol. I, pp. 1-205, Delhi 1973.

5. *lCags 'grel*, in *Bai ro rgyud 'bum*, vol. Nga, pp. 397-453, Leh 1971.

6. *Chos dbyings rin po che'i mdzod kyi 'grel pa lung gi gter mdzod*, by Klong chen pa (Klong chen rab 'byams pa) (1308-1363), in *mDzod bdun*, Gangtok.

7. *Chos 'byung mkhas pa'i dga' ston* (*Dam pa'i chos kyi 'khor lo bsgyur ba rnams kyi byung bar byed pa mkhas pa'i dga' ston*), by dPa' bo gtsug lag phreng ba (1504-1566), Peking 1986.

8. *Chos 'byung me tog snying po sbrang rtsi'i bcud*, by Nyang ral Nyi ma 'od zer (1124-1192), Bod ljongs mi dmangs dpe skrun khang, Lhasa 1988.

9. *sNyan brgyud rdo rje zam pa'i lo rgyus 'bring po gdams ngag dang bcas pa*, in *bKa' ma, The redaction of rDzogs-chen rGyal-sras gzhan-phan mtha'-yas*, vol. 18, pp. 284-415, Delhi 1969.

10. *Theg mchog mdzod* (*Theg pa'i mchog rin po che'i mdzod*), by Klong chen pa (Klong chen rab 'byams pa) (1308-1363), in *mDzod bdun*, Gangtok.

11. *Theg pa chen po'i tshul la 'jug pa'i bstan bcos*, by Rong zom pa Chos kyi bzang po (1012-1088), in *Rong zom bka' 'bum*, Delhi 1974.

12. *mDo bcu* (*Chos thams cad rdzogs pa chen po byang chub kyi sems su 'dus pa'i mdo*), in *rNying ma rgyud 'bum*, mTshams brag edition, vol. Ka, pp. 352-499, Thimphu 1982.

13. *'Dus pa mdo dbang gi bla ma brgyud pa'i rnam thar ngo mtshar dad pa'i phreng ba*, by Pad ma 'phrin las (1640-1718), Leh 1972.

14. *rDo rje sems dpa' nam mkha' che* (*Man ngag lung di rtsa ba rdo rje sems dpas gsungs pa*), in *Bai ro rgyud 'bum*, vol. Nga, pp. 383-395, Leh 1971.

15. *Pad ma bka' thang* (*U rgyan gu ru pad ma 'byung gnas kyi skyes rabs rnam par thar pa rgyas par bkod pa*), *gter ma* of O rgyan gling pa (1323-?), Si khron mi rigs dpe skrun khang, Sichuan 1987.

16. *Bai ro 'dra 'bag* (*rJe btsun thams cad mkhyen pa bai ro tsa na'i rnam thar 'dra 'bag chen mo*): xylographic edition, Lhasa; edition contained in *Bai ro rgyud 'bum*, vol. Ja, pp. 405-605, Leh 1971.

17. *Byang chub kyi sems kun byed rgyal po'i don khrid rin chen gru bo*, by Klong chen pa (Klong chen rab 'byams pa) (1308-1363), *sNga 'gyur bka' ma*, vol. Tsa, pp. 329-371, Sichuan.

18. *Byang chub kyi sems shes bya mtha' gcod kyi rgyud*, in *rNying ma rgyud 'bum*, mTshams brag edition, vol. Ka, pp. 288-352, Thimphu 1982.

19. *sBas pa'i rgum chung* (*The small collection of hidden precepts*), by Namkhai Norbu, Arcidosso 1984.

20. *Ma rig mun sel* (*Yo ga gsum bla ma nor bu dang bcas pa'i lo rgyus bab bzhi'i rim pa gser gyi nyi ma ma rig mun sel*), by sTag sham nus ldan rdo rje (17th c.), in *rTsa gsum yi dam dgongs 'dus*, vol. 3, pp. 2-127, Delhi 1972.

21. *Man ngag bshad thabs*, in *Bai ro rgyud 'bum*, vol. Ka, pp. 134-172, Leh 1971.

22. *rDzogs pa chen po byang chub kyi sems kun byed rgyal po'i rgyud kyi dum bu*, in *sNga 'gyur bka' ma*, pp. 287-298, Sichuan.

23. *rDzogs chen sems sde'i khrid yig nyang lugs*, by Sog zlog pa Blo gros rgyal mtshan (1552-1624), in *sNga 'gyur bka' ma*, vol. Tsa, pp. 371-412, Sichuan.

24. *Zangs gling ma* (*Slob dpon pad ma'i rnam thar zangs gling ma*), *gter ma* of Nyang ral Nyi ma 'od zer (1124-1192), Si khron mi rigs dpe skrun khang, Sichuan 1987.

25. *gZhi lam 'bras bu'i smon lam*, by 'Jigs med gling pa (1730-1798) in *Klong chen snying thig*, vol. 2, pp. 445-447, Delhi 1973.

26. *Ye shes gsang ba sgron ma rin po che man ngag gi rgyud*, in *rNying ma rgyud 'bum*, mTshams brag edition, vol. Ka, pp. 810-837, Thimphu 1982.

27. *Ye shes gsang ba zhes bya ba'i rgyud*, in *rNying ma rgyud 'bum*, mTshams brag edition, vol. Ka, Thimphu 1982.

28. *Rig pa rang shar chen po'i rgyud*, in *rNying ma'i rgyud bcu bdun*, vol. 1, pp. 389-855, Delhi 1989.

29. *Lo rgyus rin po che'i mdo byang*, belonging to the *g.Yu yig can* section of the *Bi ma sNying thig*, part two (Ja), pp. 162-233. In *sNying thig ya bzhi*, edited by Klong chen pa (Klong chen rab 'byams pa) (1308-1363), vol. 8, Delhi 1971.

30. *Sems sde bco brgyad kyi dgongs pa rig 'dzin rnams kyis rdo rje'i glur bzhengs pa*, in *sNga 'gyur bka' ma*, vol. Tsa, Sichuan.

31. *Sems sde ma bu bco brgyad kyi dgongs pa ngo sprad pa'i thabs rig pa rtsal dbang bco brgyad bskur ba'i chog khrigs bla ma'i zhal gdams*, in *sNga 'gyur bka' ma*, vol. Tsa, Sichuan.

32. *gSang sngags snga 'gyur la bod du rtsod pa snga phyir byung ba rnams kyi lan du brjod pa nges pa don gyi 'brug sgra*, by Sog zlog pa Blo gros rgyal mtshan (1552-1624), in *The Collected Works of Sog-zlog-pa Blo-gros-rgyal-mtshan*, vol. 1, Delhi 1975.

33. *bSam gtan mig sgron* (*sGom gyi gnad gsal bar phye ba bsam gtan mig sgron*), by gNubs chen Sangs rgyas ye shes (9th c.), Leh 1974.

34. *Lhun grub rdzogs pa chen po'i ston pa dang bstan pa'i byung tshul brjod pa'i gtam nor bu'i phreng ba*, by Chögyal Namkhai Norbu, manuscript.

WESTERN WORKS

35. Dudjom Rinpoche. *The Nyingma School of Tibetan Buddhism. Its Fundamentals and History*. Two volumes. Translated and edited by Gyurme Dorje and M. Kapstein. Wisdom, Boston 1991.

36. Karmay, Samten G. "A discussion on the doctrinal position of rDzogs-chen from the 10th to the 13th centuries," in *Journal Asiatique* 263, Paris 1975, pp. 147-155.

37. ——. *The Great Perfection: A Philosophical and Meditative Teaching in Tibetan Buddhism*. Brill, Leiden 1988.

38. Longchenpa. *You are the Eyes of the World*. Translated and edited by K. Lipman and M. Peterson. Lotsawa, Novato 1987. (Contains a translation of the *Kun byed rgyal po'i don khrid* by Klong chen pa.)

39. Mañjusrimitra. *Primordial Experience*. Translation by Namkhai Norbu and K. Lipman. Shambhala, Boston 1987. (Contains a translation and commentary of *rDo la gser zhun*.)

40. Namkhai Norbu. *Dzog-chen, The Self-Perfected State*. Ed. Adriano Clemente. Snow Lion, Ithaca 1996.

41. Neumaier-Dargyay, E. K., *The Sovereign All-Creating Mind, The Motherly Buddha*. State University of New York Press, Albany 1992. (Contains a translation of the first part of the *Kun byed rgyal po*.)

42. ——."A Rnying ma text: The *Kun byed rgyal po'i mdo*," in *Soundings in Tibetan Civilization*. Ed. B. Aziz and M. Kapstein. Manohar, Delhi 1985, pp. 282-293.

43. Tulku Thondhup. *The Tantric Tradition of the Nyingmapa*. Buddhayana, Marion 1984.

44. ——. *Hidden Teachings of Tibet, An Explanation of the Terma Tradition of the Nyingma School of Buddhism*. Ed. H. Talbott. Wisdom, London 1986.

45. ——. *Buddha Mind, An Anthology of Longchen Rabjam's Writings on Dzogpa Chenpo*. Edited by H. Talbott. Snow Lion, Ithaca 1989. (Recently reprinted under the title *The Practice of Dzogchen*.)

46. Reynolds, J. M. *The Golden Letters*. Snow Lion, Ithaca 1996.

47. Yeshe Tsogyal. *The Life and Liberation of Padmasambhava*, parts I and II. Dharma Publishing, Emeryville 1978. (Contains a translation of the *Pad ma bka' thang* by Orgyan gling pa.)

48. ——. *The Lotus-Born, The Life Story of Padmasambhava*. Translated and edited by Erik Pema Kunsang. Shambhala, Boston 1993. (Contains a translation of the *Zangs gling ma* by Nyang ral Nyi ma 'od zer.)

Index

This index contains most of the Sanskrit and Tibetan names and terms that appear in the text.

K

L

M

T